Bad for Democracy

Bad for Democracy
How the Presidency Undermines
the Power of the People

Dana D. Nelson

With a New Preface

University of Minnesota Press
Minneapolis
London

Published by the University of Minnesota Press
111 Third Avenue South, Suite 290
Minneapolis, MN 55401-2520
http://www.upress.umn.edu

Library of Congress Cataloging-in-Publication Data

Nelson, Dana D.
    Bad for democracy : how the presidency undermines the power of the people / Dana D. Nelson.
        p.   cm.
    Includes bibliographical references and index.
    ISBN 978-0-8166-5677-6 (hc : alk. paper)—ISBN 978-0-8166-5678-3 (pb : alk. paper)
    1. Executive power—United States.   2. Presidents—United States.
    3. Democracy—United States.   I. Title.
    JK516.N35 2008
    320.973—dc22

                                                        2008024047

Printed in the United States of America on acid-free paper

The University of Minnesota is an equal-opportunity educator and employer.

17 16 15 14 13 12 11 10   10 9 8 7 6 5 4 3 2 1

Contents

Preface
The Winter of Our (Presidential) Discontent

ARCHETYPES TEACH THAT THE SEASONS REFLECT THE CYCLE OF life and life experiences. As the literary critic Northrop Frye memorably schematized, spring, a period of renewal and rebirth, is the season of comedy. Summer, the season of triumphal growth, is romance. Fall, when light and life wanes, is the season of tragedy. Winter, with little light and warmth, is associated with satire.

The U.S. presidential calendar reorders those apparently natural affinities. In the waning of fall, we elect a new president, full of sprouting hopes for our resurgent political future. At the crest of winter's ringing cold, that president is inaugurated, buoyed by warming ceremonies of unity and a nation's effulgent confidence (reflected in typically sky-high "job approval" ratings for the entirely untested president). Then comes spring—the first evaluation, the 100-day mark, report cards—usually matched by a new hesitation, an equivocation about the nation's newest knight in shining armor. Finally the hot months of summer roll in, August recess, and with it the first real signs of disappointment in (and for some, despair over) the nation's newly elected savior, who, with Congress, goes on vacation. Then begins the regular cycle, where the second winter's cold more than compensates for the warmth of the first: by the anniversary of the inauguration, we can expect a slide in public approval once voters have had a year to see how and what their dream candidate will really do in office. Over and over, these cycles repeat. And magically, every time, we forget how the cycle goes, believing, with every quadrennial election, that if we manage to see our chosen candidate take office, we'll live in the perpetual glory of that wintertime inaugural summer.

If only.

When I completed the first edition of this book for publication in February 2008, then-candidate Obama was still months away from winning his party's nomination. The months that followed were surprising, energizing, and (despite notable differences) familiar. The excitement of the election year combined with Barack Obama's particular grassroots organizing appeal to citizens to revivify their engagement with the U.S. democratic process, his progressive rhetoric on the campaign trail, and the hope that he might be the first to break the centuries-old color line in the White House to make him a seemingly incomparable presidential candidate, which is surely what his supporters claimed. They were confident his election (and the Democratic sweep across the board) boded not just change but historically salvific transformation—of the petty racism that for too long has marred U.S. cultural life and structured its institutions; of the war in Iraq so many felt should never have been launched; of the U.S. government's official willingness to flout treaty agreements, international conventions, and law in the execution of its "war on terror"; of the torture and endless detention of prisoners; of the economic recession that decades of deregulation and Wall Street "exuberance" had forced on us; of executive branch arrogance and the de facto line-item veto of the signing statement (denounced in 2006 as a threat to constitutional government by the American Bar Association); of a punishing and expensive health care system that leaves so many without a safety net; of the vicious politics that for decades now has characterized Washington; of cronyism, insiderism, and the influence of the Big Money lobby on U.S. politics and policy-making; of the formal disregard for environmental protections so needed in an era of global warming; of the homophobia that punishes members of the U.S. armed forces and in society more generally. Most of all, Obama's supporters knew his election meant a new birth for democracy—of citizen equality and involvement, of democratic access and input on law and decision-making, of meaningful political belonging and efficacy we all yearn for as members of the world's leading democracy.

If only.

In the early months after the inauguration of our nation's forty-fourth president, pundits and ordinary Americans—at least those not worrying about whether he is a "real" American—engaged in a frenzy of president-savior comparisons. Obama's leadership was like FDR's. His vision was like Lincoln's. His aims were like Johnson's. Or, he was a hero: in a January 2009 Harris Poll, adults (age 18 and over) named him as their hero in response to a question that did not provide a list for respondents to choose from (he beat out Jesus and Martin Luther King Jr.). The nation's new hero was also a superhero: knowingly witty and nevertheless deliciously unself-conscious comparisons of Obama to Superman flew across the Internet—for instance, Jib Jab's "He's Barack Obama" ("He'll leap a building, run industry, save a kitten from a tree . . . He's come to save the day!")—and were marketed as bobblehead dashboard dolls and T-shirts. He was a culture hero, too: his name became slang for *cool,* as in "that's so Obama." Jon Stewart's *Daily Show* offered a tongue-in-cheek and simultaneously overawed tribute to Obama's "insanely glamorous" romantic skills after he took the First Lady to New York City in late May for dinner and a musical ("What the f***? . . . How do you compete with that?"). And when he was not being described as a culture hero or superhero, well, then, a rock star, as in "Barack Star" T-shirts, videos, and musicals.

The historic nature of his presidency may have helped elevate the nation's forty-fourth president, at least temporarily, to a nearly untouchable level. An April 2009 Pew Research Center study of the media coverage of the first hundred days of his presidency documented that the press had been notably easy on him (despite his repeated complaint about Fox News: "one television station that is entirely devoted to attacking my administration"). Journalism.org summarized the report: "As he marks his 100th day in office, President Barack Obama has enjoyed substantially more positive media coverage than either Bill Clinton or George Bush during their first months in the White House . . . Overall, roughly four out of ten stories, editorials, and op ed columns about Obama have been clearly positive in tone, compared with 22 percent for Bush and 27 percent for Clinton in the same mix of seven national media outlets during the same first two months in office." The study showed that up to the 100-day mark, far more coverage of Obama had focused on his "personal and leadership qualities" and on his relationship with American citizens than on his policy agenda.

A second April study, by the Center for Media and Public Affairs, corroborated the Pew's findings. Interestingly, neither report earned much immediate notice by the press, as reporter Robert Samuelson editorialized in his May 31 editorial in the *Washington Post*, "The Obama Infatuation." The media's lack of willingness to criticize a popular president matters, Samuelson insists, because the so-called fourth estate can serve as an important check on relatively unchecked modern presidents. As he put it: "In the campaign, [Obama] claimed he would de-emphasize partisanship—and also enact a highly partisan agenda; both couldn't be true. He got a pass. Now he claims he will control health-care spending even though he proposes more government spending . . . Journalists seem to take his pronouncements at face value even when many are two-faced" and when they do, they fail their public, which deserves help in sorting through both difficult policy issues and the political smokescreens erected to obfuscate their costs and benefits. In the same month, Peter Baker of the *New York Times* observed that the Obama administration, fronted by a president who daily performs an "above-it-all disdain for the impatience and fecklessness of today's media culture" is unrivaled in its ability to spin the media cycle, citing Obama's four-day tour in July of "exclusive" interviews with PBS, CBS, NBC, and the *Washington Post,* along with his special invitation offering White House access to *Nightline.*

In the early months of Obama's presidency, his positive achievements and his distinction from the previous administration were lead news (except on Fox, which manages to find something distasteful and even sinister in every action from Obama and his administration). There was some thoughtful critical coverage in mainstream media, but it was typically buried. A June 2009 *New York Times Magazine* cover article emphasized the former Senator's determination to "win over" Congress, featuring the current president as a Congressional compromiser, quite different from his more adversarial and unilateralist predecessors, and meanwhile Obama's more understated but no less significant executive unilateralism went relatively unremarked—for instance, in his continued use of the signing statements he denounced George Bush for utilizing. Obama's first signing statement, attached to the March 2009 spending bill, came just days after he instructed government officials not to enforce any Bush signing-statement provisions attached to laws without consulting his administration's attorney general, Eric Holder. Obama's statement nevertheless expressed his administration's interest in preserving expansive executive powers (at least, his own) and went so far as to contest a Congressional whistleblower provision that established protection for federal employees who give information to Congress, asserting basically that as president he could override any such legal protections at his discretion. By July, Obama had issued enough signing statements declaring his authority to bypass legal provisions to provoke the House into issuing an official rebuke (voting 429 to 2 in favor). In a follow-up letter, Democratic Congressmen Barney Frank and David R. Obey reminded the president of statements he had made as a Senator during the Bush administration: "During the previous administration, all of us were critical of the president's assertion that he could pick and choose which aspects of Congressional statutes he was required to enforce. We were therefore chagrined to see you appear to express a similar attitude." But Obama's change of heart on the subject of expanding executive powers should not come as a surprise—rather, he's staying true to a long historical trend.

Obama seems to register signing statements on the general principle of marking out areas where the executive's power should not be challenged, whether or not he intends to enforce particular legal provisions, making his specific approaches to executive policy difficult to discern beyond his rhetoric of transparency, counterbalanced by his practice of opacity. His ongoing use of signing statements promises to entrench them as a means to expand presidential powers and essentially to continue asserting the line-item veto the Supreme Court has explicitly disallowed. He has sought other putatively constitutionally principled ways to bypass Congressional lawmaking and democratic accountability—for instance, a bill introduced in February 2009 by Senators Leahy, Specter, Feingold, and Kennedy that aimed to provide guidance to federal courts considering cases in which the executive has asserted the state secrets privilege. The Obama administration's response to the proposed State Secrets Protection Act seemingly appears, as Dan Fejes of the blog Pruning Shears observed in August 2009, in the odd conclusion to a July Department of Justice amicus brief. This was offered in response to the appeal of a suit filed by an employee fired for refusing to recant a complaint about his company's practice of hiring illegal immigrants. The Obama administration's filing mainly concerned arcane issues about attorney–client privilege, in essence arguing that an employer victory before the Supreme Court would undermine district court judges' ability to control the discovery process. Yet the brief spends numerous final pages addressing the question of state secrets, an issue only tangentially raised by the case at hand, arguing that the president's right to invoke state secrets protection is rooted in the Constitution. As Adam Liptak summarizes in his *New York Times* coverage of the amicus brief, that argument "is controversial, and the brief's account of the relevant decisions was incomplete."

It's clear that the Obama Department of Justice does not want judicial or democratic limits put on the authority the executive can claim under the rubric of state secrets protection. Early on, the Obama DOJ was invoking the doctrine to prevent courts from reviewing the same warrantless wiretapping program that candidate Obama had so forcefully condemned when the Bush administration was overseeing it (for example, on his campaign web site's "Plan to Change Washington," where he listed as one of the "problems" to be solved by his administration the "secrecy" that "dominates government actions"). While early DOJ filings in February and even March 2009 could be interpreted as transitional caution, as early as April it was evident that the Obama-staffed DOJ was hewing closely to and even exceeding the desire for government secrecy that characterized Bush's administration. The Obama DOJ even outdid Bush-era arguments on behalf of expanding executive powers in favor of secrecy, inventing an entirely new category of "sovereign immunity," which, in Glenn Greenwald's summary, claims "that the Patriot Act bars any lawsuits of any kind for illegal government surveillance unless there is 'willful disclosure' of the illegally intercepted communications." As Greenwald elaborates on Salon.com:

> In other words, beyond even the outrageously broad "state secrets" privilege invented by the Bush administration and now embraced fully by the Obama administration, the Obama DOJ has now invented a brand new claim of government immunity, one which literally asserts that the U.S. Government is free to intercept all of your communications (calls, emails, and the like) and—even if what they're doing is blatantly illegal and they know it's illegal—you are barred from suing them

unless they "willfully disclose" to the public what they have learned . . . This is a brand new, extraordinarily broad claim of government immunity made for the first time ever by the Obama DOJ—all in service of blocking E[lectronic] F[rontier] F[oundation]'s lawsuit against Bush officials for illegal spying.

Despite a prolonged uproar about the Bush administration's unilateralism and secrecy, and its frequent assertion that the executive was above the law, surprisingly little outrage has made headlines about the Obama administration's staking remarkably similar views—its unwillingness to give up military tribunals, or to relinquish the powers claimed by the Bush administration with regard to a president's right to indefinitely imprison military detainees, or to support any Congressional hearings reviewing the legality of the Bush administration's conduct in the "War on Terror" (the White House expressed its desire to "look to the future" when Attorney General Holder announced his appointment of a special prosecutor to investigate CIA detainee abuses). Supporters who later would profess themselves enraged about Obama's domestic and economic policies hardly lifted an eyebrow about his claims to what are in essence royal powers for the presidency.

Meanwhile, conservatives concluded with genuine delight that Obama's actions (despite his unwillingness to speak on the subject) prove him a solid supporter of Reagan's "unitary executive theory." This theory of executive power, as I detail in this book, encourages presidents to act with all available secret and public tools to expand the purview of executive power, even extralegally. The more modest legalistic claims of the theory—related to the president's control over agencies—do little to check the unilateralist psychology and administrative culture it has fostered since its articulation under Reagan. Its practical effect, as law professor Peter M. Shane summarized in his analysis of unitary executive theory's effects on government, *Madison's Nightmare*, has been to undermine U.S. constitutional democracy. Obama's support for that theory and its deep influence on ongoing policy decisions deserve discussion and debate among citizens on the right and left. But how do we get there? Media and cultural hyping of Obama's incomparability made it all the more difficult critically to evaluate how his executive aims and policies impact both constitutional government and citizen democracy.

Whether or not our society can deliberate the merits of unitary executive theory to the ongoing health of our nation's democratic experiment is a question entirely unrelated to whether mainstream America would take off the rose-colored glasses regarding its current president. Obama is (as the nation discovered in the dog days of August) like most other presidents in the typical cycle of his approval ratings—the crest and then the inevitable fall of supporter hopes. But health care reform had begun floundering. Obama tried briefly to invoke the old magic of his campaign to inspire voters to renew their enthusiasm for his "plan" (still without offering a specific plan), and headlines read "Faith in Obama Drops," "Obama's Trust Problem," and "Obama's Just Not That Into You." When politics as usual—acrimonious and uncompromising as ever—went on summer recess, reporters turned instead to town halls featuring citizens with loaded guns. People hoping for real change—in health care, in Washington gridlock—might have been indulged in a week or two of regret. But no. Get over it, recognize "he's just not that into you," and move on to the next guy urged the allusive Salon headline, sidestepping the very point on which reporter Mike Madden allows Obama to finish the article: the necessity of citizen activism. The president reminded his supporters at a conference call and video forum on August 20 sponsored by his postelection Organizing for America that in 2008, rather than giving up when McCain and Palin surged to the head of the polls, they "kept on working steadily, deliberately, sensibly, knocking on doors, talking to your coworkers, just giving people the facts . . . and that's what we're going to have to do today."

He labeled the problem in a nutshell, as anticlimactic as it is. In the United States, we expect the president to do the work of democracy. When he disappoints, as the Salon title suggests, we write him off and regretfully get busy looking for the next one who will do the trick, right the ship, win the day. One of the (many) problems with the belief that the president is both the leader of democracy and its central agent is that it trains people to put all their energy into electing the right president, then they can settle back into their "regular" lives, waiting for him to get the(ir) job done. As Bonnie Adkins, an Iowan organizer for the Obama campaign who subsequently tried to rally the troops to assist with his health care reform agenda, summarized for a *New York Times* reporter about one of the most active set of supporters in campaign history: "The enthusiasm is not there like it was a year ago. Most people, when they get to November 5, put their political hat away and it doesn't come out for three years."

One intelligent August criticism of Obama was that instead of leading the reform he was operating like an organizer—bringing interested actors to the proverbial table and leaving it to Congress, the health insurance industry, doctors, hospitals, the pharmaceutical companies, and, perhaps unexpectedly, to the regular Americans who mounted massive grassroots campaigns to reach the ears and votes of their Congressional representatives to wrangle out how reform should go. In this critique, health care reform was floundering because President Obama left the ship without its rudder. Michael Moore, in a *Rolling Stones* roundtable in August 2009 (with David Gergen and Paul Krugman), swiftly turned that point on its head: "I want to ask people reading this conversation, 'What have you done today, what did you do yesterday, what do you plan to do tomorrow to make sure we have universal health care in this country, to get those troops out of Iraq and Afghanistan?' We need to see a mass mobilization like we did last year, and it can't all be on Obama for that not happening. We have to take responsibility for that ourselves."

That's a great point, one Obama prepped his supporters for during his campaign, during his acceptance speech, during his inaugural address. He knew better than his supporters that his candidacy was exciting an enthusiasm that he as president would be unable to meet, an enthusiasm for democratic involvement. Citizens were bound for disappointment in their expectation that Obama would deliver that change. Not two weeks after his inauguration, Chris Bowers posted a letter on Open Left titled "What Does Obama Want Us to Do?" Seemingly immobilized in the aftermath of inauguration ("should we be holding more cocktail parties and/or dinners with Republicans in our neighborhoods, as President Obama himself is doing?"), Bowers spoke for many of Obama's supporters when he castigated the new president for fostering "a major leadership vacuum right now." His letter is alarming in the level of its civic passivity and the extent to which Bowers gets the representative relationship exactly *backward*. It's not the president's job to tell *us* what to do or how to represent his agenda: it's our job to tell the nation's "number one" representative—and all our other representatives—what we want him and them to do.

In August, as Congress wrangled with health care reform, some people began doing that, both on the right and the left; for instance, the well-covered Tea Party campaign, a grassroots effort to fight for fiscal responsibility, limited government, and the free market; or FDL Action, which organized supporters to call progressive members of Congress demanding their support for a public option as Obama and the Senate's so-called Gang of Six express their willingness to abandon it; the street-theater tactics of the Backbone Campaign, a Seattle grassroots organization whose public actions aim to embolden regular citizens to demand government accountability to citizens and not just corporations; or the fifty-state grassroots organization Equality Across America, which organized an October march in Washington, D.C. on behalf of LGBT civil rights to forward the demands Washington seems perennially willing to back-burner. Democracy, as these and many other groups grasp, is about the people's sovereignty: our power, not the president's. It's ours to shape, to grow—and to lose.

By September, a new report from the Center for Media and Public Affairs had announced that media coverage of Obama had distinctly "soured" in the months since its rosier April report. Studying thousands of articles, the researchers concluded that the trend of favorable coverage had entirely reversed, with positive stories plummeting from highs of 59 to 43 percent, and negative coverage similarly reversing from 41 to 57 percent. Thus in the dog days of summer begins the winter of our presidential discontent. Citizens, it seems, hate facing that their president is susceptible to human failure, that he can't singlehandedly pass legislation or save the nation. As Homeland Security grappled with the system breakdowns that enabled the "underwear bomber," Umar Farouk Abdul Mutallab, to board a plane bound for Detroit on Christmas Day 2009, and as Massachusetts electors filled Ted Kennedy's storied seat with the Republican Scott Brown, breaking the Democrats' filibuster-proof Senate majority and virtually ensuring the end of this round of health care reform, the media and citizens on both sides of the partisan divide warmed their rage by blaming Obama (and he presidentially agreed that "the buck stops here"). The press celebrated the anniversary of his inaugural by marveling at his low approval ratings (only Reagan's were lower at the one-year mark, which you would think would at least caution the pundits), and political bettors began gambling that the president would not be viable for a second term. Ridiculing his scholarly cool, Maureen Dowd accused Obama of missing "the moment to be president—to be the strong father who protects the home from invaders, who reassures and instructs the public at traumatic moments"—in short, of failing to be the very superhero her editorial lead mocked ("Captain Obvious Learns the Limits of Cool").

But Obama detractors, right and left, might usefully cool off a bit and consider that the failures we seek to attribute to the president could as easily be dropped at our own feet. The cycle of the four seasons evoked by our quadrennial presidential election might encourage us to believe that democracy will perpetually renew itself, a gift of nature reminiscent of the seasons. In the seasonal rendition, the energies of democracy wax and wane; like the winter freeze that coaxes seeds from their hulls and gives roots the rest they need to thrive again in the summer to come, this "natural" cycle is a good thing. We become energized in the democratic summer of the election cycle and involve ourselves in selecting a new president. Then we cozy into our couches during the democratic winter and wait for him to perform the magical work of democracy, preferably with a cinematic flourish that will keep us happily spellbound.

The ever-renewing cycle of seasons might be a comforting myth, but it's not democracy's reality. The real radicalism of the U.S. revolution for independence came in its advancement of the ideal and the practice of the people's sovereignty, the idea that regular people were qualified and capable of self-rule if they worked at it vigilantly, thoughtfully, and hard enough. The Constitution structured a balanced government, and we have for centuries regarded its scheme of checks and balances as the clarion of democracy—without really paying attention to how those checks are holding up. Here's what the Framers got wrong: the three branches are not in fact equally suited to protect their own self-interest. The one headed by the single person—the executive—is best suited for that. Consequentially, over time, the presidency has expanded its symbolic and practical powers to the point that, as I argue in this book, the presidency is jeopardizing the fundamental premise of democracy: the self-rule *of the people.*

As we stew in the cold of winter, once again blaming the president for not fixing everything we see wrong in our nation (and indeed, the world), we might want to consider that we are unthinkingly surrendering our own democratic power and agency, both as a form of government and as our most precious cultural and political heritage. Corazon Aquino, the Philippine politician who led her country into what many regarded as a democratic revolution against the corrupt Marcos government, died in August 2009. Reflecting on the optimism of that revolutionary moment, and what came after, many Filipinos expressed a sense of regret not just for the loss of Aquino but for their country since her landmark election— for lost opportunity, the failure to capitalize on the possibilities opened up in that moment of change in the face of continuing poverty, inequality, and corruption. Teresita I. Barcelo summarized in *The New York Times*: "We thought all we needed to do was remove the dictator and do nothing about it. We thought the problem was just the dictator. I say the problem is us. We did not change."

As Barcelo understands, what the president does for us can be good or bad—but either way, it isn't democracy. *Bad for Democracy* urges that we learn from her wisdom that democratic change does not come like the change of seasons, a gift of nature or the president, but rather from our own efforts at self-governing. Democracy is not "natural"; rather, it's a habitat we build together. It won't be easy, but if we care about our nation's democratic experiment, we must seriously rethink the relationship of citizens to our form of self-government. We must find ways to involve ourselves in that project among those with whom we disagree, within a government that is far friendlier to corporate than citizen interest, and within a society that has for too long considered "democracy" something that only "government" does.

January 2010

Bad for Democracy

Introduction
The People v. Presidentialism

IN THE RUN-UP TO THE 2004 PRESIDENTIAL ELECTION, A BUSH
administration official memorably asserted to *New York Times* reporter
Ron Suskind, "We're an empire now, and when we act, we create our own
reality. And while you're studying that reality—judiciously, as you will—
we'll act again, creating other new realities, which you can study too, and
that's how things will sort out. We're history's actors . . . and you, all of
you, will be left to just study what we do." Suskind's article "Without a
Doubt" framed this assertion as the administration's assessment of Left-
leaning intellectuals, and it predictably outraged Bush's political opposition. His administration was widely seen by Democrats as heedlessly
unilateralist: this bald assertion of power seemed concisely to summarize
Bush's own philosophy and his scorn for those who disagree with him.

But this is not just a simple summary of the Bush–Cheney–Rumsfeld–
Wolfowitz philosophy for dealing with political opposition. Rather, it
draws on a deep and relatively unnoticed tradition of expanding presidential powers that began in the age of George Washington. This expansion
has come at times through the ambitions, machinations, and moxie of individual presidents—some of them impressively gifted governmental and
political leaders. It has also come through the active and passive consent
of citizens, the courts, and Congress. Because the president has come to
symbolize both our democratic process and our national power, we tend
to see him simultaneously as democracy's heart (he will unify the citizenry) and its avenging sword (he will protect us from all external threats).
Those beliefs, inculcated in us from our earliest days in school, reinforced
by both popular culture and media coverage of government, politics, and

Youthful patriotism: we learn as schoolchildren to treasure the signs of our democracy—
Constitution, flag, and president. Verner Reed, "Fourth of July, North Danville, Vermont, 1952."
Photograph from the Verner Reed Archive at Historic New England; courtesy of Historic New England.

foreign affairs, make us *want* to give the president more power, regardless of the constitutional checks and balances we also learned to treasure as schoolchildren.

Every now and then, a president reaches too far. Then Congress, or the judiciary, or the citizenry reacts, mobilizing to take back some of the powers of the presidency. The habit in such moments is to blame the individual president who provoked the immediate reaction, ignoring history and turning a naive eye to the future. The fact is, ever since the office was invented, presidents have been appealing to how it serves as a symbol of national strength and domestic unity, and to its function as a focal point for foreign policy, to claim more powers for the office than those it was explicitly granted by the Constitution. Especially since the administration of Franklin D. Roosevelt, when the executive branch and federal bureaucracy underwent a massive expansion, *every* president has worked to extend presidential powers in ways that the Constitution's framers would likely have viewed as alarming and profoundly compromising to their ideals and aims. When citizens and government officials focus their response to presidential power grabs by aiming it at a single president, they effectively fail to check the problem because the next president will (as history tells us) repeat the grabs—and will almost surely keep the powers. Whenever a president succeeds at a power grab, he establishes a precedent that the next president can refer to as he (and maybe someday, she) makes yet another incremental grab for powers that the framers allocated to another branch.

The Bush administration, although pushing for powers with more openly ideological and brazenly partisan purpose than its predecessors, is not inventing new maneuvers. It is just staying on the track of U.S. history. As citizens, we absolutely should be alarmed. But we need to stop focusing our anxieties and anger about presidential overreaching solely on George W. Bush and his administration if we want to do something to reverse this trend. The Bush administration's theory of presidential power, the "unitary executive," forwards without apology a set of strategies for building the power of the executive that supporters of Ronald Reagan began promulgating in the early 1980s. And every president since—both Bushes and Bill Clinton—has built on and strengthened the executive unilateralism advocated by the unitary executive. This theory of leadership for government and democracy explicitly challenges the balancing and mixing of powers that the framers believed would ensure a healthy check on each branch. And its proponents reject prior notions that the president's leadership depends on his abilities to negotiate and compromise. Insisting that the president should control *all* administrative power, with an unchecked right to determine how laws are implemented, the unitary executive maneuvers with preemption and unilateralism. Indeed, the most ambitious advocates of this model argue that the president has coequal power to interpret the Constitution and therefore is not bound by Supreme Court decisions. While the Court has not yet ruled on this theory, four of the nine justices (John Roberts, Samuel Alito, Antonin Scalia, and Clarence Thomas) have explicitly supported this model in court decisions or other writings and speeches. If the theory is upheld, the president will be granted uncheckable powers that he can confidently claim are "constitutional"—even though they will be in direct defiance of the Constitution our framers created.

How has our democratic project in self-governance reached this point? And even more important for those who object, how can we feel so helpless and resigned in the face of this looming possibility?

Presidentialism, or The Consent of the Powerless

As the country's only nationally elected representative, the president, as the wisdom goes, stands for democratic power. But there's a kind of shell game involved in this act of representation: the president substitutes the trappings of national power for the power of the people. The president's sovereign power and the people's sovereign power are not the same thing at all. One is primary (the legitimating democratic sovereignty of "We, the People") and the other secondary (a *representation* of the primary power). But the mesmerizing power of presidentialism—the way we look to the sitting president for national strength and unity—encourages citizens to believe that their democratic agency depends on presidential power, instead of the other way around. Thus, when people begin to feel uncomfortable at their diminishing political agency, they can be reassured by the quadrennial ritual of electing a president. If only this time we get the right one in power, we can feel as if we were able to do something, as if we had some say.

This once-every-four-years hope for the lever-pull sensation of democratic power blinds people to the opportunities for democratic representation, deliberation, activism, and change that surround us, in local elec-

---

tions, in school boards and town halls, on the streets with our neighbors, at work, in daily life. Believing that democratic power happens only in the moment we act to hand it over to the next president, we neglect to cultivate and exercise a broader democratic agency by staying attentive to local politics, by engaging with civic projects, or by practicing democracy as the art of making possibilities out of disagreements in many avenues of daily life and not just by proxy in elections. Believing that democratic power is for the president to wield, we succumb to the lethargy of people waiting to be led, rather than remember that democracy is about self-governing.

How did this single elected office become a holy trust for democracy, instead of what the framers conceived it as, an office for executing the laws passed by Congress? How does a citizenry so proud of its government's fabled checks and balances (celebrated recently, for instance, when the Rehnquist Court handed down its 2006 decision on *Hamdan v. Rumsfeld*, which found that President Bush did not have authority to set up the war crimes tribunals and declared special military commissions illegal under both military justice law and the Geneva Conventions) habitually get its own sense of proportion so wildly distorted when it comes to the presidency? What is it about this office that makes its singular occupant—and not the people who elect him—the symbolic center of democracy and national power?

I argue in this book that our historical presidency became attached to a powerful logic that works to condition how citizens feel toward the president. I call this developing logic *presidentialism*. Presidentialism shapes how citizens unconsciously feel about both the president and democratic practice. Unexamined, these trained feelings can pull us in powerfully antidemocratic directions. Crucially, they can confuse us in moments when we have legitimate and pressing questions about the democratic ethics of presidential behavior or about the devaluation of citizen power within our government. By keeping our democratic hopes oriented toward the salvific and powerful president (if not this one, maybe the next one can deliver us), these unconscious feelings keep us from recognizing, remembering, imagining, and exercising the democratic work we can do ourselves and the democratic work that is otherwise going on—and that we too often actually scorn—all around us.

Presidentialism at Work

The Islamic radicals who turned U.S. domestic aircraft into weapons on September 11, 2001, woke the entire United States to the reality and continuing threat of terrorism, branding an enduring moment of historical recognition for a country that had long considered itself collectively exempt from the terrors and violence that have afflicted many other countries in the world.

Looking back, Americans remember how shaken we each were on that day. And if we are fair, even those who now revile George W. Bush and his policy choices since that date remember his thrilling leadership at Ground Zero. As President Bush began his September 14 speech at the site of the collapsed towers, workers at the site's outer limits protested their inability to hear the president. Bush started again, and again workers interrupted: "Can't hear you!" The president then famously went off-script: "I can hear YOU," he responded. "I can hear YOU. The rest of the world hears YOU. And the people who knocked these buildings down will hear from all of us soon." His speech was widely heralded by the press as a defining moment of presidential leadership. This, seemingly, was the moment Americans had been waiting for. Those who feared Bush wasn't up to the job evidently decided he was: his job approval rating, according to media polls, skyrocketed from the mid-50s to over 90 percent, the biggest bump ever received by a president in the polls, and in fact the highest approval rating for a president in documented history.

As I have noted, Americans have come to expect two somewhat contradictory symbolic roles from the president. In one aspect, Americans look for a sense of democratic connection and recognition—a heartwarming unity delivered by the "soft" president who can "feel our pain." In the other, Americans look for an avenging protector, a steely sense of safety that comes through the toughness of the "hard" and unforgiving president. In his improvisation, George W. Bush, with genuine leadership skills and perfect intuition, delivered on both aspects. He united domestic recognition and presidential caring with the promise that his leadership would deliver protection and a strong national response. In this literally iconic moment, the president's words recognized the efforts of the brave New Yorkers, collecting their energy and passion into a strong and focused response. In this moment, Bush stood as the symbolic heart of national unity and democratic agency.

This moment also recuperated a good deal of gathering discontent in the days following the attack, and, interestingly, it effaced another trend—the recognition of the power of ordinary citizens to address the calamity. By all accounts, President Bush's immediate response to 9/11 did not inspire confidence. He seemed strangely slow to register the emerging threat facing the nation, continuing awkwardly to read from a school book and to question the second graders in a Sarasota, Florida, classroom for more than five minutes after the second plane hit. Finally leaving the classroom, he gave a rushed statement to reporters, promising that "terrorism against our nation will not stand." Then he hurried to Air Force One and spent the day flying away from New York City and Washington, D.C., offering the nation only a two-minute, grainy statement with poor sound quality from an airbase in Louisiana, reporting (somewhat behind the point) that "freedom itself was attacked this morning by a faceless coward."

Even his staunch Republican supporters were disturbed by how the president seemed to be running away instead of leading during the nation's crisis. It was nighttime—at the end of a long day of network television replaying the horrifying collapse of the first, then the second, tower over and over, as rumors, fear, and grief grew—before the president made it back to Washington, D.C. At 8:30 p.m., from the Oval Office, Bush delivered another short, poorly coordinated, and unmemorable address, promising only that the day would not be forgotten, that "we go forward to defend freedom and all that is good and just in our world."

But in the gap of presidential leadership, it turns out that the United States had no shortage of heroes and leaders. Mayor Rudy Giuliani sprang into action, collected and focused. But far more memorably than Giuliani, it was the people of New York City, the extraordinarily brave and resolute firefighters, police, emergency workers, medical staff, and citizens who emerged as the heroic actors in this moment of crisis. People all over the nation dropped what they were doing and found their way into the city to offer aid and support. In this calamity, the People instantly

Carly Levy *(right)* hands out water and cookies she bought herself to people waiting in line for up to six hours to donate blood at a temporary center set up in the immediate aftermath of the 9/11 attacks. Photograph by Kathy Willens; courtesy of AP Photo.

emerged as the lifeblood and force of the country, risking their lives, rescuing strangers, coordinating shelter, relief, and recovery. Those outside New York City watched with awe and pride as ordinary people manifested themselves as American heroes. The nation faced a crisis, and the response was democratic power in action: the People took the lead. Frustration and disappointment with the president's awkward and uncoordinated response was outweighed by the growing admiration for the many nameless people acting on the ground in New York City. Flags popped up everywhere, representing a resurgent pride, not just abstractly in "America" but, far more specifically, a rightful and altogether too rarely experienced pride in the abilities and courage of the American *people*.

One brilliant aspect of President Bush's speech on September 14 was to unite the two symbolic modes of the president: at Ground Zero he was both the democratic heart and the national avenger. Another brilliant aspect came in the way that the president stepped into his presidentially ordained role as the symbolic hero. In that moment, President Bush emerged as the central figure for national power, symbolically overshadowing the extraordinary efforts of the men and women at Ground Zero even as he spoke to honor them. In that moment, he activated the powers of presidentialism, signaling that we could all stop worrying and go home, that he would now be taking care of things. Soon, he would make this message literal, telling American citizens that the best response to this extraordinary act of terror and the crisis into which it threw the country was simply to conduct business as usual: go to work, go to school, go on trips, go shopping. As the nation's symbolic hero, President Bush soothingly and effectively *deactivated* citizen heroism and civic agency. And his job approval ratings, pollsters emphasized, went sky-high.

Perhaps there is no surprise in the apparently high approval for Bush in the immediate aftermath of the attacks. But there are some good questions that we should ask ourselves and maybe some useful lessons. The president has historically been at the center of national power in foreign affairs. It's obvious that the nation needs the president to demonstrate leadership in times of crisis, and it's normal for people to want to see that the person elected to the office can act wisely and decisively in a national emergency. But we need to ask why job approval ratings could go sky-high on the basis of a simple speech. Whatever our feeling about the antideliberative nature of public opinion polling, this numerical certification of Bush's abilities to lead provided a measure that guided Congress, which, four days later, handed the president a raft of unilateral powers in the Authorization for Use of Military Force against Terrorists. In so doing, they skated right past the Constitution's provision that such powers belong not with the executive branch but with Congress. The resolution was extraordinarily vague and open-ended, and many members of Congress have come to regret their vote for it. Many citizens are apparently regretting their support, too, as Bush's job approval ratings, based on actual evidence of what he could and would do on the job, plunged in 2007 to lows exceeded only by Richard Nixon in his final days in office. Now, years later, many people want to dissociate themselves from the moment of unity that the 90 percent approval rating reflected to us—"I didn't vote for him"; "I've never trusted him"; "I can't stand the sound of his voice."

So here is a genuinely nonpartisan question worth asking (and I assure you nonpartisan, because as I show, it's not hard to find other such incautious moments in the history of American citizens and their presidents): how is it that American citizens can need so much from the president and can look, according to public opinion sampling, near-entirely satisfied that they're getting it, with so little evidence? Or to put this another way: in the four days that preceded President Bush's visit to Ground Zero, the nation saw *only* national unity on their television sets and in their streets, evidenced by thousands of ordinary citizens helping with relief efforts in myriad ways. So why does that national unity feel most real when the president assumes the role of heroic leader? Why is it somehow less real when it is enacted by thousands? Why do people feel better and safer when the president says he is at the helm and manning the ship, rather than when we are so evidently doing that work ourselves?

The Power of the Presidency

It's probably better to start with something more basic—for example, what is the president's role in democracy? That seems relatively obvious to most: he's our nation's chief executive; our commander in chief; our only generally elected representative. He's the voice of the people, the leader of the free world and democracy, and for that, the most powerful man in the world. When we approve of particular presidents or their actions, we feel the exhilaration of democracy—of feeling connected in one self-governing national community. When we oppose them, we feel they are an embarrassment, a dishonor to the nation and to the office itself, the office that stands for us. When we find ourselves unhappy with our current president, we long for the next opportunity to elect a president we can admire, a president who will rectify the mess this one is making and be the leader the nation deserves.

The present book aims to question this democratic common sense. It argues that we citizens have a powerful, civically and presidentially trained *misunderstanding* of the relation of the president to democracy. The president, cast from the early 1800s as the "leader of democracy," has often been either a bad surrogate for or downright antagonistic to the self-governing interests, abilities, and efforts of the people. The president's *anti*democratic function in U.S. democracy has become normalized both symbolically and structurally. It has gained wider acceptance—and with that, momentum—over time. The more that individual presidents have successfully arrogated power to the executive branch (and most have), the more potentially severe the conflict between the presidency and democracy—the self-governing sovereignty of the people—has become (and, ironically, the more difficult to identify and name as such).

Political historians and commentators in the twentieth century have demarcated "the modern presidency" and have argued that especially since the Great Depression, the demands of modernization and the entailments of bureaucratization have together necessitated enlarging the president's role in the nation's democratic government. But important and underacknowledged aspects of the executive branch's historical proclivity toward self-aggrandizement were incipient in the original constitutional design and were enhanced by emerging U.S. cultural and political practices in the early nation. These proclivities were accelerated by foreign and economic interests and hot as well as cold wars of the twentieth century. Now, as Bush administration lawyers and other sympathetic legal thinkers outline rationales for the unitary executive to justify both public and secret actions that Bush has authorized in the war on terror (like military tribunals, brutal interrogation techniques for prisoners, and unwarranted domestic wiretapping), the executive branch is taking yet another hard turn away from the principles of democracy, if by democracy we mean something closer, rather than farther away from, self-government by the people. Bush is doing it—ironically—in the name of "democracy," for one key argument offered by unitary executive advocates is that the president represents the people, and the people, as they observe, have never objected to power grabs by presidents.

Of course that argument is incorrect: people have *always* objected to power grabs by the president, from Washington onward. Citizens objected to Washington's suppression of the Whiskey Rebellion, and they complained against Andrew Jackson's arrogance with the veto, as well as his handling of the U.S. Bank. They excoriated Abraham Lincoln for his wartime suspension of habeas corpus. They reacted to FDR's Court-packing plan by calling him a "dictator." They condemned John F. Kennedy, Lyndon Johnson, and Nixon for secret wartime maneuvers. They reviled Nixon's abuses of power, lambasted Clinton's, and are condemning those of George W. Bush. Sure, they've never massed at the White House to throw a president physically out of office, but presumably this should not be what it takes to register citizen disapproval. And yet proponents of the unitary executive theory are only half wrong. As often as citizens have objected, they have also enjoyed and celebrated manifestations of presidential power, starting with Washington. While people resent the power assumed by presidents they personally dislike, they tend *in general* to approve of presidential power. As I will show, this is precisely because our expectations of what the president can and should do both domestically and internationally are so unrealistic. Typically, when people are dissatisfied with a president's performance, the most reliable answer has been to give the office *more* power, the power that promises to allow the occupant to "get the job done." It has come to seem that the better the president is at getting his job done, the more powerful our experience of democracy.

Democracy and Disagreement

So what do we mean when we say "democracy"? Self-rule is one of the most radical, fundamentally innovative political aspirations in human history. But however much democracy is celebrated in theory, it's not a set formula—it's not even clearly a form of government. There have been many different forms of government that stake a claim to the title of democracy. No one system gets democracy exactly right: it has always been a struggle figuring out how to enact it, let alone keep it going. In the early years of the United States, the framers famously rejected democracy as a model, insisting that the face-to-face negotiations between (at least some) citizens prescribed in classical models like fifth-century Athens, and increasingly practiced in town meetings across the young nation, were im-

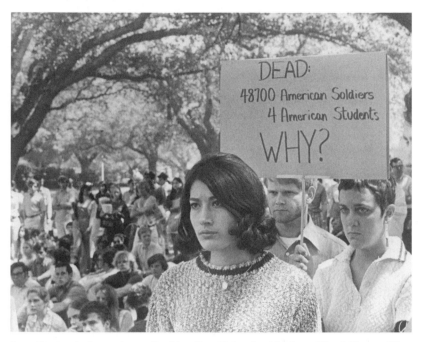

Luana Perea and other students at Louisiana State University objecting to Nixon's Vietnam War policies and the Kent State massacre in 1970. Courtesy of Office of Public Relations, Records, RG #A5000-0020.1, Louisiana State University Archives, LSU Libraries, Baton Rouge, Louisiana.

practical for a geographically and economically expanding nation. The framers engineered a representative system to accommodate the energy, aims, and needs of a diverse and growing nation. Their system took democracy out of the hands of the *demos*—the many, the people—and put it into fewer, presumably more efficient and qualified, hands: their elected representatives. But the people, while ratifying the Constitution's representative system, did not forget the democratic power that they had begun consolidating in the fight for national independence or the democratic practices that they had participated in before and during the war. They have never stopped fighting through one avenue or another for democracy, and these struggles, as many Americans proudly remember, have resulted in key expansions of citizen power and civic rights throughout the United States' history.

We treasure the democratic spirit of our nation's founding and its expansions of access and rights. But every such expansion has taken years of political struggle. Sometimes it has taken lives. Democracy is notoriously difficult to institute, and it's just as hard to maintain. Because of the effort it takes—because people have to take responsibility for it, fight for it, watch over it, nourish it—many buy the argument that a participatory democracy is an impractical ideal, and we therefore shouldn't be too worried about letting our leaders govern for us in the best ways they see fit. I don't agree, either in principle or in fact. My definition of democracy is the simple one, taken from the original Greek: *demos* (people) + *kratia* (power). Democracy is happening when the people have and can use the power of self-governance. Simple to say and hard to realize, especially so because we don't ever get to struggle for democracy in ideal conditions—democracy is the art of making something decent together out of whatever we've currently got. And what we have now are "representative institutions" that most people don't feel are working for them, as seen by presidential and congressional approval ratings. What we've got now is precious little public trust—which is undeniably bad for democracy.

Yet it may be that we've been wrong to attach our hopes for democracy to institutions. This is not to say that formal institutions can't support democracy; it is simply to point out, as political theorist C. Douglas Lummis wisely observes, that institutions can only be a *means* to democracy: they cannot be democracy itself. Rather, we might more fruitfully think of democracy as a spirit we the people guard and nurture, a goal that we are always working toward, and that democracy won't exist if we stop guarding, nurturing, and working at it. In other words, democracy is neither the government's shape nor its responsibility: the responsibility for democracy belongs to us, the people, together. Then the question becomes (and it's the BIG question): how do we effectively guard and nurture that spirit, and measure and maximize its presence in our government and in our lives, in the midst of our ongoing disagreements and differences?

U.S. citizens have always been attached to democracy and for good reason: because we like to play a part in shaping our own destiny; because it's better to do the hard work of self-governing than to be ruled by even benevolent despots; because, as difficult as it can be, it can also be very satisfying to do this work together. I don't take as an accident or a sign of bad education that most Americans describe the United States' political system as a democracy when in fact it is more accurately a *republic*—a form of government based on representation and the consent of the governed, rather than on the daily involvement of a self-governing people. This habit of misnaming is a residue of the ongoing struggle for and appreciation of the principle of the people's sovereignty in the United States. It's a way of holding on to what the United States' formal government charter, the Constitution, starts from ("We the People") and then puts at a certain representative distance from its citizens.

Liking democracy in theory and liking it in practice, though, are two different things. The difficult distance between the two might have something to do with the way we're content to keep calling our system a democracy as it becomes less and less evidently so. Self-rule means navigating never-ending disagreement among a diverse people. It's about figuring out how to put deliberation together with action. It's not work we can do alone, as individuals. Self-rule is a project we do together in public, as a people: The People. That is hard, often messy, sometimes downright ugly work and adds on to the things we already have to do to manage our lives from day to day, where self-rule at an individual level seems like enough of a project. Democracy is the best political principle human history has yet discovered for navigating the difficulties of fostering, building, and maintaining community—*if* we want to deal with the people we live among. Democracy says that people are smart enough to figure things out together, but it doesn't map how to resolve anything or how to get along in the meantime. Thus the problem and discomforts of disagreement are perpetually present with any project associated with democratic self-rule.

In our nation, it's become easy to scare people away from the work (as opposed to the ideal) of democracy by threatening them with disagreement. For instance, the media often describe heated democratic deliberation and deal making in Congress with terms like "nasty," "ferocious," and "scathing" (Jon Stewart's *Daily Show* hilariously mocked this habit on its January 24, 2008, episode). This makes democratic disagreement sound like a *danger*. And so we learn to retreat from such dangers—as indeed, we have. Bill Bishop documents in *The Big Sort: Why the Clustering of Like-Minded America Is Tearing Us Apart* how we are more and more politically insulated, choosing workplace environments, church communities, leisure activities, and neighborhoods where people do not challenge our political beliefs. This notable, nationwide trend over the past thirty years toward political self-enclaving adds to and is perhaps symptomatic of the presidential depoliticization I describe here. This cocooning aims to protect our political values. But it does so only by hermetically sealing them off from the bracing challenges of deliberation, from the oxygen that disagreement and reconsideration offer to our political being and knowing. It cordons off our political values, ironically, from the very politicalness that democracy depends on, which political theorist Sheldon Wolin describes this way: "By politicalness I mean our capacity for developing into beings who know and value what it means to participate in and be responsible for the care and improvement of our common collective life."

It's not incidental to my observations about the growing depoliticization of our democracy that the president, as the nation's only nationally elected representative, quadrennially promises to take care of our conflicts and end partisan "rancor." His singular resolve contrasts appealingly with the uglier contending personalities and agendas that characterize our disagreements on the ground or that we see playing out in the so-called democratic branch: the legislature. (Indeed, presidents habitually portray legislative debate—Congress's never-ending disagreements—as a sign of its governmental *weakness*. President after president has scolded members of Congress, asking them to set aside their differences in the name of "bipartisanship," implicitly contrasting their propensity for childish disagreement with his more adult determination.) The president knows how much we dislike disagreement, among ourselves or among our political representatives. Every four years, he promises that if we elect him by defeating his opponent, he'll unify the nation and make the unpleasantness of political disagreement go away. He'll lead the nation into a more compassionate, unified, and stronger future.

That's an attractive offer (at least, when it's your candidate who is doing the talking—we tend to feel revulsion when we hear the other candidate saying the same thing). What is fascinating about the presidency, from its constitutional inception to this day, is that it appeals to primal desires within ordinary humans—a desire for strong leadership (someone who will put an end, at least temporarily, to our problems, who will relieve us of the work that comes with responsibility) and a desire for unified community. These are not in themselves undemocratic desires, but if they become so strong or habitual that they overpower other key democratic desires—a desire to exercise responsibility within our political system and society, a desire to create and sustain working community, a desire to find positive solutions out of our differences, a desire to grow the civic commonwealth—they begin to work against democracy, turning us toward something more like demagoguery or a plebiscitary presidency (let's sketch the difference: democracy means self-government; representative democracy means government through elected representatives; demagoguery means having popularly supported rulers). The symbolics that quickly arose around the presidency with its founding in 1789 cultivated and continue to cultivate feelings that work against our democratic politicalness, teaching citizens to abjure political disagreement, and—importantly—to feel most democratic in the moment that we cede our self-governing agency to the president. We might more properly call this pseudodemocracy, in which the citizen's presidentially conditioned habit of feeling "democratic" in the moment of voting for the president's power imperils the vitality of our nation's vaunted political system and its democratic future.

Bad for Democracy does not make a party-based argument: neither Republicans nor Democrats should be blamed for this predicament. Nearly every president, regardless of party affiliation, has as a candidate denounced the presidential power grabs of the current officeholder. And every president since FDR has attempted to overpower the judicial and legislative branches. This pattern can start to seem like the normal working of our fabled constitutional design of checks and balances. But the presidency's steady success at accumulating more and more power for the executive branch despite occasional setbacks might clue us in to look away from individual presidents and examine the history and structure of the office itself, as well as the dynamics between the presidency and the citizens in whose name, and with whose power, the president governs.

Does Democracy Need a Commander in Chief?

The first part of my argument is simple enough: it's not particular presidents who are a problem for U.S. democracy, it's presidentialism. Presidentialism characterizes the unconscious power that the presidency works on citizens, and it describes the gravitational symbolic and institutional place that the presidency assumes within U.S. government. We understand the president's strength to be the strength of U.S. democracy. Although the hallmark of constitutional democracy is the separated and balanced powers of the three governmental branches, executive, legislative, and judicial, the fact is, when we think democracy, we think of the president. Legislatures and judges alike are factually more likely to assist than to impede the president. On the rare occasions that they set up a roadblock, they are often depicted by media and understood by citizens to be *interfering* with the president's power and the democratic process.

Presidentialism has trained us for this conclusion, and insofar as it succeeds, it works to undermine our democratic proclivities and skill building. Baldly put, presidentialism has been bad for democracy. Despite the particular virtues and leadership skills of some presidents, presidentialism works against peoples' civic cultivation of democratic skills. It trains us to want the president to take care of democracy for us instead of remembering that democracy, properly defined, is *our* job. Presidentialism depoliticizes citizens, making us less inclined to think and, thus, less likely to participate in self-governing. Presidentialism encourages people to see democracy as a winner-take-all endeavor in world politics as well as in the domestic sphere, an arena where presidential candidates go *mano a mano* and then when the winner ascends to office, the losers (and his supporter-constituents) fade from view. This teaches citizens to see negotiation and compromise as the weakness, not the strength, of democracy. Presidentialism trains people to see democracy as being both led and symbolized by a single person, a strong leader standing for a strong consensus, instead of remembering that disagreement is a productive working principle for democracy. In this way, presidentialism makes people fundamentally uncomfortable with one of the most important motors for political freedom and agency. It leads us to see and thus to overemphasize democracy as unity, instead of helping us remember that a decently functioning *dis*unity can provide better solutions and make an even stronger nation.

The civically trained desire to see the U.S. president as "the most powerful man in the world" has had the effect of allowing individual presidents incrementally and steadily to increase the power of that branch, most recently in the aftermath of 9/11, when Congress gave to the executive their branch's right to supervise war powers (a constitutional power that Congress has in fact not exercised since December 8, 1941). In this sense, presidentialism is colonizing democracy for its own powers and purposes, depending on the people to keep believing that the executive's power is somehow our power instead of recognizing that the truth is exactly the opposite. Whether particular presidents are good or not, the increase of presidential power concretely diminishes our democracy, by taking prestige as well as power from what was historically denominated the "people's branch," the legislature, and ultimately by taking it away from the people. No single person can make democratic decisions, since democracy gets its vitality from people negotiating their differences to find positive solutions. And even if we account for the fact that presidents seldom make decisions without drawing on the resources and counsel of their cabinet, the fact is, members of their cabinet are neither elected by nor accountable to U.S. citizens.

Using our Constitution as a measure, presidential analysts argue that the executive branch has steadily encroached on the powers of the other two branches—although they differ in their opinion of the effects of this redistribution of power. As political scientists Matthew Crenson and Benjamin Ginsberg summarize in a recent essay, "Downsizing Democracy, Upsizing the Presidency": "September 11 may have represented a lethal landmark for international terrorism, but in fact it was just another milepost in the expansion of presidential power." The Bush administration's appeal for presidential powers in the aftermath of the al-Qaeda attack was by no means unprecedented but part of a steady trend by presidents to expand executive powers that began with Thomas Jefferson's Louisiana Purchase. This trend accelerated rapidly in the twentieth century, and especially since the Reagan presidency, such that we have moved decisively away from our constitutionally organized congressional government to something the framers neither aimed at nor, seemingly, even anticipated: the twentieth-century innovation of presidential government.

Despite the breathtaking accumulation of presidential power during the twentieth century, many presidential analysts continue to highlight the president's *lack* of power, competing, depending, and cooperating as he must with the two other branches. These scholars may be using a corporate executive as their comparison. Corporate executives have more unilateral control of their company than the founders seemingly intended the president to have. George W. Bush, with an MBA degree from Harvard, recognized the power of this analogy and staked his appeal in his 2000 campaign on his qualifications to meld the national executive office with his qualifications as a corporate executive, asserting that, as *New York Times Magazine* reporter James Bennett summarized in "America, Inc.: The M.B.A. President.": "Good management . . . makes good politics." Bush underlined and drew on this analogy to corporate management to frame his job as our nation's executive officer. His emergence as our "nation's first M.B.A. president" correlates with a notable expansion of executive office powers in the business community. Organizational behavioralist Rakesh Khurana outlines how in the 1990s, corporate culture developed a preference for outsider CEOs with star appeal rather than insiders with functional expertise or industry qualifications. This growing—and in Khurana's account, irrational—preference for charisma over experience has created a cycle where CEOs are handed higher salaries, unparalleled power, and ever higher shareholder expectations. Their inability to meet these expectations has somehow only fueled the trend, which has been, as Khurana outlines, increasingly costly to businesses, workers, shareholders, and consumers. The many and various failures of this so-called corporate savior have accelerated corporate instability. While analysts have begun thinking about the costs of such myths for corporate and business culture, we have not yet pursued the implications of such behavior for our common political culture. This behavior fits hand in glove with the increasing political powers that corporations have over citizens, not just in work life but in political, that is to say, democratic, life. As corporations can now buy more voting and lobbying power than ordinary citizens, as corporate shareholders now seemingly have disproportionate shares of economic and political power, we might want to start thinking about how the economic modeling of presidential power functions as a shell game, offering a kind of oligarchic feudalism tricked out as democracy's future.

To return to more properly political analogies: while many presidential scholars compare the president's powers negatively with those of prime ministers, whose agendas are not impeded by the distribution of power to other legislative branches, others observe that the U.S. president has far more power in setting foreign policy agendas. While he may be more hamstrung domestically by Congress's legislative capacity, the president does not bear the responsibility—and therefore the limits on power and agenda—that being leader of his party entails for the prime minister. Presidential scholars and analysts often describe how the separation and balance of powers keeps the president comparatively weak (especially with regard to domestic policy), and how demands put on his office by public and international expectation combine with his structural dependency on the other branches to create a lot of "frustration" for individual presidents. Scholars call this the "paradox" or the "ambiguity" of presidential power.

But the fact is, as comparative political scientist Arend Liphart frames it, no one seems very committed to the idea of executive checks and cooperative government. *Everyone* wants the president to have power: the president, the legislature, journalists, analysts, scholars, citizens. Our expectations for leadership are powerfully and unconsciously shaped by even mythical expectations of what leaders—and especially presidents—can do. Citizens expect the president not just to oversee the execution of laws passed by Congress but to *fix the nation's problems*. We feel betrayed—personally—when he doesn't and punish him accordingly in the polls. The inability of the executive to fix all our problems is partly what presidential historians mean when they call him comparatively weak. The word *weak* makes it sound as if the president should ideally have *more* power rather than lead us to consider that our expectations for what presidents can and should do are both deeply unrealistic and counterproductive to the democracy we say we treasure. Rather than question our own expectations, though, we are encouraged by such analyses to see more power for the president as the solution to his—and our—problems. After all, who wants a weak president?

Organizational behavioralists and business analysts have described these inflated and unrealistic expectations of organizational leaders in the corporate world as the "myth of leadership," a paradigm we might apply to our analysis of democratic culture. The myth of leadership becomes more pronounced in times of social or political uncertainty. In societies that consider hierarchies necessary, people turn to leaders when they feel out of control, looking to them to put things in order. Leadership, then, has both factual and symbolic dimensions, which are often wildly misaligned. Our habit of expecting superhero qualities from leaders may help explain why voters find candidates attached to powerful fictional characters (like Reagan's Captain Casey Abbott, or Arnold Schwarzenegger's Terminator) compelling candidates for executive office. What is perhaps more difficult to explain and as important to account for, though, is that these fantasies about presidential power condition not just how citizens vote but also how political analysts and historians describe the president and, even more consequentially, how political leaders (like members of Congress) in Washington respond to him.

The book that follows does not pose the expected polemic solution to its polemic analysis. The second part of my argument is also simple, although admittedly more challenging: we are not powerless about this. Democracy's sovereign power comes from us and manifests in the political world we make together. So there's a great deal that regular citizens, working together, can do about the problems I ascribe to presidentialism. But we don't need to dump the president so much as we need to de-center the presidency from its place within our own political needs, action charts, and voting preferences. My ambition for change is thus arguably simple, yet could have important effects (including, I ardently hope, a significant take-back of powers habitually granted to the executive office). We can and should work to give the office of the president both less symbolic and less actual power in our day-to-day relationship with democracy. The aim of this book is to reveal presidentialism's perennially problematic relationship to democratic self-governance and to encourage citizens to rethink our relationship to the presidency, resuscitating and reenergizing our democratic agency and involvement.

Why focus solely on the president if I care so much about democratic participation? Why not focus on other problems, like voter apathy or campaign finance reform? Such questions highlight exactly why I want us to start rethinking our relationship to democracy by getting over our obsession with the necessity of presidential leadership for it. If we stopped obsessing over getting the right person into office, by the right means (getting more people to vote, getting different candidates by altering the balances of economic power), we would have a good deal more interest and energy to give to all kinds of democratic reforms. In other words, such questions assume I'm asking my readers to do the opposite of what I'm suggesting and provide a precise index of the problem I'm analyzing. I'm not saying "let's stay obsessed with the president." I'm saying the opposite: let's *dump* our obsession with him. Let's get over the president and imagine and create a democratic politicalness that doesn't play straight into his hands. However counterintuitive it sounds (and exactly insofar as it does sound counterintuitive), I believe that if we stopped putting so much of our energy into getting the right president, we would have surplus energy for the hard work of negotiating the problems that face our democratic system. We could accomplish voter reinvigoration and campaign finance reform through other avenues than finding the president who might support such agendas. Our project in self-governance can become more vital, robust, and accommodating. If we stop expecting so much from the president and fixating on our dissatisfaction with what he does and does not accomplish, we will be able to see that our democracy is *already* far more vital than we have been imagining, rich in civic possibility and citizen activism all around us.

Bad for Democracy

This book is about how the presidency came to be so powerful and why that's bad, both for democratic government and for *us* as citizens of the world's "leading" democracy. It's about why we don't have to surrender to our presidentially trained civic powerlessness, and what we can do instead of surrendering. This book differs significantly from other recent critiques of executive branch power in its willingness to analyze the institution of the presidency rather than blame particular actors, and in its optimism about our ability to challenge these powers and change our democratic future. It asks readers honestly to confront our less rational hopes and desires not so much for any particular president but for the *presidency,* to think critically about what these hopes and desires contribute to the democratic history we are making together, and to consider possible ways that we can help democracy recognize its power as an open system, a project that doesn't look for leaders but instead toward catalysts and toward broad and varied routes for participation.

Several questions guide my project:

- Why do we think democracy needs a leader?
- What are the costs of presidentialism for democratic culture, imagination, and practice?
- How did the idea of democratic self-government become reduced to its thinnest version: voting for the president?
- What happens when we sign off on the idea that the president is our nation's commander in chief?
- What happens if we "stay the course" and let presidentialism, now in the form of the unitary executive, have its way?
- What are concrete steps we can take, if we care about this problem, to stop it and change the course of our nation's experiment with democracy, such that we can participate more fully in its future?

I develop the first part of this book's argument, about the history of presidentialism and its current tendencies, over four chapters. The first chapter looks at how the president became the nation's symbolic hero, taking us from Washington to Reagan. It starts with some issues surrounding the Constitution's framing, then turns to a pivotal and famous text, Mason Locke Weems's "I cannot tell a lie" biography of Washington. This enduring work presented Washington in terms of what people would come to know more familiarly in the twentieth century as a "super-hero," and studying it helps us see how presidentialism, from early in the nineteenth century, begins converting democratic energies aimed at the public sphere into private feelings aimed at an idealized president. Next, this chapter turns to the dramatic, crisis-driven presidency of FDR and looks at how the emerging popularity of cartoon, radio, and television superheroes—from Superman and Wonderman to Tarzan and the Lone Ranger—coordinated with political events of the period and the expansion of the media, allowing people to accept FDR's often questionable expansions of presidential powers and executive bureaucracy as just the heroic rescue democracy needed. During this period we can see how an American myth about the presidency broadens. This myth teaches that regular Americans, passive, disorganized, and in distress, need to depend on the extraordinary (and possibly extralegal) interventions of the president, who, like a superhero, will wreak a satisfying vengeance for their wrongs and save the day—and the nation. Both Kennedy and Reagan would successfully elaborate on this formula to cement their popularity later in the twentieth century. It's made for a satisfying story, but, unfortunately, it leaves us stranded in real time. Believing that the solution for democratic problems can come only through the intervention of a "great president," we invest our best political energy into supporting his power rather than cultivating our own powers as citizens.

Chapter 2 studies how democratization in the United States became idealized as voting for the president and how this link is not so much democratic as *pseudo*democratic. It studies how voting for the president came to be so central in U.S. democracy and tries to account for why the presidential campaign season leaves so many of us feeling dissatisfied and democratically powerless. The chapter begins with some attention to the late eighteenth century, when Americans were experimenting—passionately—with democracy and reformulating their renounced support of the king as enthusiasm for the United States' new president. It then focuses on the controversial and popular President Jackson, to study what is known as the democratization of the presidency, and to ask whether Americans actually got more democracy as a result of getting the right to vote for the president. Jackson invented the notion of the presidential mandate (although the Princeton-educated President Woodrow Wilson would name it), and he wielded it in the name of the "common man." But what, besides a more focused sensation of representation, did the common man gain? The chapter follows these questions into the Progressive Era of the early twentieth century, when, again appealing to the interests of the common man, Wilson reconceived the president as the main agent for democracy. His arguments have become the textbook rationale for what we now know as "presidential government"—something other than what the framers designed—and supplied the logic that FDR would use in his massive expansion of the executive branch. During this era, voter participation began to fall precipitously. It has never since achieved the levels witnessed in the late nineteenth century. The remainder of the chapter is devoted to probing that problem: if we think democracy culminates in the right to vote, why are fewer and fewer of us bothering?

Chapter 3 analyzes the presidency's developing wartime ambitions and how the president's constitutionally authorized foreign power has accumulated over time to legitimate his *domestic* function as "commander in chief." The chapter begins by looking at how debates about presidential war powers were framed in the Constitutional Convention, then studies the crucial shift in the understanding of war powers that Lincoln initiated during the Civil War. It examines how twentieth-century presidents eagerly seized on war powers as a way to expand other executive powers, necessitating their reliance on a strategy of overplaying crises—the historian Arthur Schlesinger memorably summarized this strategy as "scaring the hell out of the country." Presidents have faced Supreme Court repudiation for their war-funded overreaching, but they have also received crucial supports, and thus the president's association with wartime command has most recently culminated in President Bush's early-term refusal to explain himself to the American public. Offering explanations is not something commanders have to do, he famously opined to Bob Woodward. But this notion—that our president is also our commander in chief—has nothing to do with and indeed perverts the framers' intentions. This assumption functions to militarize our political and social culture, and, worse, it accomplishes a crucial reversal of the location of sovereignty in a democracy, attributing sovereign powers to the president—as though they originate in him and his office. Thus people are encouraged to forget democracy's most revolutionary grant: the power lies with the people.

The fourth chapter concentrates on the development of what scholars are calling "presidential power tools"—unilateral presidential powers that remain largely unknown to the general public—and studies their implementation from Reagan to George W. Bush. It pays particular attention to rationales for a theory of the presidency that began to be articulated during Reagan's years in office, known as the "unitary executive," a theory about and strategy for accumulating presidential power that every president since has protected and supported. It details how this business, or CEO, model for the presidency reframes democracy in oligarchic terms, giving business interests greater agency within democracy than its putative citizens. Unitary executive theory is frank in its bid for government supremacy, nowhere more clearly than during the Bush–Cheney years in office. This is not, it's important to understand, something that President Bush and Vice President Cheney have cooked up on their own. It is an organized movement that will not disappear after this administration takes its curtain calls. Its most enthusiastic proponents since the turn of the twenty-first century have harnessed the reversal of sovereignty accomplished by presidents' parading as commander in chief, to argue for expansions of presidential powers that would put their prerogatives on par with that of kings. So far, the theory has received only minimal press coverage—mostly around the time that Chief Justice John Roberts and Justice Samuel Alito were undergoing Senate questioning prior to their confirmation. If I began this book as a contrarian exercise, trying to get people to realize the difference between a democratically organized government (which might need a president) and democracy itself (which, I'll argue, doesn't), I now have reason to make a much more urgent plea. This book is not so much a thought experiment as an appeal for people to pull back on presidential powers before it is literally too late. It's time for those of us who care about democracy to pay attention to the well-organized push for the unitary executive and to mobilize against it.

In the closing chapter, I develop the second part of my argument: we're not powerless. Democratic power belongs to us. But we're way out of practice, not in the least because of the extent to which we've all participated in political self-enclaving—surrounding ourselves with like-minded people, news sources, and forms of entertainment that support instead of challenge our ideals. I outline my ideas about what democratic practice might become if citizens could junk the idea that we need the president to lead democracy, as well as the idea that it only works with people who already agree with us. Democracy is a project for independence, but it also depends and can thrive on our *inter*dependence. Drawing on energizing examples of open systems projects—on the Internet and in activist culture—this chapter asks readers to reimagine and retake democracy as a project we lead together, amid and out of the synergy of our many differences. It asks readers to invest in a democratic project in self-governance that recovers the often forgotten, crucial middle clause of Lincoln's resonant formulation: of the people, *by* the people, for the people.

Chapter 1
How the President Becomes a Superhero

WHAT MAKES PRESIDENTS—USUALLY AGING, AND NOT ALWAYS physically fit, men—good models for action toys? Type "presidential action toys" into an Internet search, and you might be surprised at how many of our nation's leaders have been fitted out as action-adventure playthings. For example, BBI (Blockbuster, Inc.) proudly describes its Elite Force President George W. Bush action-figure toy:

> This limited-edition action figure is a meticulous 1:6 scale recreation of the Commander-in-Chief's appearance during his historic Aircraft Carrier landing. On May 1, 2003, President Bush landed on the USS Abraham Lincoln (CVN-72) in the Pacific Ocean. . . . While at the controls of an S-3B Viking aircraft from the "Blue Sea Wolves" of Sea Control Squadron Three Five (VS-35), designated "Navy 1," he overflew the carrier before handing it over to the pilot for landing. Attired in full naval aviator flight equipment, the President then took the salute on the deck of the carrier.

At the routine action-figure price of $24.99, this presidential action figure takes its place beside other superhero figures, like Arnold Schwarzenegger's Terminator (as with Bush, Schwarzenegger is available in a three-piece-suited "executive" version, too), as well as jokier ones, like the "You don't know Dick" Cheney action figure (complete with "shotgun and retractable kick spike shoes"). BBI's Bush and his friends can help kids re-create cinematic portrayals of the president as an action hero, for instance, Harrison Ford's President Jack Marshall in *Air Force One* (whom *Variety*'s Todd McCarthy summarized as a "kick-butt action hero").

Even more, the U.S. president naval aviator hero can hope to measure

The Lonely Decider Making Heroic Decisions and Keeping Democracy Safe. *The Daily Show* spoofs President George W. Bush for his superhero rhetoric. The Decider artwork by R. Sikoryak; courtesy of *The Daily Show* and Comedy Central.

up someday to the life-size reinvention of our nation's first president at Mount Vernon. According to an AP story dated October 28, 2006, worried that George Washington was being perceived as "a dour, stodgy historical figure," Mount Vernon officials raised $110 million to revamp his image. So along with many other multimedia improvements to the facility, they paid forensic scientists to create a life-size figure of Washington and to cast him as the "nation's first action hero." That might sound like a pathetic attempt to catch our first president up with contemporary popular culture, but Mount Vernon officials are not innovating as much as news coverage might lead us to think. Washington was created as an action hero within a few years of his death. The idea that the president has superhero powers is one of the office's most enduring associations, a durable folklore that has witnessed significant enhancements over time. This chapter outlines how the president came to be a superhero and considers how—and to what ends—the presidential superhero becomes the leader of our democracy.

Inventing the President

Washington is so enshrined in our national memory that it surprises most people to realize that our country's first organization for government, the Articles of Confederation, did not provide for a president. In fact, the nation did not have one until thirteen years after declaring independence. If we learn anything about the first organization of the United States, it is that the Articles of Confederation led to weak government. Discovering that it lacked an executive office certainly reinforces that picture. The Constitution, we know, was designed to remedy the flaws of the nation's original organization of government. The solution, a federally structured "strong government," was emblematized by the president: the executive office was both a structural fix and a symbol for strong federal reorganization.

It's worth pausing to rethink some of this historical shorthand about "weak" and "strong" government. The 1780s are commonly represented as a time of crisis in national history that necessitated the formulation of a strong national government: this is precisely how participants in the Constitutional Convention represented the case. But this is a description that historian Gordon Wood has characterized as "incongruous":

> On the surface at least the American states appeared remarkably stable and prosperous. . . . Both the Confederation government and the governments of the separate states had done much to stabilize the finances and the economy of the country. The . . . Confederation deficit could not be considered serious. Despite a temporary depression in the middle eighties . . . the period was marked by extraordinary economic growth. In fact . . . it was a period of high expectations, clearly reflected in the rapid rate of population growth.

Whether or not there was a definable crisis, the Constitution's advocates effectively harnessed the notion to emerging political diversity and class dissent in the newly formed United States. Federalist proponents used "crisis" to deploy a political counteroffensive against what John Adams, James Madison, and others castigated as democratic or popular despotism: developing local traditions and reconceptualizations of equalitarian practice increasingly manifest throughout the United States.

Under the first organization of government—the horizontally organized "firm league of friendship" entered into by the coequal states under the Articles—citizens began insisting locally on participatory practices of representation along with more direct modes of democratic self-governance. This movement was expressed in new, strict residency requirements for representatives; expanded suffrage definitions framed to ensure structures for electoral consent; and a model of equally weighted electoral districts that reflected the one-state one-vote rule of the Articles of Confederation. Citizens began showing up at legislative sessions to deliver instructions to their delegates, and even more pointedly, some stopped sending delegates to the state legislatures, preferring to conduct government closer to home. This growing democratic involvement was amplified in the increasing phenomenon of extragovernmental organizations of people: county assemblies, watchdog committees, radical associations, and other "unofficial" out-of-door actions. We typically remember these self-organizations of citizens in the framers' hostile terms, as a threat to orderly government. This might sometimes have been true. But from another vantage, we can just see them as people excited about and experimenting with new practices of participatory self-government. This is not to advocate that democracy should be run by mob action; it's simply to point out a historically documented surge of enthusiasm for the possibilities opened up by the ideal of democracy and let us remember the excitement of this period of historical and political innovation, when people took up the work of self-governing.

It was this democratic excitement that the new office of the president was designed, in part, to calm. This office was built to transcend the local enthusiasm and contradictory positions of disagreeing citizens (remember that in its original design, the Constitution allowed for the popular election only of congressional representatives, not senators or presidents). According to the authors of the *Federalist Papers,* the president, chosen by electors delegated by state legislatures, would reflect a refined and rational version of "the sense of the people." The distance pyramidically installed between the people's general, "disorderly" interests and the president's judicious distillation of their singular interest designated the president as the nation's supremely objective representative agent. Thus this new office was presented as a means for cleaning up the messiness and unpredictability of interpersonal, local democracy: the president was the symbolic guarantor for the Constitution's scientific, impersonal system for representative national politics.

Our democracy is unthinkable now without the president. But this office was not immediately popular or even commonsensical. We of course easily recall that the colonists who banded together to throw off British power opposed the monarchy. So it's unsurprising that they opposed vesting a single person with power over government and thus supported the Articles of Confederation for how it envisioned each state as a coequal player in the project of self-government. (In fact, in each session Congress elected a person to preside over that body as its executive officer, so it's not as though Congress under the Articles had no principle of organization or point man.) The not-so-recently former colonists of the late 1780s continued to be suspicious of anything that smacked of monarchical powers, having already developed some affection for the privileges and responsibilities of self-governance.

Indeed, many commentators of the period and historians in years since argue that the notion of such an office or of the executive branch might not have sold at all, except for the widespread assumption that General Washington, the military hero of the Revolution, would assume its duties. The framers may well have consented to give the office the scope that they did, despite their own anxieties about reinstalling anything that smacked of monarchy, only because they imagined it through the lens of Washington's well-known humility, restraint, and commitment to republican principles. Pierce Butler, a delegate from South Carolina (and author of the Constitution's fugitive slave clause), later reflected on the important influence that the delegates' knowledge of Washington had on the job description for the executive:

> I am free to acknowledge that his powers (the President's) are full great, and greater than I was disposed to make them. Nor, *entre nous*, do I believe they would have been so great had not many of the members cast their eyes towards George Washington as President; and shaped their ideas of the powers to be given to a President by their opinions of his virtues.

Washington's extraordinary reputation and his own presidential history have managed to overshadow the interesting debates about the executive office that developed during the Convention itself. For instance, the framers discussed having Congress elect the executive, like a prime minister. They debated forming the office so that it would be shared by several people: a multiple executive. Supporters liked the idea of having men from different regions to balance the presidency's political representation across the differing interests of the country. This idea was debated seriously, but it is not clear from available records of the proceedings why the topic was dropped. It was abandoned perhaps in favor of arguments like those made by the Federalists, that a single executive would offer more "energy" and "vigor" (notions connected to the idea of governmental strength) as well as readier accountability. For unknown reasons, the notion of the multiple executive lost—maybe for the good. But it is worth pausing over its appearance in the debate and considering the different emblematic resonances of these two conceptions of the office. While a singular president could effectively symbolize and perhaps more effectively enact "energy," "vigor," and "unity," the multiple executive promised something different: to model representative democracy as the process of creating plus-sum solutions out of disagreement. This model for the executive might have slowed the political process—and it might well have changed the course of U.S. history. It would have offered an entirely distinct symbol for national leadership, creating a substantively different correspondence between the role of the executive office and the work of democracy.

Yet even in the face of their admiration for Washington and their an-

---

BAD FOR DEMOCRACY

ticipation that he would agree to serve the nation as its first president, the framers did not in fact give the executive branch the kinds of sweeping powers we associate with the office today (or that proponents of the unitary executive theory currently claim for it). In the language of the U.S. Constitution, the president is not the leader of democracy. Quite differently, he is the executive of the institutions that are designed to support representative democratic self-government. He is, in the somewhat vague description of our founding document, a *functionary* of republican government, albeit with the strength of his own branch.

The Constitution, as we know, both defines and limits the power of the three branches. Its description of presidential powers, however, is both less extended and less precise than its description of the scope and limits of the legislative and judicial branches—a vagueness within which claims to executive power have found traction. Why would the founders have been so vague about such a controversial office? Some historians attribute their imprecision to the reassuring presence of Washington, whose example, the framers may have anticipated, would define and set a tone for future officeholders. Others ascribe it to the framers' inability to reach agreement on the scope of presidential power.

It also seems possible that understandings of the founders' "intent" have changed with the times. To take a prominent example of such a historical shift, the Constitution denominates the president as "commander in chief." This is a title that seemingly decrees wide powers over democracy for the president. But most governmental historians agree that the title—invented by King Charles of England in 1639 and regularly granted to the British colonies' governors—was a simple and hollow formality, not a signal that the president was to be vested with supreme constitutional agency (as current proponents of the unitary executive theory claim). The framers gave the legislative branch, not the executive, the power to declare and fund war, to call up the militia, to provide for the common defense, and other powers associated with national defense and wartime aggression.

Even the most prominent spokesmen on behalf of the Constitution and its innovation of the executive office, the authors of the *Federalist*

Papers, were quite explicit that there was no intent in the design of the Constitution to give war powers to the single figure of the president. For instance, John Jay emphasizes in number 4 that

> absolute monarchs will often make war when their nations are to get nothing by it, but for purposes and objects merely personal, such as, a thirst for military glory, revenge for personal affronts, ambition or private compacts to aggrandize or support their particular families, or partisans. These and a variety of motives, which affect only the mind of the Sovereign, often lead him to engage in wars not sanctified by justice, or the voice and interests of his people.

And in answering antifederalist charges that the framers intended to grant the president monarchical powers, Alexander Hamilton (the federalists' most outspoken advocate for monarchy) somewhat impatiently explained the framers' deliberate purpose to keep such powers from the president, underscoring in number 69 that the president's militia powers as conceived by the Constitution pale in comparison both with those of the British monarch *and* with those of the governor of the state of New York! It is Hamilton, as well, who clarifies the intent behind assigning the executive the title of commander in chief: "The President is to be Commander in Chief of the army and navy of the United States. In this respect his authority would be nominally the same with that of the King of Great-Britain, but in substance much inferior to it."

The Constitution gives the president only a thin framework of explicit powers that belong solely to his office: for instance, the power to grant reprieves and pardons, and to fill governmental vacancies during any Senate recess. His other enumerated powers are either shared—he is given the power to make treaties but only "by and with the Advice and Consent of the Senate"; he has the power to make judiciary and diplomatic appointments, but only "by and with the Advice and Consent of the Senate"—or secretarial and advisory: he is obliged "from time to time to give to the Congress Information of the State of the Union and to recommend to their Consideration such Measures as he shall judge necessary and expedient," and he is obliged to "take Care that the Laws be faithfully executed." The framers, for the most part, except for his charge to ensure the execution of laws passed by Congress, explicitly gave the president only such power as the Congress was willing to delegate to him.

If we return to the Constitution, then, we can see that the framers did not create a *presidential* government—which is what analysts agree we have today. What the framers created was a deliberative government that drew its power from the "great body of the people." The branch that represented that body—Congress—was the branch that was vested with the most actual and symbolic power. Elaborating on the principle of separation and balance of powers, Madison observed in *Federalist* number 51 that "in republican government the legislative branch, necessarily predominates." The framers of the Constitution gave the executive almost no power that was independent of the legislative branch, the branch they intended to represent "the people." As political scientists Theodore Lowi and Benjamin Ginsberg amusingly frame the point, while the founders may have denominated the officeholder as "chief executive," the powers that they specified for him rendered him "chief clerk."

From very early in presidential history—since Adams succeeded Washington—presidents and analysts alike have been debating how to negotiate the discrepancy between the scope of powers seemingly signaled by the title for the office, the "vigor" and "energy" that the authors of the *Federalist Papers* attribute to it, and the constitutionally mandated dependency of the president on the legislative branch. In this continuing struggle, proponents of presidential power have managed to expand the purview of the office by appealing to "informal powers"—powers that are staked to the symbolics of the office. They argued that the president must have powers commensurate with his leadership role in representing a figure of national strength and unity.

The Leader of Strength and Unity

Most historians agree that the transition from congressional to presidential government—and thus the most formal effects of what I describe in this book through the term *presidentialism*—began with Franklin D.

Roosevelt's New Deal presidency. But the symbolics of the office—its looming power to focus and train citizens' democratic aspirations—began developing long before the twentieth century. That symbolic force helped pave the way and perhaps even created a certain inevitability for a presidential government the founders neither called for nor seemingly anticipated in their forwarding of the presidential office as a unifying icon and agent for national government.

Citizens were not very interested in the presidency as a political office during the years of the early nation. We see this when we contrast the lavish ceremonies prepared for Washington's inaugural journey from Mount Vernon to New York City with continuing voter preference for local over national political contests. For instance, in the 1796 election, historian Roger Sharp notes that in Pennsylvania, "Thomas Mifflin ran virtually unopposed for governor . . . and the election drew almost 32,000 voters to the polls, in sharp contrast to the 24,487 voters Jefferson and Adams attracted"—this in the state where Philadelphia was still the seat of national government.

Before citizens began directing their political preferences toward the presidency, they were rehearsing feelings of national belonging through rituals that celebrated Washington. The historian David Waldstreicher outlines how federalists began to summon and direct the newness of national feeling by tailoring monarchical rituals for displays of republican sensibility. In Waldstreicher's summary, national celebrations "made it possible for ordinary citizens to act politically between elections," and celebrations of Washington's birthday, as well as those in response to his tours of the eastern and southern states in 1788 through 1791, gave citizens a way to attune their national feelings, if not necessarily their political beliefs, through the theatrical celebration of the president. Washington, it may be surprising to realize, was no less attentive to the symbolics of office than our recent media-age presidents. As Waldstreicher recounts:

> On approaching a town, Washington would leave his carriage and mount his famous white horse. At least a few miles out he would be met by a deputation of militia or local dignitaries, who would then guide him into the state, country, or city. Virtually all the residents of the surrounding areas gathered in town to get a

Early presidential image control: George Washington on his famous white horse. Engraving by William Holl after painting by John Faed. Courtesy of Library of Congress. Original painting: John Faed, *George Washington Taking the Salute at Trenton,* circa 1900; oil on canvas, 77½ x 55½ inches.

glimpse of the war hero president. Often a full-scale civic procession followed. In the evening Washington attended dinner parties with the local elite, at which the standard thirteen national toasts would be offered.

Such celebrations encouraged citizens to set aside political disagreement in a unifying exercise of national feeling, where carefully coordinated theatrics gave participants a chance to experience citizenship as the thrill of spectatorship. But these civic exercises could not quell swelling political disagreement during the 1790s. And indeed, political opposition staked its public expression by modifying federalist celebrations: their demonstrations featured the *people* as democracy's actors instead of the president.

Despite the broad popularity of what Waldstreicher calls Washington's "sentimental journeys," even the venerated Washington could not avoid stirring some heated disagreement in the new nation. The persuasive power of living presidents would always be temporal. But the dead president? That's a different story.

Dead Presidential Powers

Washington died in 1799. Just one year before, President Adams and his federalist colleagues, seeking to squelch public opposition, had pushed through the Alien and Sedition Acts. The electoral college responded by electing Adams's Republican opponent, Thomas Jefferson. This "second American Revolution," the peaceful transfer of power from one party to another, did not consolidate political unity in the United States or resolve anxieties about political disagreement among politicians or between the U.S. government and its citizens. So when the itinerant preacher and traveling book salesman Mason Locke Weems began marketing his wildly popular "I cannot tell a lie" biography of Washington in the early 1800s, he offered the American public a chance nostalgically and *fictionally* to recapture a sensation of national unity that could offset their anxieties about ongoing political disagreements.

It seems that the American public in 1809 understood Weems's folksy fictions about the president for what they were: moral embellishments. It wasn't long, though, before moral fiction had turned into sacred national fact. (Try telling a schoolchild that the "I cannot tell a lie" story is itself a lie!) Weems delivered to the nation a founding father with superhero qualities—one they would never let go of. We continue to embrace and rehearse the exemplary figure of Washington today because the fabled presidential father balances deeply contradictory civic desires. These desires are for the kind of connectedness that enables democratic negotiation and for the kind of strong protection that wards off disagreement. The president's symbolic resonance can become—at least after he dies, when his living actions won't disrupt his idealization—a container that manages and promises to resolve those countervailing needs. As Weems popularized this dead president, he started consolidating the emotive force of presidentialism.

Let's look at how Weems's mythical Washington played out these contradictory desires. Recounting Washington's part in the defense of Fort Necessity during the French and Indian War, Weems presented to his readers a warrior with a magically armored body:

> By this time . . . Braddock had fallen—his aids [sic] and officers, to a man, killed or wounded. . . . Washington alone remained unhurt! Horse after horse had been killed under him. Showers of bullets had touched his locks or pierced his regimentals. But still protected by heaven—still supported by a strength not his own, he had continued to fly . . . where his presence was most needed, sometimes animating his rangers; sometimes striving . . . to rally the regulars.

This Washington was completely impermeable: bullets couldn't pierce him. But like the superheroes who would emerge in the twentieth century, General Washington also had a soft side. The hard warrior who defended the country grew up, readers learned, from a boy with a miraculously sensitive heart. The childhood that Weems recounted was sprinkled liberally with Washington's tears, as, for instance, when one fall his father chidingly reminded him of his selfish refusal to share an apple with his brothers and sisters the spring before. Then the father convinced George to do so only by promising that God would deliver a bigger apple harvest in exchange for little George's generosity. Confronted with the loaded trees and his father's reminder, "George looked in silence on the wild wilderness of fruit . . . then lifting his eyes, filled with shining moisture . . . he softly said, 'Well, Pa, only forgive me this time; and see if I ever be so stingy any more.'"

Washington's mythical status is such a commonplace that we don't often question the mythological work of such a story. What does it mean for Weems to create a president at once so impenetrable and so sentimentally permeable, so hard and yet so soft? It seems that Weems was reworking the Elizabethan doctrine of the king's two bodies to negotiate the newer tensions of representative democracy in the United States. If, as historian Michael Paul Rogin summarizes, the doctrine worked in two directions, making the political realm "independent of the body mortal who governed it" and at the same time allowing the officeholder to absorb the realm into his "personal identity," the president's hard and soft bodies offered a symbolic solution to some central political conundrums facing the United States under the Constitution: How do you have both unity (what the nation was built on) and political difference (what democracy depends on)? How do you defer to representatives (thereby gaining the comfort of their protection) and still maintain democratic contact (which inevitably carries with it the discomforts of disagreement)? If, as I've suggested above, the federalists offered the president as an emblem of national unity that would *replace* the messiness of the routine disagreements fundamental to democratic engagement, Weems seems to have insisted that our first president actually delivered the best of both: he protected us and he cared about us—so much that he *cried*. Weems's Washington met people's desires for protected patriotic unity and their desire for the interconnections of living democracy.

Thus the charisma we habitually look for in presidential candidates now consolidates first in relation to a dead president. Living presidents unavoidably remind citizens of political conflict and partiality. But the mythology of the (dead) president promises to absorb those many conflicting desires so that we don't have to negotiate them. This reorganization of citizen desire toward the dead president thus encourages a loss of public imagination about self-managing democracy. It encourages us to focus our feelings of loss—feelings that could have to do with diminishing opportunities for citizen agency—not on our governmental system or our own beliefs and habits but on the funereal memory of the "perfect" president. Thus it substitutes a regretful patriotic nostalgia for an active resourcefulness about our current conditions. Read from this angle, Weems's biography of Washington can help us think more about the symbolic work of presidentialism. It can help us understand how presidentialism, from early in the nineteenth century, begins converting democratic energies aimed at the public sphere (energies for negotiating with each other) into private feelings aimed at the president (desires for protection and individual recognition).

Weems's depiction of Washington made its strongest appeals to privately oriented feelings, and it proposed these private feelings as a *replacement* for public, confraternal energy and action. The chapter that recounted the "birth and education" of the man Weems denominated our nation's "political father" foregrounds little George's relation to his own father, the grandfatherly Mr. Washington. Mr. Washington endeavors to give George a liberal education, teaching him to share with his friends, to labor always for generosity and, above all, truthfulness. The famous cherry tree anecdote documents the successful inculcation of Mr. Washington's long lesson on truthfulness. Describing it to George as the "loveliest quality of youth," "Pa" explains how he "would ride fifty miles . . . to see the little boy whose heart is so honest, and . . . lips so pure, that we may depend on every word he says." By contrast, he offers up "the case with the boy who is so given to lying, that nobody can believe a word he says!" Rather than see his dear George turn into this boy, Mr. Washington avers that "gladly would I assist to nail you up in your little coffin, and follow you to your grave." Mr. Washington delivers his lesson to a tearful and anxious George:

> I rejoice in the hope you never will [lie]. At least, you shall never, from me, have cause to be guilty of so shameful a thing. Many parents, indeed, even compel their children to this vile practice, by barbarously beating them for every little fault: hence, on the next offense, the little terrified creature slips out a lie! just to escape the rod. But as to yourself George, you know I have always told you, and now tell you again, that, whenever by accident, you do anything wrong, which must often be the case, as you are but a poor little boy yet, without experience or knowledge, you must never tell a falsehood to conceal it; but come bravely up, my son, like a little man, and tell me of it: and, instead of beating you, George, I will but the more honour and love you for it my dear.

Weems summarized this episode as "the sowing [of] good seed"—a manly lesson with manful results.

While we typically associate openly expressed feeling (sentimentalism) with women, it's worth dwelling a moment on how this scene elaborated a developing masculine variant of sentiment (we could call it patriotism) in the early nation. In this scene Mr. Washington directed the desire for connection (in this instance George's intense desires for his father's love) toward a disciplinary aim. The immediate aim seems to be "truth telling," but subsequent passages emphasized a subtle additional dimension to the lesson. Here and elsewhere, the loving truths rewarded by male recognition—what Weems calls the "spirit of a brother"—lead to the "right order" of male self-subordination to a higher, fatherly authority. And this is a lesson little George successfully absorbed. For instance, in his school years, George's sentimental identification with fatherly authority led him often shamelessly to tattle on his schoolmates for fighting among themselves. Weems offered a former classmate reminiscing about how George would upbraid his classmates:

> Angry or not angry, you shall never, boys, have my consent to a practice so shocking! shocking even in *slaves* and *dogs*; then how utterly scandalous in little boys at school, who ought to look at one another as brothers. And what must be the feelings of our tender parents, when, instead of seeing us come home smiling and lovely, as the JOYS OF THEIR HEARTS! they see us creeping in like young blackguards, with our heads *bound up, black eyes,* and *bloody clothes*! And what is all this for? Why, that we *may get praise*!! But the truth is, a quarrelsome boy was never sincerely praised!

In this speech, George invokes brotherly feeling—fraternity—by appealing to the "tender" feelings of *parents,* not brothers. It is by this same logic, one that substitutes hierarchy for equalitarianism, that George rationalizes hauling in the master to end conflict rather than allowing boys to settle their disagreements among themselves. Weems's schoolboy George thus prefigured the work that presidentialism, according to its federalist proponents, would perform for the disorderly habits of democracy. The president promises to circumvent the messiness entailed by equalitarian negotiation. He reminds "boy" citizens to preempt their own disagreements by subordinating themselves unquestioningly to the higher wisdom of their loving master, teacher, father, or president, who has their better interests at heart. Thus symbolically, Weems's beloved dead president offered to convert the sometimes fractious self-governing equalitarian energies of political fraternity into a loving desire for self-subordination within a neatly and hierarchically ordered political system.

Explaining his narrative approach to the biography, Weems insisted that "private life is always the real life," that it is the life "behind the curtain" where one discovers the true worth of a patriot and a man. His biography monumentalized Washington as a man who was most a patriot in the privacy of his own home. Here Weems underscored President Washington's own lessons in his Farewell Address, suggesting that citizens can best exercise their citizenship not together in the public square but at home, in their worshipful and private remembrance of the president. In Weems's lesson, the aim was not to see your own political desires represented in deliberative government but to model your personal desires on those of the Ideal President: "Since it is the private virtues that lay the foundation of all human excellence . . . give us his private virtues! In these, every youth is interested, because in these every youth may become a Washington." Weems offered a lesson that insistently substituted the private for the public—or, more correctly, redescribed the public "We" ("We, the People") as the private "I"—thus relocating democracy's desires for a changed *world* to presidentialism's liberal containment of a changed (self-disciplined) *heart*.

The biography aimed to teach Americans how to feel about their ideal president and about their presidentially ordered federal government, by encouraging them to model their own behavior and feelings on that of Washington. In a highly emotional scene where little George was witnessing his father's death, Weems offered to readers George's agonized cry: "O my father! my father!" Weems summarized this exquisitely painful moment in a jarring way: "The happiest youth! Happy in that love, which thus, to its enamoured soul strained an aged, an expiring sire. O! worthiest to be the founder of a just and equal government lasting as thy own deathless name!" Washington's deathbed mourning for the loss of his father provided the key emotional moment for Weems to drive home the lesson of how to be a patriot. Weems idealized a self-subordinating patriotism, a patriotism that clings for its guidance to the expiring father figure in the same way that citizens should cling to the ideal (dead) president.

It's this reverence for our dead first president that has been instilled in schoolchildren, helping condition civic expectations for the office and democratic practice ever since (most of us learned quickly that our "citizenship" grade in primary school depended vitally on how quiet and mannerly we were in class, not on how intelligently we questioned authority).

President Washington monumentalized as the patriotic master who will end democratic disputes. The sculptor Horatio Greenough modeled his subject after Zeus, the supreme Greek god of Olympus. Courtesy of Smithsonian American Art Museum and Art Resource. Horatio Greenough, *George Washington,* 1840; marble, 136 x 102 x 82½ inches.

As political scientists Marc Hetherington and Michael Nelson observe of our own era: "The significance of the chief of state role has little to do with the insignificant formal powers that accompany it or the activities it requires. Rather, it lies in the emotions the role arouses in citizens. Long before they have any knowledge of what the president does, young children already have positive feelings about his seemingly boundless power and benevolence." We are taught in childhood to cede our revolutionary grant of sovereign power as a self-governing democratic People to a fantasy about the president's "boundless power," his superhuman ability to protect us, and "benevolence," his endless capacity to feel our pain (whether or not he can do something about it). Like the president who cannot tell a lie, or the Terminator who always comes back to rescue us, he will come back from our past or perhaps from our future to rescue us from whatever mess we find ourselves in, so that we don't have to do the dirty work ourselves.

Superheroes and the Media

In the nineteenth century, schoolchildren were taught to adore the nation's first president. Around this time, Andrew Jackson did a great deal to glue (and reduce) the idea of democracy to voting for the president. Beyond Jackson, the only president citizens so revered was Abraham Lincoln, but it wasn't during his lifetime: rather, his heroic status was cemented by his assassination, after which everyone seemingly forgot how divided they were about the policies of his presidency. Rather, in the nineteenth century, political *parties* exerted more practical pull on voters' imaginations than the run-of-the-mill president. And local politics and Congress had more political influence on their lives than the president. That would change in the twentieth century with the tenure of Roosevelt. The long era of FDR's presidency (1933–45) marks the turning point from congressional to presidential government. Despite occasional public, legislative, and judicial pushback, the years of FDR's presidency saw widespread popular and official acceptance of a new logic for the executive in a vastly expanded federal government, making the executive less a separate branch to administrate the laws passed by Congress and reviewed by the Supreme Court than the apex of government management. As Lowi summarizes, "The presidency grew because it had become the center of a new . . . theory of democracy based on the president's capacity to govern." FDR's years in office ushered in the institution known as the "modern presidency."

The era also marked a definitive amplification of the superhero associations of the office. In the nineteenth century, Washington and Lincoln functioned posthumously, as quasi-religious symbols of national unification. In the era that FDR accomplished the transition to the modern presidency through the crises of the Great Depression and World War II, the nation also began its pop-culture love affair with superheroes of every order, in novels, cartoon magazines, radio, television, and movies. The mythical associations of iconic dead presidents fused to real-world crises and popularly trained desires to transform civic expectations for real-world, living presidents.

Philosophers Robert Jewett and John Shelton Lawrence describe, drawing on Joseph Campbell's definition of the "monomyth," what they term the *American* monomyth:

> A community in a harmonious paradise is threatened by an evil: normal institutions fail to contend with this threat: a selfless superhero emerges to renounce temptations and carry out the redemptive task: aided by fate, his decisive victory restores the community to its paradisal condition: the superhero recedes into obscurity.

Jewett and Shelton argue that many of U.S. culture's most popular stories, from Owen Wister's novel *The Virginian* ("*smile* when you call me that") to the *Star Wars* and *Rambo* series, are driven by the logic of this nationalist mythology. They are critical of the monomyth's antidemocratic message: the people, passive, disorganized, and in distress, await the extraordinary and extralegal interventions of the hero, who wreaks a satisfying vengeance for their wrongs and saves the day. Jewett and Shelton date the consolidation of this myth to the late 1920s and 1930s, when superheroes of every variety emerged in droves, from Superman, the Shadow, Batman, and Wonderman to Tarzan, the Lone Ranger, and figures who have faded now from popular memory like Prince Namor the Sub-Mariner, the Human Torch, the Angel, and the Shield (whose star-spangled suit was a model for Captain America's). These solitary redeemers cultivated and fed a national appetite for endangerment and rescue plots, just as the nation teetered into an era of domestic and international crisis.

Superhero characters had an uncanny resemblance to the developing symbolics of the presidency. Solitary, sympathetic figures burdened with responsibility, presidents, like superheroes, are lonely crusaders for justice in an unjust world. As the political scientist Barbara Hinckley summarizes, "The Lonely Man in the Whitehouse is burdened—with the government *and* with moral leadership. If the president is powerful, unique and morally good, then the nation he symbolizes is secure in its power, mission and morally correct course." It's arguable that popular culture—

its escalating love affair with the fabulous rescues of solitary heroes—primed civic willingness to accept FDR's massive progressive revisions to the structure and business of national government and the presidency's place in it.

FDR used emergency powers during his first term to create such agencies as the Farm Security Administration, the Federal Housing Administration, the National Labor Board, and the Social Security Administration, and to remodel existing ones. Federal bureaucracy mushroomed, as New Deal policies began exerting an unprecedented control over business and individual life. As Lowi notes, the significance of the New Deal came not in the volume of legislation and governmental relief programs but in how it restructured the relation between citizens and government. Previously that relationship depended on the adequacy of political representation, how government represented the will of the People, emphasizing due process in its aim to maximize personal liberty. The New Deal replaced this "hands-off" posture with a willingness both to regulate individual behavior and to provide individual services.

FDR created new agencies right and left, and expected to exert executive control over them without interference from Congress. Very quickly, the Supreme Court checked FDR, overturning some of his new agencies and ruling that their establishment unconstitutionally delegated legislative power to the president. In frustration, FDR tried another tactic: he initiated a project that would restructure the executive branch's administrative organization in order to gain this authority. He appointed the Committee on Administrative Management (also known as the Brownlow Committee) to give his power grab for the executive the sanction of objective, nonpartisan principle. The committee, obligingly, recommended a massive restructuring of the purview of the executive office and patterned their reforms for administration on the modern corporation. They reenvisioned the president's role as that of a CEO, depicting the president as a capable manager. They urged the expansion of the presidential staff and the development and strengthening of central management agencies. As importantly for FDR's interests, they proposed overhauling the dozens of independent agencies, boards, authorities, and commissions, insisting that what many were terming the "headless fourth branch" be brought under executive authority. Countering the first article of the Constitution, which decrees that "all legislative powers herein shall be vested in a Congress of the United States," the Brownlow report advocated that Congress should hand over to the president the authority to reorganize, abolish, or restructure functions within the executive departments. (As I show in chapter 4, presidential control of the agencies continues to be controversial: because many of the agencies effectively assume legislative duties, members of Congress believe the Constitution gives *their* branch the privilege of agency oversight.)

FDR introduced a bill to Congress in 1938 based on the recommendations of the Brownlow report, which was roundly defeated as "presidential dictatorship" (coming as it did in the same moment FDR was trying to pack the Supreme Court in order to force more favorable rulings). The following year, FDR earned passage of a trimmed-down version, containing only two of the report's many suggestions. But the Brownlow vision for executive reorganization, centralization, and strengthening would survive its initial hostile reception. Under the guidance of two Herbert Hoover commissions, appointed by presidents Harry Truman and Dwight Eisenhower, the Brownlow plan would be substantially approved. A succession of such committees has continued supporting the principle of presidential centrality and supremacy to this day, and Congress continues piecemeal to delegate powers away from itself to the executive branch.

Just as FDR's presidency marked a watershed accumulation of domestic executive powers, so too did it herald expansions for the presidency's foreign powers. While FDR displayed a caution many historians have actually faulted him for in the years leading up to the United States' involvement in World War II, once the country entered war, he energetically assumed the role of commander in chief. (His secretary of state commented that FDR liked that title more than "president.") Reelected in large part because of citizens' confidence in his foreign policy, FDR's successes — and even his failures — expanded and consolidated the power of the executive branch. Most notoriously, FDR issued an executive order to inter Japanese and Japanese Americans (but not German or Italian Americans) — an order confirmed by Congress and upheld in a number of Supreme Court decisions. Doing this, FDR effectively imprisoned more than sixty-five thousand U.S. citizens who had been charged with no crime or act of disloyalty. Following on the heels of his internment order, FDR claimed unrestrained executive authority, warning that "I cannot tell what powers may have to be exercised in order to win this war."

And yet, while claiming and assuming extraconstitutional powers, FDR did not expect to hold them permanently. As he put it in his September 7, 1942, fireside chat:

> The American people can be sure that I will use my powers with a full sense of my responsibility to the Constitution and to my country. The American people can also be sure that I shall not hesitate to use every power vested in me to accomplish the defeat of our enemies in any part of the world where our own safety demands such defeat.
>
> When the war is won, the powers under which I act automatically revert to the people—to whom they belong.

FDR promised that the extraordinary powers he claimed would automatically return to the people. Despite his promises, there would be nothing automatic about it. FDR's heroic presidential leadership through the Depression and World War II, in the era that birthed the pop-culture superhero, had the effect of permanently rewiring American expectations for the office. The American public demonstrated in the following years that they now saw such presidential power not as extraordinary but as *routine*. They expected the president to be an active reformer and leader both nationally and internationally, in regular times as well as crisis. The new attitude, in Lowi's summary, was that "the president is the government and ought to have the capacity to govern." FDR's long crisis government, along with his carefully crafted production of charismatic leadership, had solidified American desires to see presidents function as national saviors, expecting them to be, as political scientist Michael Genovese puts it, "the knight on the white horse." It was no longer dead presidents like Washington or the Civil War martyr Lincoln who would be looked to as heroes: citizens now began to expect living presidents to perform superheroic deeds—daily—in office.

No small part of this crucial transformation in public expectation came because of media's expansion from print into radio, and soon, television.

Unlike his immediate predecessors, FDR's administration gave reporters a seemingly easy and informal access to the president. In this, FDR improved on his uncle Theodore Roosevelt's cagey facilitation of the press's White House access for consolidating his own famed "bully pulpit." FDR actively courted reporters' goodwill, cultivating his ability to influence the news agenda in ways that would advance his legislative agenda. He seized on the relatively new media of radio—one that carries the human intimacy of voice. With his famed fireside chats, FDR consolidated message control through his straightforwardly accessible and reassuringly familiar style. He had some of them filmed for movie-theater newsreel footage, which allowed more Americans to experience his reassuring presence and to hear his message over and over. FDR's use of the media helped him firm up public support for his domestic and international initiatives and also began shifting the work of executive government toward something more akin to campaigning for office, as the executive office now labored to control its agenda in Congress by packaging and selling it for the *public's* approval. And his ability to promulgate his image and his message through more intimate media led citizens to feel they had a personal and immediate relationship with him—a relationship that could leave them inclined simply to ignore newspaper opinion columns that criticized and warned about FDR's policies and strategies. FDR also used the new "science" of opinion polling to influence how he was received by the public. He was not only the first, as the political scientist Melvin Holli notes, to make "systematic use of public opinion polling for campaigning," he consistently used polling throughout his long presidency, a fact only recently registered by historians and political scientists who have attributed to John F. Kennedy this "first" status.

Polling, like the media, is another technology that promises more neutrality than it has ever delivered. Before the advent of polling, the government discovered public sentiment through the political *behavior* of citizens: through the actions of citizens groups and the voices of their representatives. Polling allows government to bypass activist groups, who feel passionately about the subjects that organize them to action, drawing instead a more "scientific" and putatively representative picture of "opinion" from individual people who are no longer required to do anything other than answer their phone when a pollster calls. Thus people who don't care or know much about particular issues and who often easily form the statistical majority in any given sample end up rationalizing government inaction in response to civic agitation. Moreover, polls do not simply mirror public opinion: they can shape it, as for instance FDR's pollster Emil Hurja did when he pioneered the practice that political scientists now call "priming." Priming is the practice of steering polling questions toward only the issues a candidate is prepared to discuss and can draw a competitive advantage from. The publicity that ensues from these polls sets the terms for the representation of "public opinion" and for the political agenda. Survey polls don't allow citizens to create their own agenda; rather, they respond to the representation of "their opinion" through terms, language, and issues established by political leaders, who often use such techniques not because they're interested in being responsive to public opinion but because they want to shape and control it. This happened, for instance, when FDR sought opinion polling angles and trend reports that would allow him to justify supplying military support to England during World War II to a public that ardently opposed a U.S. entry into war.

Following FDR's example, subsequent presidents began using media and polling to campaign over the heads of Congress, directly with the American people. This innovation folded new media and polling *into* governance, allowing the president to manufacture power for his agenda through opinion leadership, as the so-called number-one newsmaker. The political scientist Jeffrey Tullis observes that today "it is taken for granted that presidents have a *duty* constantly to defend themselves publicly, to promote policy initiatives nationwide, and to inspirit the population. And for many, this presidential 'function' is not one duty among many, but rather the heart of the presidency—its essential task."

For their part, the news media increasingly looked toward the president—and away from Congress—as they portrayed U.S. government for their audience. Since the FDR presidency, the media, government, scholars, analysts, and the public alike have expected the president (not citizens and not Congress) to drive the nation's agenda. Any president who is perceived to share this responsibility with the congressional branch is characterized as a "weak president," a failure at strong leadership rather than a success at cooperative (we could say "democratic") leadership. Effectively, then (and whether or not he intended it), FDR cast a mold for the president who now must be visibly and expansively activist—publicly asserting the superordinance of his representative agency over that of Congress—in order to be considered "great." "Great" leadership has come to mean for presidents, as much as anything, managing their image and message in order to control public opinion.

Managing Presidential Image

FDR cultivated real-time power in part by making a new relationship between the president and the people through the media. Presidents who followed had a hard time living up to his legacy—the expectations for "great leadership" that his political strategy and media and polling savvy combined with pop-culture superhero plots cultivated among ordinary Americans. Truman and Eisenhower concentrated, each in their own way, on strategic and rhetorical leadership, but often at the expense of cultivating the media and polling techniques that FDR so effectively utilized. It wasn't until JFK—who won the 1960 election, it's worth remembering, by one of the tiniest margins in U.S. history—that American citizens would once again have a president who understood how much power he could cultivate for the presidency by managing his image.

Even before Kennedy ran for Congress, he had become fascinated, through his Hollywood acquaintances and visits, with the idea of image. Friends attested that he spent hours talking about the subject, analyzing how actors like Gary Cooper cultivated his so-called magnetism, trying to gauge whether he himself had it or how he could create it. Many historians and biographers have commented on Kennedy's conscious manufacture of his own image (with his father's assistance) and on how he experimented with and developed the successful television persona that was so triumphant in, for instance, his September 1960 presidential debate with Richard Nixon. But Kennedy was, it seems in retrospect, working to craft something far more durable and substantial than the mere notion of image connotes. The literature professor John Hellman has analyzed in rich detail how Kennedy drew on the power of myth as he framed his experience during World War II, when his PT boat was sliced in half by a Japanese cruiser. In the expert hands of John Hersey, a writer for the *New Yorker* and soon-to-be Pulitzer Prize winner, the story "Survival," told in the style of what would come to be known as the "new journalism," featured the young Kennedy in classic mythical terms—terms that tap neatly into the American monomyth that Jewett and Lawrence described in relation to the superhero.

In "Survival," Hersey (a family friend) represents Kennedy as a lonely and determined hero. He is importantly a democratic hero: when the survivors first turn to him for leadership, Hersey's Kennedy replies, "There's nothing in the book about a situation like this. Seems to me we're not a military organization any more. Let's just talk this over." But it's quickly evident the troops can't productively deliberate: instead, their ensuing arguments signal to their leader that "they would never survive in anarchy." Kennedy wisely and of necessity retakes command, standing alone as the leader of this microcosm of a democracy imperiled both without and within. He subsequently braves multiple solo rescue attempts, and it is finally his daring persistence, his dogged refusal to quit looking for avenues to rescue, that saves the men on the PT, who in Hersey's story have been left for dead by the other PTs (a detail contested by other survivors and accounts). Kennedy's father lobbied successfully to overturn the *New Yorker* editorial policy against allowing condensations of their stories and got a version of "Survival" into *Reader's Digest,* and then he papered the congressional district in which his son was running with reprints of the story. Kennedy subtly drew on the story's motif of heroic liminality in his public speeches during and after his congressional campaign, confident that most of his auditors had at one point been captivated by a reading of the dramatic tale. Hellman summarizes the power of this image creation:

> Kennedy the politician thus incorporated into his image Kennedy the literary character, an entity that was the product of a triangular encounter of dreams, the site where the deep psychological experiences of Kennedy, Hersey and the reader met. In each case the dreams concerned the self and the community, alienation and

longing, love and death. Kennedy, flesh and blood, was now also a dreamlike image to be viewed, collectively, as other and yet as interior to each self. The emergence of John F. Kennedy as a political figure of liminality—of potential and transition— was complete.

In his 1955 Pulitzer Prize–winning book *Profiles in Courage,* the now senator Kennedy profiled historic Senate figures, associating himself with their political courage. Here, amplifying on the heroic image Hersey had crafted for him in "Survival," Kennedy (and his writing team) lauded senators who stood bravely and alone: democratic leaders whose heroism was defined by their ability to resist the unreasonable demands of their quarrelsome constituents, rescuing them, as it were, from their own anarchic habits and bad decisions. And in his 1960 campaign for president, Kennedy drew explicitly on the mystique of the lone western hero (some thirty of the roughly ninety television series then airing during prime time were westerns) to craft his appeal for the "New Frontier." Hellman again concisely summarizes: "The gunfighter western, the most visible context and the most immediate source of resonance for the metaphor of the New Frontier, was a mythological space within which Kennedy's audience had been prepared for the idea that they could somehow join a romantic hero in returning to the primal scene of American origins to heal the wrong done by their forebears."

Self-consciously and intelligently, Kennedy offered himself to the U.S. public as a lone and selfless spiritual redeemer for a national fantasy: a quintessential American hero—and a quintessential *television* hero (Norman Mailer wryly described this aspect of Kennedy's candidacy in his 1960 essay "Superman Comes to the Supermarket"). His televised press conferences offered American citizens a chance to rehearse their intimate identification with his dashing representation of the nation as a heroic and youthfully athletic individual. He presented himself as just the man to lead the nation through Cold War predicaments like the Bay of Pigs invasion and the Cuban missile crisis. Historians and psychobiographers have speculated that he manufactured crises during office to enhance his heroic image. Even setting such perhaps ungenerous speculation aside, it's clear the Kennedy administration worked relentlessly at tailoring his

BAD FOR DEMOCRACY

media representations, including the photographic images they released to the press. Through pictures they portrayed him insistently in two ways, as a lone and restless leader, and an engaged and nurturing father. Thus they offered the public a living, modern-day distillation of both of Weems's Washingtons: the loving, family-oriented Georgie and the impenetrably tough general.

Kennedy was a heroic leader whose policies proliferated new frontiers and heroes to populate them: in his creation of the Peace Corps, in his support for space exploration, and in the Green Berets he sent into Vietnam (when it could still be represented as a frontier for new American heroism). Thus the living Kennedy, like Weems's superheroic posthumous Washington, modeled the hero who could pass it on, teaching citizens how to find the qualities that might allow them to become heroic, like their president. Then, before an adoring public could begin finding fault with the living Kennedy, he was assassinated and transfigured into the quasi-religious realm of dead presidents. There, he did not just join Washington and Lincoln; he also joined King Arthur, in Camelot.

The Kennedy family formally disavows association with the Camelot myth. But it was Jacqueline Kennedy who went, shortly after Kennedy's assassination, to the Pulitzer Prize–winning journalist Theodore White, to tell him how her husband had loved listening at bedtime to the 1960 hit musical *Camelot,* and especially the lines: "Don't let it be forgot, that once there was a spot, for one brief shining moment, that was known as Camelot." The image of Camelot invoked a magical fantasy of utopian possibility—of an idyllic government, and of a romantic, visionary, cosmopolitan leader. It worked quickly and powerfully to cement a folklore around Kennedy that seemed to reflect the magnitude of the nation's loss.

But, again, let's probe the folklore. If King Arthur's contribution was to share power with the Knights of the Round Table, Camelot's government is still a monarchy, and the myth's most important lesson is that the self-governing project of sharing power *did not work: the people needed a strong king.* The Camelot mystique continued feeding the superhero associations of the presidency that JFK had carefully crafted just as it fed the American monomyth and its antidemocratic energies. Here it's worth returning to Jewett and Lawrence's assessment of the American monomyth

The image of Jacqueline and John F. Kennedy as royalty in Camelot invoked a magical fantasy of utopian possibility: idyllic government by a romantic, visionary, cosmopolitan leader. Courtesy of John F. Kennedy Presidential Library and Museum.

for its resonance with Camelot's entailments: "Whereas popular myths ordinarily sustain the leading values and institutions of a culture, the American monomyth consistently undermines the democratic ethos. . . . the American monomyth is an escapist fantasy. It encourages passivity on the part of the general public and unwise concentrations of power in ostensible redeemers. It betrays the ideals of democratic responsibility and denies the reliance on human intelligence that is basic to the democratic hope." Kennedy's Camelot continues to provide citizens an escapist fantasy even today: although historians and political scientists rate his abilities and accomplishments as president as average, the U.S. public consistently rates Kennedy as one of our nation's greatest presidents. As the writer Gretchen Rubin summarizes, "A 2004 Gallup poll ranked Kennedy as the second most outstanding president, and a 2003 Gallup poll showed Kennedy and Lincoln tied for first place. Kennedy's stature isn't a recent trend: a 1970 Harris poll showed Kennedy to be by far the most popular president, as did a 1983 Gallup poll, and in *New York Times*/CBS

News polls for 1980 and 1996, Americans picked Kennedy as the president they'd choose to run the country today."

In death, President Kennedy, mythically regal and fantastically telegenic (never aging!), transfixed the civic gaze. In the immediate aftermath of his assassination, presidents could not live up to the fantasy that accumulated around his memory. And the very media that Kennedy played to his advantage exposed Johnson's and Nixon's attempts to game the electorate through Vietnam and Watergate. Although the Johnson and Nixon administrations are commonly credited with "diminishing" the power of the modern presidency, the dimming of its power was only temporary— and relatively insignificant to the enormous power, legitimacy, and size it had accumulated over the course of the first three-quarters of the twentieth century. Too, this temporary lull might have been avoided entirely but for Gerald Ford's pardoning of Nixon. The amiable centrist was welcomed into the presidency with real enthusiasm by a relieved Congress and a Watergate-weary American public. As Hinckley has observed, it is regularly true that presidential scandals adhere to the officeholder and not the office. Had Ford not pardoned Nixon, thereby adding fuel to the public's growing suspicion that *all* living presidents were supercrooks, the disgraces associated with the Nixon presidency might have attached only to Nixon. Instead, Ford's pardon rolled out the carpet for a broader backlash. Politicians in Washington and voters at home questioned their prior support for a strengthened executive. Congress reasserted its power as the "first branch" and passed a variety of laws aimed at keeping presidents more carefully moored to democratic accountability. Scholars cautioned in chorus about an "imperial presidency."

But caution did not last long. The U.S. public elected a denim-dressing Washington outsider from Georgia, and just as rapidly became disenchanted by Jimmy Carter's resolute refusal to play the part of the hero, with his dour pragmatism, his desire for Americans to face limits, his need to diagnose and seemingly share with citizens their "crisis of confidence." With the reality-defying optimism of Ronald Reagan to turn to in 1980, the U.S. public would rediscover its desire for a charismatic and powerful leader, tossing the incumbent antihero out on his keister.

Presidentialism's Happy Ever After

Reagan became interested in politics early in his career in Hollywood. He spent studio breaks finding people to talk with about his opinions and interests. He regularly impressed his interlocutors with his apparent command of fact—even when they weren't sure whether he might be making it all up (his longtime political adviser and eventual press secretary Lyn Nofziger admiringly remarked in his memoir on Reagan's legendary ability to "convince himself that the truth is what he wants it to be"). An assignment to U.S. military media during the war seems to have expanded Reagan's political interests. Shortly after his discharge, California Democrats approached him about running for Congress. He became more involved in professional and labor union politics, and it seems that the battles of this era—during which he became president of the Screen Actors Guild—initiated his momentous political shift toward anticommunist conservatism. He explained in his 1965 autobiography, *Where's the Rest of Me?* (the title is taken from the dramatic line his character Drake McHugh spoke in the 1942 movie *King's Row*) that he left acting for politics because as an actor, he had lost his freedom to be fully heroic. Organized politics, he hoped, would give him full scope to pursue his ambition to "bring about the regeneration of the world." Hollywood, as Rogin summarizes, "deprived him of the idealized self he wanted to enact and gave him parts that exposed his weaknesses instead." Becoming a politician allowed Reagan to disavow the gray zones both of Hollywood plots and real life, instead sticking to and fighting for his black-and-white vision of the world.

A Goldwater conservative, Reagan believed in a moral order that opposed absolute evils with absolute good, built out of individual responsibility and enterprise. It was this view of the world that Reagan mobilized in his late-1970s radio addresses, where he attacked Carter's presidential policies and emphasized, in the biographer Jules Tygiel's summary, "the threat of worldwide communism, the importance of bolstering national defense and intelligence agencies, the failures of arms control." Depicting the threats looming over the United States in broad and insistent strokes, and portraying the virtues of the United States with equal vigor, Reagan presented himself as just the man to defeat the one and strengthen the

Reagan left acting for politics, which, he hoped, would enable him to "bring about the regeneration of the world." Courtesy of Ronald Reagan Library.

other. His optimism was indefatigable: his favorite story, relates Tygiel, "depicted an optimistic boy, digging through a room full of manure, confident that 'There must be a pony in here someplace!'" And he was most optimistic about the providential future of the America he treasured, its free market, its individualistic enterprise, its status as a beacon of freedom, and its worldwide moral mission to spread democracy.

If Reagan's 1980 campaign tactics aimed to activate the broad contours of the so-called American monomyth, exit polls of the 52 percent of the electorate that voted indicated that Reagan was elected not so much because people were attracted to his conservatism but because they rejected Carter's seeming pessimism. Reagan's good mood about America, less than his political convictions and proposed strategies, seemingly won him office. But despite Reagan's impressive timing and charm, combined with the legendary ability of his chief of staff Michael Deaver and his director of communications David Gergen to spin the media positively, his goal of cutting taxes as part of installing his supply-side economic system—what would come to be termed "Reaganomics"—seemed unlikely to win congressional approval. Then came John Hinckley's assassination attempt, just sixty-nine days into Reagan's administration. The president's courage, physical fortitude, and sparkling wit impressed an anxious public, and his approval ratings surged. Reagan did not miss the chance to harness the symbolic potential of the episode in his nationally televised address to a joint session of Congress on April 28, just weeks after his hospitalization. In this address, as Rogin notes, Reagan summoned the royal symbolism of the "king's two bodies," identifying the body of the leader with the political body of the nation. After introducing the topic of his speech, a new economic recovery program, Reagan asked indulgence for a digression:

> I'd like to say a few words directly to all of you and to those who are watching and listening tonight, because this is the only way I know to express to all of you on behalf of Nancy and myself our appreciation for your messages and flowers and, most of all, your prayers, not only for me but for those others who fell beside me.
>
> The warmth of your words, the expression of friendship and, yes, love, meant more to us than you can ever know. You have given us a memory that we'll treasure forever. And you've provided an answer to those few voices that were raised saying that what happened was evidence that ours is a sick society. . . .
>
> Thanks to some very fine people, my health is much improved. I'd like to be able to say that with regard to the health of the economy.

Reagan evocatively harnessed the healing of his body to his political plan for the nation's economic recovery. Reagan suggested his ability to extend the salvific healing of his mortal body—a healing importantly delivered by the American people—to the body politic of the nation. Drawing on a powerful theory that legitimated the sovereignty of the monarch, Reagan implicitly presented himself to the nation as a spiritually sanctioned leader, imperiled and resurrected, and promising a similar resurrection for the nation's imperiled economy.

In its dramatic context Reagan's performance worked its magic. The president's approval ratings soared, and his tax and budget plans passed Congress. Reagan would soon return to powerful symbolic appeals to help win approval for his plans to defeat the communist agenda of the

Soviet Union, otherwise known as the "Evil Empire." Reagan's nationally televised Strategic Defense Initiative speech in March 1983 surprised not only the public but most of his administration. Drawing on satellite technology and referring to secret intelligence, he depicted a flourishing and expanding communist empire, one that needed to be countered in order for Americans to protect their "hope for the future" and to "preserve freedom and peace." Against those who advocated cutting and not expanding the defense budget, Reagan recalled that defense cuts in the 1930s invited the disaster of World War II. As Jewett and Lawrence observe, "True to the selfless and strictly defensive image of superheroism, he promised that this system would be shared with the Soviets once it was developed, thus producing the peace everyone dreams about." Neither experts nor politicians believed that it was possible to create a protective "umbrella"—by laser or missile—to protect the United States from a communist nuclear attack. But Reagan believed in the superiority of American enterprise and technology, and with dogged persistence (and the help of a rigged Pentagon demonstration of a ground-based laser striking an airborne missile in 1984), he continued to promote his plan. Eventually polls indicated that a majority of the public—despite the cartoonish "Star Wars" moniker applied by its detractors and possibly because of the vociferous Soviet opposition to the plan for its *offensive* capabilities—were persuaded by its touted benefits.

Reagan's political world vision was, quite simply, the American monomyth. His America was pure and innocent, and he himself was just the man to identify and forestall the threats of the Evil Empire. Americans, who reelected him to office in an impressive landslide victory, seemingly liked the message even though they consistently and frequently disagreed with his policies, that is, when they could actually learn the difference between what he was saying and what his administration was doing. Reagan, as we know in the aftermath of the Iran–Contra hearings, relied on covert operations to accomplish many of his goals. When Reagan publicly denied knowing about the weapons–hostage trade, polls showed that virtually no one believed him—less than 15 percent of those polled thought he was telling the truth. But curiously, it hardly mattered: a public primed for the extralegal salvation of superheroes was similarly willing, it seems, to accept and forget about the extralegal maneuvers of the Great Communicator and the agents who acted at his behest, like Ollie North, whose patriotic scorn for Congress, the State Department, and wimpy laws won him surprising popularity with Americans during the Iran–Contra congressional hearings.

By the time Reagan left office two years later, his approval ratings stood between 63 and 70 percent. In his farewell address to the nation on January 11, 1989, Reagan continued invoking the theory of the king's two bodies. Simultaneously denying and claiming his moniker, he said, "I wasn't a great communicator, but I communicated great things, and they didn't spring full bloom from my brow, they came from the heart of a great nation—from our experience, our wisdom, and our belief in the principles that have guided us for two centuries. They called it the Reagan revolution. Well, I'll accept that, but for me it always seemed more like the great rediscovery, a rediscovery of our values and our common sense." Like a superhero, Reagan accomplished his economic revolution at home and the dismantling of the Soviet Empire abroad, then withdrew into private life and into a privacy that discreetly shielded his descent into Alzheimer's. His death in 2004 inspired journalists to laud him, here in the ABC anchor Elizabeth Vargas's words, as the "most popular president ever to leave office." The *Washington Post* remembered him as "one of the most popular presidents of the 20th century." His passing launched a television marathon, with memorials to his life, his presidency, and his movie career. Just a year later, in 2005, Reagan won the Discovery channel series contest to select the "Greatest American." (Interestingly, Kennedy here took a distant sixteenth place, behind Albert Einstein, Oprah Winfrey, Billy Graham, Bill Clinton, and Elvis.)

As Fairness and Accuracy in Reporting (FAIR) was quick to point out, Reagan was *not* factually the most popular president of the twentieth century: "Through most of his presidency, Reagan did not rate much higher than other post World War II presidents. And during his first two years, Reagan's approval ratings were quite low." As FAIR summarizes the point, the media itself seemed entranced by Reagan's storytelling abilities and "determined to show that any criticism of Reagan could be turned upside down." FAIR quotes from Dan Rather's June 6, 2004, commentary on

CBS's *60 Minutes*: "The literal-minded were forever troubled by his tendency to sometimes confuse life with the movies. But he understood, like very few leaders before or since, the power of myth and storytelling. In his films and in his political life, Ronald Reagan stood at the intersection where dreams and reality meet, and with a wink and a one-liner, always held out hope for a happy ending."

Rather's comments highlight an interesting phenomenon of Reagan's presidency—the lack of alignment between approval for Reagan and disapproval for his policies, a durable disjuncture that polls tracked throughout his two terms in office. In the Reagan era we see the severing of presidential "charisma" from an evaluation of factually effective leadership: it started to seem that voters prefer being enchanted to being politically represented (something James Conaway predicted in his 1980 profile of Reagan in the *Atlantic*: "Reagan was no throwback, but something new in presidential politics—the public receptacle of fifty years of myth-making. Movies are the most nostalgic medium, infinitely comfortable. . . . Reagan's performances are unimportant compared to his association with our most ubiquitous and powerful form of pleasure and relaxation"). This trend toward a preference for unanchored charisma in leaders is intriguingly, if sadly, antipolitical: it flags the knowing cynicism of the U.S. electorate, their lack of trust in politicians, but also their simultaneous culturally and educationally trained desire to be rescued from this cynicism.

Rather's rhapsodic eulogizing of Reagan actually demonstrates a significant degree of self-consciousness about this substitution of enchantment for political representation. It can help us think about a key aspect of charisma, which people generally tend to consider a rare attribute or power of a particular leader. Political anthropologists Douglas Madsen and Peter Snow call charisma a "relational phenomenon," where the particular special attributes of a leader mesh with or are sought out by those who want to follow. As organizational behavioralist Rakesh Khurana summarizes, we might usefully rethink charisma as "a desire to follow." Rather's paean to Reagan's storytelling abilities thus signals something larger than media or public attitudes about Ronald Reagan the president. Rather's comments, like those of so many other media and political analysts and ordinary citizens, concisely evidence the cresting of a historical trend, a profoundly childlike and antidemocratic desire to see the president as the national savior, a heroic figure who loves us, can keep us safe from the bad guys, and always holds out "hope for the happy ending." It's a *fairy tale,* as Rather seemingly knows. But it's one with a powerful grip on our democratic imagination and practical behavior, and thus it authorizes real consequences, in our name.

Leadership versus Citizenship

Presidential scholars and analysts have an oft-repeated refrain about how the constitutional allotment of power actually keeps the president comparatively "weak" and how the demands put on his office by public and international expectation combine with his structural dependency on other branches to create a lot of "frustration" for the president. Scholars call this the "paradox" or the "ambiguity" of presidential power. Such comments reflect less on the actual balance of power than on how even supposedly objective scholars take part in the national exercise that comparative political scientist Arend Lijphart isolates for attention: from the president, legislators, and journalists to scholars and the citizenry, nearly everyone seems to believe the president should have all the power he might ever need, this despite our national pride in "checks and balances." The longing for a powerful president keeps a myth alive, and it is one that, as Barbara Hinckley has argued, has actual consequences for our practice of democracy. She enumerates the key features of this myth: "Presidents are identical to nation, identical to government and powers of government, unique and alone [and] the moral leaders of nation." One key aspect of her analysis has to do with how the concentration of agency in the body of the president completely elides the cooperative efforts that produce every act of state: "Presidents, factually speaking, do not manage the economy, but it is part of the symbolism of the office that they are singularly responsible for the nation's well-being. We speak of the president's foreign policy or economic policy, collapsing a long and complex policymaking process into the work of a single individual. We use the singular—the president—in describing what all presidents do, thereby creating the impression of specialness and incomparability." That incomparability does the work of removing presidents from systematic analysis and removing the office itself from history, mythologizing its attributes and conferring them, godlike, onto individual presidential candidates. This explains how Ford, like every other twentieth-century president, can go into office with a job approval rating in the seventies before he's done a day's work.

The myth of our presidentially led democracy has mesmerized too many—not just ordinary citizens but the media, political analysts, and scholars. As a nation, we've come to fetishize presidential leadership at the expense of democratic process and citizenship. As political scientist Benjamin Barber frames the problem in his essay "Neither Leaders nor Followers":

> In traditional political theory, we customarily speak of the act of sovereign authorization by which a people empower a sovereign to govern in its name. The trouble with representative institutions is that they often turn the act of sovereign authorization into an act of deauthorization. They do not authorize but transfer authority, depriving the authorizing people of its own generic sovereignty and thus of its right to rule. A people that empowers leaders to govern for it can end by disenfranchising itself.

The-president-as-superhero myth promises all the democracy with none of the work. As such, it teaches citizens to admire rule by strong individuals and to abjure the messy workings—disagreement, slow debates, compromise, bargaining—of actual democracy. This training works against our own abilities to navigate and wield democratic sovereignty. Subscribing to the search for a nationally redemptive hero every four years makes citizens feel less, not more, powerful and therefore all the more in need of a superhero presidential rescue. Every cycle, we wind up disgusted by our leadership. And every presidential election leads citizens to the hope that this time, we've got it right. When we turn out to be wrong—again—about the salvific powers of *this* president, we helplessly put our hopes in the next. This boom–bust cycle of hope for the presidential rescue fuels the power of the presidency, if not always the actual power of individual presidents. It offers no such boon for citizens, though. Believing that the solution for democratic problems can come only through a "great president," we put our energy into exaggerated and mythical hopes for *his* agency, rather than investigate, invest in, and cultivate our own.

The president-as-superhero myth teaches citizens to admire rule by strong individuals and to abjure the messy workings of actual democracy. Every cycle, we wind up disgusted by our leadership. Dirck Halstead, "Selects," 1968. Photograph courtesy of the Dirck Halstead Photographic Archive, Center for American History, University of Texas–Austin; e_dh_0992. Copyright Dirck Halstead, Center for American History, University of Texas–Austin.

Presidential power makes us feel powerful by proxy. And once every four years, we get the power to elect the next one. Maybe it's our longing for more democratic agency that is driving the bizarre expansion of the presidential primary season. Looking to maximize the sensation of democratic power that comes with voting for the president, our states race each other to be the one that gets to decide the primary season, narrow the field of candidates, help anoint the party's winner. The race to back up the primary means that candidates now campaign as much as two years in advance of the election—which we mostly complain about, even though as Super Tuesday looms, the primary is all anyone talks about, competing with and maybe beating out the Super Bowl for attention. How did voting for the president achieve such centrality in our democracy? And why does the long presidential season leave so many of us feeling so dissatisfied and democratically powerless?

Chapter 2
Voting and the Incredibly Shrinking Citizen

VOTING IS THE RIGHT MOST FREQUENTLY ASSOCIATED WITH U.S. democratic citizenship, and voting for the president is citizenship's most frequently cited aim. Indeed, the story of U.S. democracy is often narrated as the history of suffrage: who got voting rights and when. Unpropertied white men first, then, after the Civil War, American men of African descent. Black women and white women got the vote in 1920, Native Americans and Puerto Ricans in 1924, citizens of Chinese descent in 1943. Finally, the voting age was lowered to eighteen in 1971, to match the age of Vietnam draftees, during an era of powerful civil reform designed to ensure that minority citizens were actually *able* to vote. We narrate the expansion of democracy by remembering the obstacles overcome by citizens trying to gain the right to vote.

Voting is a democratic power, and voting, as I show in this chapter, makes voters feel powerful. But it is a democratic power that takes as much as it gives. In chapter 1, I noted that while the president served from the nation's earliest days as a symbol of national unity, it was decades before citizens began associating the president with their most important political aspirations. This chapter examines how the association between democracy and voting for the president germinates in the Jacksonian era, an association that motored the expansion of the party system, then takes root and begins crowding out other democratic forms of citizen power in the twentieth. This is a companion tale to the one I narrated in chapter 1 about the supersizing of presidential heroism over the past two centuries into fairy-tale proportions. As presidential agency looms ever larger in the public imagination, citizen power has become miniaturized: the

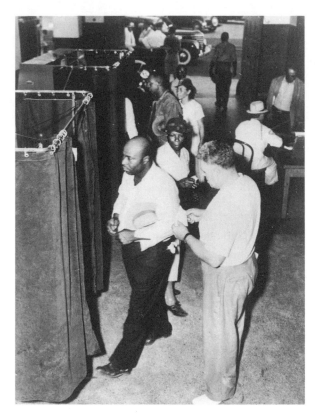

We tell the story of democracy by remembering the obstacles overcome by citizens trying to gain the right to vote. Courtesy of Library of Congress, National Association for the Advancement of Colored People Records.

democratic participation and decision making envisioned by the citizenry of the early nation has been imaginatively and practically reduced to the single act of voting for the president. This miniaturization of citizen power, intertwining with our fascination for presidential power, brings us dangerously close to the very mind-set the American Revolution so resonantly repudiated. Instead of seeing democracy as staked on the political power and agency of the People (i.e., the people's sovereignty), it brings us to the very brink of the theory that informs monarchical legitimacy: that the president's power (i.e., *his* sovereignty) is what constitutes and defines our power as a nation. Historically, these two countervailing attitudes about sovereignty have been coexisting unremarked. But we need to start thinking about their interrelation more critically, because as the president's power becomes more prominent, *democracy* suffers.

"Their Darling Democracy"

The notion that the founders "gave us" a safe version of democracy under the auspices of their carefully crafted form of representative government too easily suggests that the citizens of the early nation were a mob of political simpletons waiting for their leaders to tell them what to do, gratefully receiving the unexpected boon of the vote (for those who were property-owning white men over eighteen, at least). But as I've already shown, that's not really an accurate historical understanding. Well before the Declaration of Independence, American colonists—men and women, whites and free blacks— were developing the arts of self-governance and exercising them—in the form of committees of deliberation, demands for government accountability, published opposition, collective resistance, self-arming, and out-of-door actions both peaceful and violent. A significant number of these actions concerned property, taxation, and debt collection. And many property rebellions, like that of the North Carolina Regulators, seem to have been inspired by the religious awakenings of the mid-eighteenth century. The evangelical Protestant practices sweeping the colonies led people to believe that they did not have to defer to colonial government but could deliberate communally according to their "inner light," then *act* on what they determined together was fair. In terms of these historical property rebellions, such determinations had to do with *who* worked and improved the land. (It's worth remembering this history when we consider how religious faith continues to motor democratic political engagement, for both good and ill, today.)

Recently, historians have argued that these common people and their grassroots movements toward self-governing political participation and meaningful decision making influenced the founders' decision to declare independence. Colonial elites in Virginia, historian Woody Holton argues, were caught in the middle between a restive population of white yeomen, black slaves, and dispossessed Native Americans, and the growing British Empire. As pressures grew from both directions in the 1760s, the colonial gentry calculated that their best chances for getting the American scene under control in a way that would continue benefiting their own interests was to break free from the growing demands for tax revenue coming from

England. In so doing, they set free energies that they could only hope to control: colonial elites understood and many feared the widespread desire for popular forms of government. When the Virginian Carter Braxton described the commoners' desire to use political independence to establish "their darling democracy" in debates leading up to the Declaration, he meant it as a warning to his fellow elites.

And in fact, desire and enthusiasm for "their darling democracy" *was* difficult to constrain. Washington's administration under the new Constitution treated expressions of self-government, whether peaceful like the citizen watchdog Democratic-Republican societies that sprang up across the new states to monitor and advise state and national government, or more activist like the Whiskey Rebellion, as threats and not complements to national government. The Federalists worked to eliminate these self-governing expressions both from practice and from imagination.

The Whiskey Rebellion offers an interesting example of these early official attempts to quash enthusiasm for democracy. This event evolved rapidly in 1794, in response to renewed attempts to enforce a three-year-old federal excise tax. Because of long-standing opposition to excise taxes and especially those on distilled liquors throughout the states, the tax's collection had been thwarted. As Judge Alexander Addison, a Federalist district judge, noted in his account of the rebellion, protesters were following a long and successful tradition: their protests against similar *state* excises enacted in 1781 and 1783 had led to Pennsylvania's repeal of the taxes in 1791. But in 1794, as historian Roger Sharp notes, at "the height of the popularity and strength of the Democratic-Republican societies," Washington's administration, then based in Philadelphia, decided to enforce its federal collection. Although Kentuckians, Marylanders, and North Carolinians were also affected by the tax and indeed had joined Pennsylvanians in this protest, Washington's administration targeted only western Pennsylvania (the Pittsburgh area) for strict enforcement, calculating that it could make a swift and inexpensive example there to put down the wider resistance.

The protesters responded by organizing committees of correspondence in four counties, resisting collection through vocal, published, and action protests, even seizing the federal garrison's equipment and ammunition.

Democratic-Republican committees supported these protests, east and west of the Alleghenies, publishing letters and toasts in support of them. Careful historians of that episode observe that the whiskey tax opponents staged their opposition in ways that drew on and honored republican ideals and new constitutional processes. Washington and his administration saw a strict opposition between local (unlawful) and federal (lawful) democracy in this episode. But the rebels did not see themselves as engaged in unlawful opposition. As historian Jeffrey Davis points out, these societies appealed to those outside western Pennsylvania, publicly and lawfully explaining their opposition in terms of national principles and calling on citizens to "fraternize with us in a common cause." Their methods for staging their protest, by passing resolutions, delivering public remonstrances to officials, and electioneering, as well as their published appeals to a broader public, acknowledged their local concerns as well as their place in a larger political system.

Then events escalated. Erroneously believing federal agents were about to seize tax delinquents at the start of the harvest season and put them on trial across the mountains in Philadelphia, more than fifty armed men gathered to challenge the agents. John Neville, a widely despised tax collector, fired into the assembly of anxious and angry men, wounding several and killing one. The group responded by setting fire to his house. The local community quickly resolved to support those who had attacked Neville's property and to try to keep them from being prosecuted. Thus the "rebellion" began. Receiving news of these events, Washington gave orders to assemble thirteen thousand militia, a force larger than any he commanded during the Revolution. Pennsylvania governor Thomas Mifflin joined Pennsylvania secretary of state Alexander Dallas in calling for federal military restraint. After only a brief negotiation, President Washington, urged on by Secretary of the Treasury Alexander Hamilton, sent in the troops.

As Sharp notes, this uprising "was part of the American struggle to come to grips with republicanism and the nature of representative government." By his reading, the rebels learned a necessary lesson about civic compromise. But these so-called rebels had been asking for compromise from the start—a different form of tax on land, which would be more fairly distributed. The lesson here, from the angle of western Pennsylvanians, may have been more about which direction compromise can go: Washington's administration used this opportunity to demonstrate a federal monopoly on "compromise"—and symbolically, too, on sovereignty.

Their Darling King

After the resolution of the Whiskey Rebellion, the popularity of the Democratic-Republican societies faded. But energies for local democratic practice continued even as the imaginative centrality of federal government began taking hold. As I showed in chapter 1, this centrality began forming through the rituals of celebration—toasting and parading—that federalists encouraged under Washington's presidency. These rituals and the mythologizing of his life after his death coordinated counterintuitively with what the historian Brendan McConville has characterized as the lingering energies of royalism in the early nation. McConville argues against the trend of much historiography of the eighteenth-century colonies and early nation that has described American colonists losing their interest in British rule early in the eighteenth century, emphasizing how those colonists began developing the arts of independence long before the actual revolution. Somewhat differently, McConville insists that while American colonists lost respect for the authority of the British parliament and their local colonial governments, they remained ardently and actively loyal to the king in both political belief and social practice. This difference, he insists, is crucial, because it reveals a doubled orientation in the late colonial and early national citizenry toward both political independence *and* royalism. While the Revolution witnessed both mannerly and violent repudiations of the king's images and symbols, it's plausible that the very frenzy of reaction against the king attests to the passion through which he had for so long been regarded by the rebelling citizenry. Citizens of the early nation could be both revolutionarily independent and residually royalist, as they demonstrated in New York during the Revolution, when delegates to the Constitutional Congress—including Washington—were welcomed to the city with an "imperial" entrance procession on the same day that New York's last imperial governor was greeted with a similar procession.

As McConville summarizes, contemporaries "long remembered the bizarre day's strangest aspect. According to one observer, many of the same people who greeted Washington later 'joined in the Governor's train, and with the loudest acclamations, attended him to his lodgings, where, with the utmost seeming sincerity, they shook him by the hand.' The transition in authority had created a kind of duality in New Yorkers' minds and in minds throughout the colonies." The mythologization of Washington in the early 1800s drew on that residual desire among citizens to admire the king's power and on the long habit of seeing the king's sovereignty as what constituted them *as* a people.

Thus there are historical reasons to be at least a little skeptical about the association of democratic expression with voting for the president, with the developing national habit to see the president's power as delivering power to the American people, rather than vice versa. This doesn't mean that early citizens were mindlessly re-creating royalist fealty in their admiration of Washington, but it does signal that something more complicated than the creation of brand-new American rituals for independence was at play.

"From the Bosom of the People"

While the glamour of the symbolic president was growing in the early nation through posthumous remembrances of Washington, the habit of expecting the president to work politically for the people had not yet become established. For his part, Thomas Jefferson did nothing to contribute to the idea that citizens should look to the president for their political representation. Opposed to anything that smacked of monarchy, Jefferson moved immediately to reduce the pomp associated with the presidency and the White House established by the Washington and Adams presidencies. And—perhaps disappointingly for his political allies—Jefferson held severely to the Constitution's limits on the presidential office, demonstrating through his own behaviors that he understood Congress to be the supreme representative branch. Thus rather than try to exert executive branch power, Jefferson deployed his considerable diplomatic skills on members of Congress to persuade them toward his agendas, becoming what presidential studies scholar Michael Genovese terms an "activist leader of Congress."

To say that Jefferson did not court the people via the presidency is not to say he renounced executive power, though. In pardoning those prosecuted under the Alien and Sedition Acts, Jefferson staked an early claim for the executive branch's ability to review constitutionality. In the Louisiana Purchase, Jefferson exercised the "implied powers" (powers not specified in the Constitution that proponents say are "suggested" there) that Hamilton had claimed for Washington and that Jefferson as secretary of state had strongly contested. (As president, Jefferson felt dubious enough about their exercise that he proposed a constitutional amendment to enable the purchase. But he shortly backed away from this proposal to expedite the deal.)

After Jefferson, when Madison, Monroe, and John Quincy Adams worked to expand the powers of the office, they did so largely in coordination with the legislative branch. But Andrew Jackson, who rode to the presidency on a new tide of party activism and voter participation, brought a new conception to the office, one that would accelerate and consolidate both symbolic and political expectations for the presidency, would detach presidential power from the Constitution and prime the electorate for the twentieth-century transition from congressional to presidential government. The changes engineered by what is known as the "Jacksonian revolution" proved far more fundamental to the accumulation of power by the presidency than the evidently bolder claims for war powers that Abraham Lincoln, facing Civil War, would make.

Jefferson's transition to the presidency in 1800 is often remembered as a dramatic moment in U.S. history, what Jefferson himself referred to as a "second revolution." By this he referenced the peaceful transfer of power from one (proto)party—the Federalists—to another, the Jeffersonian Democratic-Republicans. But a more important revolution for the executive office was little more than a generation away. The next twenty years witnessed the United States' first postindependence war with Britain (the War of 1812), the first in a series of financial panics and economic depressions that would only escalate over the next quarter century, a massive acquisition of U.S. territory, and a dramatic expansion in voting rights for white men, entitling even men who did not hold property to vote in most states. Jackson became a military hero during the war, and he became a national hero to thousands of newly enfranchised, less economically privileged voters in the 1820s, a president who had started out as "one of them." When the Pennsylvania state-nominating convention met in 1824, its attendees cast their support for Jackson, declaring "Andrew Jackson comes pure, untrammeled, and unpledged, from the bosom of the people." The various economic and political convergences of this era combined with Jackson's personal history to make him uniquely viable as a presidential candidate who could, like the fabled Washington, stand as a firm defender of national boundaries even as his own humble origins and western residency allowed him to connect "personally" with nonelite voters in unparalleled ways. This connection—and its embrace by the electorate—laid the path toward what modern political scientists describe as the "personal" presidency: a popularly elected leader whose power is largely unchecked except by the "will" of the people, who signed off in advance when they elected him.

For historians and political scientists, Jackson is a highly controversial president, and they continue debating aspects of his legacy today. He is remembered for his iconic role in what is known as the democratization of the presidency, as well as for his opposition to the U.S. Bank, his unrelenting advocacy for Indian Removal, his quelling of the Nullification Controversy of 1832 (a sectional crisis and major national debate over federal versus state authority), and his hardheaded, often arrogant demeanor toward political and congressional opponents. His policies and positions as president (and also as a military general) were certainly divisive and widely debated in his own day. But he was, in a way unprecedented for presidents except for Washington, a *popular* national hero. By the early 1820s, with military biographies in circulation, Jackson was commonly and affectionately regarded both as an effective leader and as a man of the people. His popularity emerged from the stories surrounding his ferocity—on the battlefield and in diplomatic negotiations—in the Creek and Seminole Wars, and in his famous defeat of the British in New Orleans during the

War of 1812. The "Hero of New Orleans" was a national favorite well before his political allies put him forward for the presidency in 1824. The priority of his military over his presidential reputation endured past his presidency, showing up in biographies printed in the decade after his death, which devote endless chapters to his martial exploits and gloss quickly over his two-term presidency.

Jackson's family migrated to the Carolina uplands from Ireland in the mid-1760s, living among other Scots-Irish settlers attempting to scrape a living out of the clay soil. Jackson, the youngest of the family's three sons, was born on that frontier two years after the family settled. His father, who may or may not have been squatting on the land his family claimed, died just before Jackson was born, and his mother moved in with her sister, laboring to provide her son an education that might lead to his becoming a Presbyterian minister. But her youngest son's fiery temperament and his spotty education did not guide him toward ministering. Rather, at the age of thirteen, with the Revolution now raging in the Waxhaw settlement, Jackson joined up and was almost as quickly taken prisoner by the British. Here we have one of the first famous stories about the young prisoner Andrew, who, commanded to black the boots of a British officer, supposedly replied, "Sir, I am a prisoner of war, and claim to be treated as such," at which the officer reportedly drew his sword and slashed at Jackson's head. Young Andrew ducked and parried that blow with his hand, sustaining a severe injury and a tangible symbol of his early independence and sacrifice for national self-rule.

Jackson's fabled spirit of independence, then, extended from the country's Revolution into an age when its founders were dying and its citizens were becoming anxious that they could not live up to such manly exemplars. Jackson emerged as precisely such a man. His mother and both his brothers died during the Revolutionary years, and so loosed from the bonds of family, Jackson migrated to the frontier settlement of Nashville, Tennessee. Working as an attorney and public prosecutor, Jackson quickly improved his own fortune. Soon he moved into political office. In his Tennessee frontier travels, he developed a reputation as a bold and fearless Indian fighter, a reputation he would only expand as head of the Tennessee militia during the Creek and Seminole Wars. Even before Jackson became famous as the "Hero of New Orleans," he was earning a reputation not just as a ruthless military strategist but also as a ruthless diplomat, extracting draconian concessions first from the Creeks, then the Cherokees and Seminoles, in treaty negotiations.

It was as a general who snatched victory from the jaws of defeat in the War of 1812 that Jackson captivated national attention, though. The war that barely registers in popular memory today was an important symbolic turning point for the young nation. In what is often termed "the Second War of Independence," war hawks in the Democratic-Republican Party finally won their way, persuading Congress to declare war on Britain for its many years of seizing American ships and impressing sailors. The decision to declare war looked like a bad one from the start, as the United

States' multipronged attack on Canada resulted in losses on every front in 1812 and again in 1813. Things got even worse in 1814, when the British invaded Washington, D.C., forcing President Madison and Congress to flee. The British burned the new capital's public buildings—including the White House. The nation teetered toward bankruptcy, and worse.

But then England failed in an attempt to invade Baltimore and was defeated by U.S. forces in a battle at Lake Champlain. The tide began to turn. Losing interest (as had happened during the Revolution) in a war that now seemed unwinnable, England signed a treaty with the United States in late December 1814. But the slow relay of information meant that Jackson had already inflicted a humiliating loss on British troops in early January before he received news of the Treaty of Ghent. For citizens in the United States, this past-the-point victory was better than good. If the war had begun with a sense that England was damaging U.S. commerce and emasculating its honor, then Jackson's humiliating routing of British forces in Louisiana resuscitated that honor. It added victory to the treaty with England and fueled a surge of national pride.

Jackson's popularity was fanned with military biographies that appeared in the late 1810s and early 1820s. These celebrations of the "Hero of New Orleans" appeared at the crest of a key historical transition. States began expanding suffrage for white men after the Revolution, a trend that accelerated in western states in the early part of the nineteenth century and spread eastward. The popular vote for the first time played a key role in the presidential election of 1824. By the mid-1830s, nearly every state had lifted restrictions on white male voters, and parties began holding national nominating conventions. States regularized their elections to coordinate the first national voting day on November 7, 1848. National citizenship in this era became firmly linked to white manhood, and democracy to the vote. No matter their social or economic rank, these men had won their "rights." These new rights were symbolically associated not just with the men's ability to vote for members of town council but more especially for the man-of-the-people president, Andrew Jackson.

This transition in the criteria for civic entitlement was neither smooth nor inevitable. Many during the founding era associated political participation with the economic stability of property ownership. These political elites were not happy with the notion of expanding the franchise to men they considered "dependents" (i.e., economically dependent on *employment* for their living). Even before the Declaration of Independence, political elites had become concerned about the contests over property from among such underlings. As evangelical religion swept through the colonies in the 1740s and again through the states in the 1820s, preaching a theology that redeemed without discriminating, and as working-class sentiment consolidated in the years following the Revolution, more and more nonelites began suggesting that political democracy would depend on an equitable redistribution of property. They contested the hereditary claims of the landed elite at the same time they fought off onerous taxes, debt foreclosures, and the speculation claims of the wealthy to lands they did not occupy in the west. The political enfranchisement of nonproperty holders threatened to foreground these battles over the traditional claims of property, just as the War of 1812—and Jackson's role in forcing massive land cessions from the Cherokee and Chickasaws—auspiciously opened up huge tracts of land for triumphant occupation by white men agitating for ownership rights.

The Era of the Common Man?

Jackson, then, was just the man for such a moment. His self-made background and his spectacular military record made him the popular—and electorally denied—candidate in 1824, the first election where the popular vote played a significant role. Jackson pulled in nearly forty thousand votes more than John Quincy Adams, who would become president by brokering a deal for electoral college votes with Henry Clay, the third runner-up. Under the Constitution, of course, each state decides how it chooses its electors. Because the office of the president is *indirectly* elected, in the early nation, one-quarter of the states did not even allow a popular vote on the presidency. This trend diminished rapidly after Jackson's controversial 1824 denial: by the early 1830s, every state but South Carolina chose its electors according to the results of the popular vote. The people may have been thwarted in their popular choice that year, when just more than one-quarter of eligible voters showed up at the polls, but in 1828 they swept Jackson into the presidency. That election saw the proportion of eligible voters casting ballots swell from 27 percent to an astonishing 57 percent, with the total vote increasing from just more than 350,000 to more than 1 million. Jefferson's "second revolution" pales in comparison with this moment as a political transition. Jefferson's election came through an electoral college controlled by the states' political elites; Jackson's in 1828 was the accomplishment of a newly enfranchised public. Thus President Jackson was the first to represent the popular vote's new power; he stood for the triumphal presence of the "common man" in the voting public. Common men and women celebrated this landmark moment by visiting the White House, which Jackson (most scandalously, in the eyes of the elites) opened to all comers for his first inaugural. This apparent political expansion—the democratization of the presidency—explains why the Jacksonian era is known as the "era of the common man," despite how carefully historians have documented that common men faced *more* economic instability and downturns than ever during those years.

Jackson did not miss the political significance of this symbolic expansion and his connection to it. In his first annual message to Congress, he declared: "I consider it one of the most urgent of my duties to bring to your attention the propriety of amending that part of our Constitution which relates to the election of President and Vice-President. Our system of government was by its framers deemed an experiment, and they therefore consistently provided a mode of remedying its defects. To the people belongs the choice of electing their Chief Magistrate." Jackson argued that the House of Representatives could not in fact be relied on to represent the choice of the people: there "it is obvious the will of the people may not always be ascertained, or, if ascertained it may not be regarded." Ignoring the federalists' careful arguments about protections for minority interests, Jackson argued that the "first principle" of the U.S. system is *"that the majority is to govern"* and thus on this basis, the president must serve as the direct representative of that majority.

Jackson's call for the constitutional removal of any "intermediate agency in the election of the President and Vice-President" went unheeded (as we were well reminded during the 2000 election). But he would more successfully seize the momentum of this election for a related cause, insisting that this landmark election accrued a special new authority for his presidency—what would be called in the twentieth century a "mandate." By this theory, only the president can represent the will of the entire electorate; once elected, the president is de facto authorized by the people in *all his decisions*. Thus to disagree with the president, in his casting, was to insult the *People*. Jackson was guided by this imperative as he proceeded to wage war on the Second Bank of the United States and to veto more bills than all his predecessors combined. He exercised his veto power in unprecedented ways: not because he thought legislation was unconstitutional but simply because he disagreed with it, and thus as the single representative of the whole people, he felt entitled to act against it on their behalf. His notion that presidents were uniquely authorized by all the people for political action put the president's representative authority symbolically on par with that of Congress, and presidents who followed were happy to elaborate—and expand—on this theory of executive power.

Significantly, the notion of the mandate suggests that the basis for presidential power comes not through the Constitution but directly through the people—both the particular people who voted for him and, more abstractly, "the sovereign people" whom the elected president then claims to represent. This idea, combined with the ambiguity of the Constitution itself with regard to the specifics of executive power, installed a creative new logic that presidents could exploit in defining the office's scope and reach. If the people had previously conferred their abstract and multiple sovereignty onto the less abstract but multiple body of Congress, Jackson's innovation of the mandate encouraged citizens to see their sovereignty most powerfully condensed and unified in the singular body of the president. It offers a sensation of sovereignty to the people through their participation in the presidential election. This theory turns the indirect mode of election in the Constitution into something that *seems* more directly powerful.

Jackson's presidential legacy fundamentally changed not only the nature of the presidency as a public office but also the nature of politics. His efforts in office and the energies that emerged during this era reworked the relationship between the president and the citizens, and between citizens and the representational political process. Inspired by their success at getting Jackson into office and excited by the possibilities of their organizing for change, white male voters increasingly staked their democratic citizenship by joining a party and voting for its slate. Formal political parties made their dramatic emergence onto the national stage in the 1820s and 1830s to organize nominations and campaigns. They were a forceful new energy in the political scene, and they took over politics and political organizing during the nineteenth century, for both good and ill.

The Party System and the Presidential "Expansion" of Democracy

The appearance of Jacksonian democracy and the party system has long been seen by political historians as marking a definitive break within federal republicanism, the point at which "democracy" enters the U.S. governmental picture. There are strong arguments on the side of this theory: representative institutions did change in the wake of Jacksonianism, as legislatures and city officials were elected more directly. More offices were opened to election or to party-controlled appointment, more white men had the franchise, and more men participated in the newly open partisan political process. But from McConville's perspective, with his emphasis on the lingering civic disposition toward royalism, the party patronage system that appeared under Jackson "resembled nothing if not an eighteenth-century patronage network, formalized and made available to two emergent parties who espoused an egalitarian language in a world where the son of a president had already been elected to that same office, and the distribution of wealth was more inequitable than it had ever been before 1776."

It would be misleading, however, to assess the Jacksonian era simply through its record of party patronage and spoils abuses. As historian Mary Ryan reminds us, during this era politics in public reemerged along with many other forms of publicity like religious revivals, county fairs, cattle shows, traveling museums, and menageries. Fueled by suffrage's promises of political inclusion, men of all classes began joining public associations, holding meetings in public, and taking a stake in the local shaping of civic and political life. These associations, their public events and meetings, literally represented the people and their occupational, religious, social, and political diversity in public. This newly vigorous public life changed the structure of U.S. politics, broadening the arena of offices eligible to election. Before the Jacksonian era, city governments had little democratic accountability: all of this changed during the next forty years, as people lobbied in public for public institutions to become publicly accountable.

The influence of parties on political life literally exploded during the antebellum period, organizing and channeling these new political expressions and energies. Party electioneering became a form of mass entertainment, working in this way to expand voting rolls and political activism. While party loyalties were deeply felt and seriously pursued by some, they could be entirely diversionary for others. Voting was not yet the single-minded and surgical event of pulling a lever in the privacy of a booth, but a series of sprawling, public, carnival-like activities, where people spent hours drinking, socializing, and—usually—voting. If party activism helped create the push for democratizing local public offices, expanding the realm of democratic accountability, a significant aspect of that energy was as diversionary as it was political. Historians Glenn Altschuler and Stuart Blumin recount an episode at a New York state election in the 1840s, where a man named Nelson Hall could not remember if he had handed in a Whig or Democrat ballot. Questioned about the confusion, he testified that "he did not care for whom he voted; [he] had always been a Jackson man."

Was Hall a fool? Or do such instances—and they are numerous—offer clues about the "duality" that McConville describes in the early nation: the simultaneous emergence of democracy building *and* less democratic desires to be led by a powerful leader? Altschuler and Blumin point toward something a little more specific. They highlight how political parties developed a mode of democratic agitation that didn't particularly depend on the *political* investments of the voters they mobilized. The developing parties, Altschuler and Blumin assert, were similar in that they "demanded little of their loyal voters besides voting itself," aiming their efforts at mobilizing "large numbers of voters who did not have to care much about the outcome of the elections." In this way, parties arguably toiled to depoliticize the very democratic involvement they elicited. Thus partisan festivals or rallies would compete with and gradually even replace the meeting-place practice of democracy that had characterized the conduct of public business in towns and localities across the states, involving citizens more directly in the project of self-governing. Ironically, then, as suffrage expanded and as party membership gained public visibility, politicalness—the art of self-government—contracted. Political voice and expression began disappearing from the wider sphere of the town hall and square, and its "out of doors" counterparts, political watchdog committees, protests, and riots, were channeled toward the act of casting a ballot for a slate of candidates on a straight ticket offered by party bosses and organizers.

After Jackson, the presidency's connection to the "common man" became political common sense, if not constitutional fact. As presidential historian Richard McCormick observes, these changes took on their own logic, developing a momentum unforeseen by those who crafted the Constitution. By the 1840s, as he summarizes, "the presidential game had now become a kind of mass folk festival. . . . To a detached observer, the phenomenon defied explanation in purely political terms. Neither the charisma of the candidates nor the quality of the issues at stake could seemingly account for such an extraordinary expenditure of emotional fervor or organizational energy." McCormick underscores how the presidency "came to be the great focal point of all American politics, far transcending in intensity of concern congressional elections, or, in most states, gubernatorial or legislative contests," and argues that the intensity of this connection had more to do with cultural imperatives than political ones. From this point, the presidential contest functioned more, he suggests, as a partisan ritual of national belonging than as a democratic expression of deliberative public will. In the mid-nineteenth century, he suggests, the public did not particularly delude itself about the nature or force of the ritual: "It is not at all apparent that in the popular view the presidency was looked upon as a source of strong leadership in government."

More recently, historians have pushed harder on these suggestions about the surprisingly *un*democratic outcomes of this seemingly (and much-trumpeted) democratic expansion. Altschuler and Blumin suggest that "there is an incompleteness to the Jacksonian revolution that ought to give us pause." They note that the dramatic surge in voter participation during the 1828 election did not demarcate a trend. If this was a revolution, it was one, in their estimate, that fizzled halfway. They disagree with those who point to the emergence of modern parties and their national conventions—commonly considered the bedrock of U.S. democracy— as the importantly democratic outcome of this "revolution." They argue, differently, that the parties did not emerge in response to some popular demand for formalized political opposition but were the product of party bosses vying for power. Jacksonian era parties were about capturing and controlling, and not just expanding, popular participation. The appearance of openness in party conventions, they contend, was an illusion carefully orchestrated by party leaders. They conclude that while we should not dismiss what the parties contributed to expanding democracy, we need at the same time to be careful about overstating or romanticizing what they actually achieved.

Parties, Congress, Presidents, and the "Little Man"

Despite the growing popularity of presidential elections as festivals for enacting national belonging, Congress maintained its primary role in federal government throughout the nineteenth century. Lincoln did usurp key congressional powers during the Civil War. But Congress fought back in the years following, impeaching Lincoln's successor Andrew Johnson when he tried asserting prerogative powers. Congress preserved its constitutionally designed preeminence for the next several decades, into the twentieth century.

Political parties remained a central force in national politics through the Civil War, Reconstruction, and into the Gilded Age. The 1880s through early 1900s saw the cresting of party influence and of voter turnout—in some towns more than 100 percent! Obviously there was corruption and ballot box stuffing, but even allowing for that, participation was clearly impressively high (averaging around 80 percent of the eligible electorate), and higher than it ever has been since. Throughout the nineteenth century, parties and their "bosses" had strengthened themselves by enrolling the masses, and by the late nineteenth century, their effectiveness at enlisting support was obvious.

But in the 1880s and 1890s, goaded by the economic maneuvering of the wealthy and a financial depression that impoverished ordinary citizens, people began organizing new, "third" parties to fight both corporate *and* party corruption. These movements came in the midst of the Gilded Age, when a few entrepreneurial men and their families—like the Vanderbilts, Rockefellers, Roosevelts, and Astors—amassed enormous fortunes and built economic empires, expanding the legal definitions and entitlements of the corporation and using their growing power to squeeze government coffers as well as laborers' livelihoods. The gap between rich and poor was significant: in 1890, William Vanderbilt held the nation's largest fortune at $200 million, when the median household wealth stood at $500. The Populists, a largely agrarian labor movement that aimed for democratic reform of the economy, made a strong push for representation in local, state, and national government on a platform that called for (among its many interesting features) legal unionization, a graduated income tax, national ownership of railroads, settler ownership of land, and voter reform. They made a significant showing in the run-up to the 1896 election, earning serious attention from both parties. Democratic leadership "fused" with them, nominating William Jennings Bryan for president. ("Fusion" is an electoral strategy where two parties nominate the same candidate and thus the candidate's name appears on the ballot twice, a practice that directly registers the influence of the third party in the ballot count.) Republican leadership joined up with banking, industrial, and corporate leadership to put down the Populist threat. They were only barely able to do so: the Republican candidate, William McKinley, won by a margin of four percentage points in the popular vote.

The emergence of the Grange movement, agrarian Populism, and urban Progressivism, and a plethora of other parties like Labor Reform, Independent, Greenback-Labor, Readjusters, and Farmers' Alliance (to name only a few), made it clear to business and mainstream party interests that citizens were bringing the energies of labor strikes and riots into focused political action. Elites in business and government took this threat seriously and began working to gain control within the Republican and Democratic parties. As part of their own strategy, they took up the Populists' and Progressives' call for electoral (as well as other significant) reform. There is no question reforms were needed. But whom they would benefit was the question.

With the combined efforts of third-party interests, government, and big business, the early twentieth century witnessed waves of electoral cleanup maneuvers. While some of these strategies advantaged and broadened the electorate, others contracted it. Parties' sway over presidential candidates was interrupted by the introduction of the so-called Australian or secret ballot in the early 1890s. This reform allowed citizens to dodge the public peer pressures of party and thus enabled them to begin the practice of splitting their ticket—that is, voting for senators and representatives from one party and presidential candidates from another. As political scientist Theodore Lowi carefully documents, the innovation of the split ticket took power away from the parties and accumulated it for the presidency: split-ticket voters seem far more inclined to vote against their party in presidential, rather than local, state, congressional, or senate, elections. Split-ticket voting reoriented parties' relationship to their presidential candidates, forcing them to pay more attention to presidential candidates' popular appeal, rather than just their party loyalty. This gave presidential candidates an increasing leverage to develop their own personal campaign and administrative agendas, loosening their obligations to and dependency on parties.

After the 1896 election, state after state outlawed fusion, making it harder than it already was for third parties to gain electoral traction; many also installed direct primaries, forcing a "democratization" of parties' candidate selection process and loosening party bosses' control. The Populists belatedly won their appeal for the direct election of senators with the ratification of the Seventeenth Amendment (1913), and then white women and African American women won the vote in the Nineteenth Amendment (1920). In the name of cleaning up the voter rolls, business reformers initiated a series of voter reforms at the local and state levels. Business-backed reform initiated a series of improvements designed to expose corruption and make government more efficient and accountable.

Civil service reform removed key public jobs from party control and re-organized city "functions" as independent agencies so they could be run on a nonpartisan basis. By diminishing their resources for patronage, business aimed in part to weaken parties' ability to bestow favors locally, and what they couldn't do through reform initiative, they undertook with widely publicized investigations into party corruption. As sociologists Frances Fox Piven and Richard Cloward summarize, "After the turn of the century, the local parties, weakened by relentless reform assaults, were less able to reach voters by any method at all. The great spectacles and celebrations, the marching bands and parades that had punctuated earlier campaigns, faded away." As parties lost the ability (and will) to mobilize voters, and nearly every state, north and south, enacted ever-more restrictive registration and poll requirements to eliminate "irresponsible" voters, the more impressive rates of voter turnout witnessed in the late 1800s fell to below 50 percent by 1920. The fall-off in voter turnout was disproportionate among both rural and agrarian poor, including white and immigrant laborers in the north, and both blacks and poor whites in the south (e.g., voter participation in Texas fell to 30 percent by 1930; in Mississippi as early as 1900 it had fallen to a minuscule 17 percent of those eligible). This trend established a pattern that has yet to be interrupted in the U.S. electorate: the underrepresentation of the poor and the over-representation of the wealthy at the polls.

It was during this same period, near the turn of the century, when a new press for executive branch clout began. The offensive started with Grover Cleveland, whose proclivity for the veto caught the attention of a newly minted Johns Hopkins political science PhD, Woodrow Wilson, a young professor who had just published a plan for improving and focusing congressional responsiveness to public opinion when Cleveland became president. In that book, *Congressional Government*, which was published in 1885, Wilson argued that the Constitution couldn't adequately keep pace with changing historical circumstance. He proposed abandoning the fear of faction and unimpeded majority rule that led the framers to their mechanistic constitutional model, with its careful checks and balances, and called instead for a more organic model that would appreciate and cultivate national spirit and government efficiency by coordinating, instead of separating, branch powers. In this book, Wilson entirely discounted the president as an agent for this change, believing that the Constitution made him too weak and dependent on the legislative branch and his own party to accomplish the sweeping reforms Wilson envisioned: "The business of the President, occasionally great, is usually not much above routine. Most of the time it is *mere* administration." But Cleveland's reassertion of prerogative by veto, and his independence from both Congress and party politics, soon caused the young professor to begin rethinking his consignment of the executive to the government's dustbin, a reassessment reinforced by McKinley's presiding over the Spanish-American War.

The presidential assault on congressional authority that captured Wilson's interest was launched from the executive's power base: foreign policy. As the constitutionally designated point man for diplomacy and treaty negotiation, and with the power to initiate defensive war, the executive has always had an advantage over Congress in foreign relations. Presidents John Tyler and James K. Polk used secrecy and unilateralist preemption to seize both diplomatic and military supremacy from Congress during the Mexican War, blurring the line between offensive action, which the president is not constitutionally authorized to take, and the defensive action he is. The president's foreign policy powers expanded rapidly in the early twentieth century as presidents took more and more unilateral privileges that eroded congressional power and input, including expanded war powers, the increasing replacement of treaties (which require Senate ratification) with executive agreements (which don't), and the assumption of near-complete control of national security and intelligence.

McKinley launched the expansion of presidential foreign policy powers as he ignited U.S. imperialist ambitions. McKinley himself was averse to warring with Spain, but a bellicose Congress declared war, and once in, McKinley energetically assumed the mantle of commander in chief, pressing it to imperial ambitions. He presided over Cuba's eventual U.S.-sponsored independence, then swiftly engineered U.S. colonial possession of Puerto Rico, Guam, the Philippines, and Hawai'i, effectively creating the United States as an international colonial power. Then Theodore Roosevelt, with his boundless desires for both world power and publicity, increased U.S. international investments as he expanded the president's role in the eyes of the public. Roosevelt's "Big Stick" policy forced a deal for the construction of the Panama Canal, enforced an executive agreement with Santo Domingo over the Senate's refusal to ratify a treaty, and was central to brokering a peace agreement that ended the Russo-Japanese War—an agreement that included Roosevelt strategizing to cut off European support for Russia by secretly committing the U.S. military to support Japan. When opponents objected that his claims for prerogative were unconstitutional, Roosevelt confidently insisted otherwise. His principle was that broad presidential powers were implied in the "take care" clause of the Constitution ("He shall take Care that the Laws be faithfully executed") and could be limited only by explicit constitutional prohibition or congressional legislation. As he said in his autobiography of his executive agreement with Santo Domingo, "The Constitution did not explicitly give me power. . . . But, the Constitution did not forbid my doing what I did." Within a generation, during Franklin D. Roosevelt's presidency, the Supreme Court would accept and certify Theodore Roosevelt's brash and expansive interpretation, declaring executive agreements part of the presidency's implied powers and allowing future presidents to bypass the treaty process described in the Constitution when they deem it necessary or useful.

Since the Constitution structured the president as the nation's point man for foreign relations, the aggressive expansion of U.S. international interests during this period added strength almost automatically to the executive office. This international power grab coordinated with domestic developments that had, since the 1880s, been increasing national power at the expense of state politics over the question of big business's interests in interstate commerce. The importance and stature of federal government was growing nationally and internationally, and, accordingly, the size and reach of federal government began rapidly to expand.

Soon Progressive intellectuals in both the Republican and Democratic camps were elaborating on Wilson's forceful critique of the weak government they increasingly believed the framers had created. Reacting against the perception of big money's lawlessness, Progressives identified government as the agent that should intervene on behalf of ordinary citizens looking for fairness and redress. But the problem with congressional government, they argued, was that it was too beholden to the interests of the wealthy. Congress, they argued, buried the interests of the "little man" and disabled his access to genuine democratic agency in his struggle with big money and big business. They began looking for ways to give this overwhelmed and underrepresented majority a more meaningful voice and role in government than they had been able to achieve through parties and Congress.

The Presidential Mandate: Whose Power?

Wilson, now president of Princeton University and soon to mount a successful gubernatorial campaign in New Jersey, published in 1908 a significant revision to his earlier work. Nearly a quarter century of political observation had caused Wilson entirely to reverse his earlier position. In this new book, *Constitutional Government,* he jettisoned his earlier assessment of the president's mere functionality, enduringly reimagining the executive office as a far more appropriate focal point for the national will—public opinion—than the Congress, which he now regarded as hopelessly fractious and micromanagerial. His arguments for a new kind of presidential leadership became the canonical rationale for the president's expanded domestic powers. But for a book authored by a political scientist, this description of the ideal president seems more like a paean to a comicbook superhero than an objective analysis of human agency and institutional function:

> The nation as a whole has chosen him, and is conscious that it has no other political spokesman. His is the only national voice in affairs. Let him once win the admiration and confidence of the country and no other single force can withstand him, no combination of forces will easily overpower him. . . . If he rightly interpret the national thought and boldly insist upon it, he is irresistible; and the country never feels the zest of action so much as when its President is of such insight and caliber. It is for this reason that it will often prefer to choose a man rather than a party. A president whom it trusts can not only lead it, but form it to his own views.

Wilson named and expanded the Jacksonian theory of the presidential "mandate" while he gave presidential powers an extraconstitutional foundation. The presidential leadership growing out of this mandate would in Wilson's projection give citizens a broader and more unified form of representation than anything they could ever garner from their congressional representatives, and would guarantee the president powers beyond those explicitly named in the nation's governing document. Wilson urged citizens to "expand" their own sovereign authority by taking no more action than to support presidential, rather than congressional, leadership and the development of the president's influence. The president's increasing powers would be, he promised, their increasing power.

But as the last sentence in the passage quoted above signals, there is an aspect to Wilson's vision for presidential leadership that aims at something other than representing the will of millions of people. In Wilson's view, the president does not actually even try to do this. Rather, using his powerful charisma, the ideal president *shapes* the will of citizens into conformity with his own. As a leading Wilson scholar, Ronald Pestritto, summarizes, "This is a central irony of Wilson's political thinking: while his rhetoric pushed for a popularization of the American system of governance, Wilson did not maintain a terribly high opinion of the people themselves. Hence, his calls . . . rely heavily on the ability of leadership to educate and move the public through political rhetoric. The public will is to govern, but only insofar as it is led by educated elites who see more clearly than anybody else where that will is actually going." Pestritto's observation begins to highlight the problem for democracy that lies at the heart of the mandate. The president's pledge to wield the power of all the people promises to increase governmental efficiency and to make the president more symbolically prominent in the eyes of his constituents. But it does nothing to broaden the self-governing agency of the people, their ability to discover, articulate, and meaningfully advance their own agendas.

Although it was touted as advancing democratic responsiveness, political scientist Richard A. Dahl describes the effects of the president's claim of the mandate as "pseudodemocratization." He argues that the notion both counters the constitutional design of the executive office and operates under a false premise, namely, that elections indicate the majority's preference not just for the person who occupies the office but for the minutia of his policy decisions, without additional deliberation or contestation from the people or Congress. This notion of the presidential mandate has underwritten, in Dahl's view, a dangerously antidemocratic conception of executive "leadership." He labels it a "myth . . . harmful to democratic life":

> By portraying the president as the only representative of the whole people and Congress as merely representing narrow, special, and parochial interests, the myth of the mandate elevates the president to an exalted position in our Constitutional system at the expense of Congress. The myth of the mandate fosters the belief that the particular interests of the diverse human beings who form the citizen body in a large, complex, and pluralistic country like ours constitute no legitimate element in the general good. . . . Because the myth is almost always employed to support deceptive, misleading, and manipulative interpretations, it is harmful to the political understanding of the citizens.

As Dahl suggests, this notion of the presidential mandate works to squelch both disagreement and deliberation among citizens. It encourages citizens to feel that their objection to presidential policies is somehow unpatriotic, even anti-American. As the nation's "number one democratic representative," the president who claims a mandate for any particular policy is defusing democracy's most important political strength, its ability to create plus-sum solutions from differences of opinion. It teaches citizens to leave the hard thinking to the tough man, the one strong enough to win the mandate (and to feel represented when he uses it to club his opponents). It teaches citizens to practice their patriotism by identifying with the president's choices rather than deliberating, identifying, and pressing democratically for their own choices and ideas. The theory of the presidential mandate is a shell game: it garnishes the people's power (its supposed source) for the unfettered use of the president, for reinforcing the power of *his* office.

Other aspects of Progressives' well-intended reforms had similarly pseudodemocratic results. Wilson's call for presidential reform was swiftly taken up by one of the Progressive movement's leading advocates,

Herbert Croly, an influential journalist and cofounding editor of the *New Republic* whose political commentary influenced both Republicans and Democrats. Croly's critique of the Constitution, like Wilson's, was that its mechanical structure of checks and balances did more to thwart than represent the organically developing will of the People: worship of the Constitution kept citizens believing in a democracy that was less active than symbolic. Croly wanted government reforms that would make it more dynamically responsive to majority will. For Croly, one of the president's most important routes to actualizing the public will was through his oversight of an independent and "scientific" administrative bureaucracy. He advocated separating partisan politics from the objective and efficient administration of the laws and policies that resulted from the political fray. The science of administration was a topic of great interest not just within government but also in big business. Calls for an independent, expertly administered bureaucracy similarly motivated a corporate innovation in the early twentieth century of separating owners from expert managers. Progressives' visions for elaborating scientific or expert administration drew on the expanding corporate organization, even as their plans aimed to limit the prioritization of big money over the little man by finding ways to give the regular citizen a larger and more effective sphere for action in the political economy. The idea of expert policy administration would work powerfully over time, though, to prevent regular citizens from having any meaningful input into the politics of policy, and thus another reform that aimed to give greater voice to the little man effectively worked better to silence it.

Before FDR assumed office, the first two years of the Great Depression had mobilized citizens into popular movements and a variety of demonstrations and strikes (though not back into the voting booths — turnouts through the early 1930s hovered below 50 percent) against big business. Teddy Roosevelt's Progressive Party had faded from view, but his nephew, deeply influenced as much by his uncle's political goals as by Wilson's intellectual arguments, would carry out Wilson's and Croly's ideas about the presidency during his twelve-year administration, one central feature of which was the massive reorganization and expansion of the executive branch under a more "scientific" managerial model. Thus, even as the presidency was reorganized to combat more efficiently the unfairnesses of Depression-era capitalism, the logic for that reform would increasingly be drawn from the organization and mind-set of big business. This structural confluence may explain the success of corporations in the 1940s and 1950s at effectively adding a "fifth freedom" to FDR's famous four American freedoms guaranteed by government (freedom of speech, freedom of religion, freedom from want, freedom from fear): free enterprise. And as I show later, free enterprise and its partner, corporate profit, would quite effectively overtake the democratic priorities of the late-twentieth-century presidency.

In the 1930s, the electorate had been primed by national and international crises, pop-culture superheroes, and the proliferating and reassuring immediacy of the president through media to embrace FDR's massive expansion of the presidency's domestic and foreign powers, and of executive and federal bureaucracy. FDR's aggressive deployment of the federal government to reach into the lives of citizens began providing the relief they were striking and protesting for, and seemed to confirm Wilson's and Croly's earlier, salvific view of the president as the best agent for the little man. These expectations became more and more habitual. But while expectations for what the president could accomplish rose, election turnouts curiously stagnated and declined. Though voter rates during the 1940s and 1950s edged up toward 60 percent averages, they never returned to the highs of the late nineteenth century. And this was as true for FDR's charismatic presidency as it would be for John F. Kennedy's, when voting in presidential elections peaked around 63 percent and has been sliding downward ever since, dipping below 50 percent in the 1996 election. Captivated by the centrality of the president to media coverage of government (well more than half of lead stories in mainstream media since the 1970s have focused on presidential activities) and tutored by ever-present opinion polls reflecting "public approval" back at them, twentieth-century citizens have raised their expectations for the presidency's ability to represent, guarantee, and lead democracy. But as the president has become more symbolically, effectively, and administratively central to U.S. government, political participation has continued diminishing. What can we make of that?

Turning Out the Vote, or Pavlovian Democracy

As Gore Vidal quipped in 1980, the real two-party system of the late twentieth century is constituted by those who still vote in presidential elections and those, equally numerous, who don't. The fall in voter turnout over the last quarter century has received a good deal of attention from political scientists, sociologists, and government experts. Experts and citizens have debated widely how to improve participation and gain a more representative turnout. Congress implemented a series of reforms under the National Voter Registration Act of 1993 (derided as the "motor voter law" by opponents). More than a decade later, we've seen that the debates and reforms aren't working to improve turnout. Some say it's better for democracy when disconnected voters don't vote; some say nonvoters are in fact represented by the president's attention to opinion polls; some say nonvoters rationally calculate that in a mass democracy their single vote couldn't "win" the election; others say that the fault lies with presidential candidates who don't even bother pitching their campaigns to large segments of the population—the poor, youth, states that are incidental to the electoral count—and so why should citizens vote even if we can get them registered? These debates, all valuable, nevertheless pivot on the centrality of some kind of voting for the president to the vitality of democracy. But it might be worth probing that assumption.

Elections have undeniably worked to expand and democratize citizen involvement in U.S. history. We have been taught to see voting as a right, if not necessarily a responsibility. As such, it's a "freedom"—and the decision to vote is just as much a part of our democratic freedom as a decision not to vote. "Freedom" and "vote" go together in our democratic lexicon, then. But is voting just a freedom? As the political scientist Benjamin Ginsberg has observed in his book *Consequences of Consent*, historically elections have worked to train and to "limit mass political involvement by prescribing conditions for acceptable participation in political life." Without denying their democratizing aspects, we could think about how elections also work to *contract* some democratic freedoms, not least of which is our democratic imagination for political action and expression outside the vote. Ginsberg outlines three key ways that elections limit democratic participation:

1. they limit the frequency of citizen participation;
2. they limit the scope of participation;
3. they limit the intensity of political activity by converting it from a means of asserting demands to a collective statement of permission.

Elections encourage citizens to believe that voting is their only access to representative input, an input they can exercise only once every four years. It's certainly true that elections occur more frequently. But in practice, we know that precious few participate in what are called "off-year" or "mid-term" elections—labels that link *every* election to the quadrennial presidential election. The numbers are stark: in federal elections, if the presidential turnout hovers around 50 percent, in mid-term elections, the turnout hovers around 37 percent. While rates for local elections are harder to access, we do know those numbers usually tend to be even lower—from 15 to 30 percent of eligible voters.

Elections also train citizens to limit their political action to the simple—and highly private—act of voting. The voting reforms of the early twentieth century sought to diminish the power of political parties on individual voters. These were well-meaning reforms. But the technical privatization of voting has not only diminished parties' power and their ability to push for major initiatives or comprehensive and distinctive platforms, it has also worked to train citizens away from the idea that self-government is a *public* activity, something people do by coming together to deliberate, debate, and act. It is in the act of coming together with strangers in public, agreeing and disagreeing, that people begin to experience themselves *as* a public, as a citizenry, a democratic community, as the disagreeing and nevertheless collective sovereign people who initiate and certify the Constitution. As political scientist Benjamin Barber observes, modern forms of voting are alienating in the extreme and discourage precisely this understanding of public democracy:

> Voting should be an occasion for celebration as well as for choice, just as the exercise of freedom should be a rite as well as a right. In some localities the Swiss still

choose their representatives and vote on policies in daylong assemblies in which festive games, theater, drinking and camaraderie accompany the formal voting process. Rousseau notes the invigorating sense that such celebrations have on the community's sense of identity as well as on individual citizens' autonomy and capacity for action. In contrast, our primary electoral act, voting, is rather like using a public toilet: we wait in line with a crowd in order to close ourselves up in a small compartment where we can relieve ourselves in solitude and in privacy of our burden, pull a lever, and then, yielding to the next in line, go silently home.

In this pulling of a lever, voters are asked to decide, in Ginsberg's words, "who shall govern" and not "what the government shall do": their participation in the subsequent work of policymaking is not invited. Voting teaches citizens that democracy is simply the private delegation of representation, and not also the work of political action and decision making as a public.

Thus the discipline of modern voting trains citizen attention away from public freedom and its potential ability to allow people to find collective, and not just individual, political agency in a range of democratic actions, initiatives, and decision-making practices. Some argue that it's okay when the uninformed voter *doesn't* go to the polls, because they don't like the idea that people who don't know or don't much care about issues can cancel out or dilute the votes of passionate and informed people. But that isn't so much a problem presented by the uninformed voter as it is by the fact that voting is the *only* way people can have input into representative democracy. If there are few accessible routes for people to come together to discover the issues they care about, to articulate and forward them publicly for political action, then it is hardly surprising that, in the age of five-second sound bites dominated by presidential agendas, voters find themselves feeling disconnected from the very civic agency that voting supposedly represents. None of us can change the nation, set an agenda, or win the election on our own—not even the president can do this. But together, people can and have done a great deal. Voting in the bathroom privacy of our booth, we are discouraged from recognizing this. Voting trains us to endorse candidates who will decide for us like parents decide for children, rather than to regard ourselves as a sovereign and self-governing citizenry. President George W. Bush summarized this lesson in

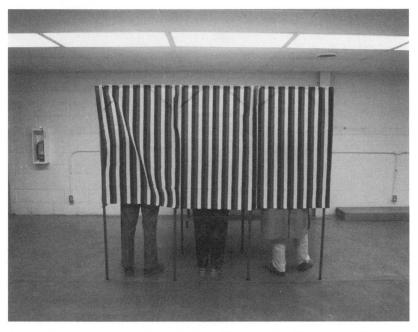

As Benjamin Barber observes, voting in the United States "is rather like using a public toilet: we wait in line with a crowd in order to close ourselves up in a small compartment where we can relieve ourselves in solitude." Photograph by Cliff Schiappa; courtesy of AP Photo.

the spring of 2006, facing news of public opposition to Donald Rumsfeld continuing as secretary of defense: "I hear the voices, and I read the front page, and I know the speculation. But I'm the decider, and I decide what is best."

U.S. elections have encouraged voters to accept that the height of democracy comes when they hand over their democratic agency to a president who will make all the hard decisions. After all, his "mandate" is to represent us all. This mandate has worked to put the president alone at the center of the drama of American politics, and although not all presidents are good at holding the stage, we continue watching our televisions as they in effect monopolize public space. The electoral drama encourages us to believe that, in political scientist Bruce Miroff's words, the "president is a surrogate for a mass public that cannot act for itself." Thus his agency is our agency, his decisions our decisions. And although we feel frustrated when we find ourselves disagreeing with the decisions of our current "decider," that doesn't seem to impact on the faith we take into the next election. Voting seemingly teaches even those who vote for the "loser" to subordinate themselves to and experience themselves as part of the "People's mandate." Voting, in other words, works powerfully, if not necessarily rationally, to incorporate citizenry into the new presidential agenda, whether or not people agreed with it going into the voting booth. As Ginsberg explains in his book *The Captive Public: How Mass Opinion Promotes State Power,* voting serves "to convince citizens that they actually control the state and thus stand to benefit from its power." Summarizing the results of two pre- and postelection polls that queried respondents on their trust in government and confidence in its responsiveness, he discovered a clear pattern of increased confidence among voters after the presidential election. Fifty-five percent of voters who felt they did not have satisfactory input into government felt that they did after they voted in the presidential election—*whether or not they voted for the candidate who won.*

Democracy as Presidential Drama

Voting, then, works like a ritual of democratic faith. When we vote for the president, we feel that we've participated in democracy, even if the candidate we voted for doesn't win. Although political scientists touting rational choice theory, a model that analogizes all human action to economic choice, tell us people have an aversion to losing propositions and that this is why many do not vote, the "losers" Ginsberg analyzes above—those who vote for the losing candidate and nevertheless feel they have satisfactory input into democratic government—probably have a different reason for voting and a different reason for feeling satisfied. It's possible that such people keep voting because voting gives them the temporary sensation of being connected with a democratic public, a sensation they get almost nowhere else in political life, a sensation that they treasure against the tide of all the expert common sense and institutional energies aimed at devaluing this ideal.

As Barber so pithily observes, our voting rituals don't foster that feeling. But the rituals surrounding the president's victory certainly do.

Civic desire for democratic community is redirected toward the victorious president. The presidency has come to dominate—even monopolize—the rituals of democracy and, thus, the democratic imagination. Clinton's inauguration, January 20, 1997. Photograph by Wilfredo Lee; courtesy of AP Photo.

Inaugurations are symbolically powerful because they ritualize the coming together of the nation for a kind of rebirth, a nonpartisan democratic baptism of sorts. In the inauguration, civic desire for democratic community is redirected toward the singular person of the victorious president. Politics is as much about ritual as it is about decision making, and there's nothing wrong with that: ritual works to bind community through the often divisive work of decision making. The problem here is, rather, how the presidency has come to dominate—even monopolize—the rituals of democracy and thus the democratic imagination. In fact, each citizen is represented by hundreds of government officials, from U.S. and state senators and representatives to mayors, city council members, state and county commissioners, school board members, electoral college members, district and county clerks and attorneys, judges, sheriffs, tax collectors, comptrollers, and more. But the symbolic dominance of the president in U.S. public imagination encourages citizens both to forget these other avenues of democratic access and representation, and to overvalue and overestimate what the president can and does do for them and the country.

Indeed, Barbara Hinckley discovers in her careful analysis of presidential speeches since Harry Truman that presidents actively encourage key misimpressions of government. Presidents are so consistent in these misrepresentations that Hinckley analyzes them as a mythical story line. In this mythical, nonfactual realm of the "symbolic presidency," presidents depict the work of government as though it were conducted solely by the president, on behalf of the American people and the nation, abstracting away all other avenues, actors, and interests. They represent themselves as working alone in government, usually with no help from Congress, their administration, or other government officials. As Hinckley summarizes, "Government is not shown to have a separation of powers. When Congress is mentioned at all, it is trivialized and dismissed." Presidents tend to conflate interest groups with the American people, and almost never portray these groups as having opposing political interests. Moreover, presidents make democratic politics sound demeaning. They deny involvement in political activism, blaming Congress for partisanship and, by extension, encouraging citizens to believe that political disagreement is bad rather than productive. Not just leaders of government, they present themselves as, in Hinkley's words, "cultural and religious leaders of the nation," with references to religion far outnumbering "those to parties and elections." They insist that they face challenges unique in the world and in history, thus encouraging citizens to see them in mythical terms.

This project is carried well beyond mere speechwriting. As I showed in chapter 1, JFK honed the art of cultivating an image that would sell to the public. Richard Nixon created the Office of Communications as what governmental historian Lewis L. Gould denominates a "quasi-journalistic operation." If in theory it was established to provide information from the White House to the public, it soon became, in Gould's words, "a means of generating popular opinion itself." Nixon's White House staff created "citizen" letter-writing and phone-calling campaigns to media outlets, presenting seemingly independent civic pressure to get the kind of coverage the administration wanted (now known as "astroturfing"—an artificial public-relations endeavor made to look "grassroots"). Under Ronald Reagan, members of the White House staff began devoting themselves to maximizing the president's time on television and "spinning" stories to his advantage. As journalist Mark Hertsgaard summarizes, Reagan's staff "effectively rewrote the rules of presidential image-making. . . . Their objective was not simply to tame the press but to transform it into an unwitting mouthpiece of the government." And while presidents have long worked to supply the most advantageous images of themselves to media, as *New York Times* reporter Elisabeth Bumiller detailed, George W. Bush's administration has worked to limit the access of non–White House staff photographers, narrowing the availability of visual images of the president whenever possible to those controlled by White House image makers. Since the 1970s, more than one-third of the White House staff has become devoted to the project of scripting, spinning, and managing the presidential drama for the U.S. public.

Savvy management of media has heightened presidential candidates' abilities to evade the demands of political parties. Many political scientists agree that this potent mix of media exposure and loosened party ties has led to our current situation, where presidential candidates run on personality and charisma, often minimizing rather than clarifying their political differences once they're past the primaries. Voters have a difficult time, for the most part, discovering what candidates actually plan to do and support in office. Instead, campaigns focus on the candidate's adoring family, ability to "connect" with voters emotionally, and ability to "unite" America through feelings like "compassion" and "hope." Lowi names this new era of presidential style the "personal presidency" and insists that its basic terms are corrupt: "No entrepreneur would ever sign a contract that leaves the conditions of fulfillment to the subjective judgment of the other party. This is precisely what has happened in the new social contract underlying the modern government of the United States."

Increasingly, tuned-in citizens understand politics as watching news about the president, in a way that mirrors (and reinforces) thinking of democracy as voting for the president. The communication studies scholar Roderick Hart argues that television offers both a false simplicity and a false sense of activity to viewers that works to divert them from a more active politics. In his words,

> Television does all of this by overwhelming viewers with the sights and sounds of governmental life and by supersaturating them with political information. All too often . . . this tumult creates in viewers a sense of activity rather than genuine civic involvement. In addition, television consistently tells the story of specific persons in specific situations, thereby producing a kind of highly individuated, cameo politics that distracts viewers from common problems and public possibilities. Television does this work, and much more, in a highly entertaining fashion and is often genuinely informative. But television also produces an overwhelming passivity in viewers even while making them feel politically involved.

The passivity of feeling politically involved while watching the president is exactly what Miroff is after when he describes how the presidency schools citizens to experience democracy as vicarious participation. As he puts it, "Taught by our 'realists' that the significant issues of our times are above and beyond ordinary citizens, who couldn't make much of a difference even if they could understand, those same citizens are offered compensation in the form of a presidential spectacle enacted in their name." Thus presidentialism discourages political participation both as voting and in broader terms: "When contrasted with presidential action, citizen participation usually looks drab and petty. It is thus easier to concentrate on private affairs and to restrict politics to conversations with friends and coworkers about the president than it is to seek out opportunities for one's own action."

The personalized and heroic dramas of presidential leadership that are the joint production of media, presidential administrations, presidential candidates, government officials, and scholars create, in Miroff's summary, a "politics whose central features stand in contradiction to the features of authentic democratic politics." Democracy becomes a drama where the lone president heroically bucks the will of Congress, the Court, and even the People ("I'm the decider"). In this symbolic saga, his successful assertion of executive will over and against the forces that oppose him constitutes not just his success but the success of *democracy*, where democracy is imagined as a singular triumph and not the hard-earned collaboration of many and diverse actors.

As Hinckley observes, ritual and symbol can substitute for something that does not exist otherwise. We need to ask whether our rituals and practices actually allow for the support and growth of democracy, or substitute something that is not democratic in the first place. If we have long been taught to believe that the highest act of democracy is voting for the president and that politics is following what the president does in the daily media, it might be time to question that wisdom and consider whether the accumulating power of the presidency in our democracy, symbolic and actual, works something more like the screen projection of the Great and Powerful Wizard in *The Wizard of Oz*. His power? Or ours? Self-government for Oz began when the curtain was pulled back to reveal the little man in the control booth.

Chapter 3
Presidential War Powers and Politics as War

THE GREAT AND TERRIBLE OZ INSISTED ON SUBORDINATION AND obedience to his commands. His dazzling media displays and intimidating style for a long time distracted his subjects from the actual powers of the little man running the show. He used his subjects' power to consolidate his own reign, all the while encouraging their sense of dependency on him. Of course he believes his lust for power, and his desire to make his people cower before it, is all for their own good. But when he's revealed to be a common man just like them, they discover that what they were lacking was not more or better executive power but an essential faith in and exercise of their own strengths and abilities.

From the beginning, Americans have loved making military heroes into presidents. The most popular presidents of the early nation, George Washington and Andrew Jackson, won their first recognition as military heroes. Citizens thus began to confuse the line between military and civilian leadership, despite the framers' careful separation of those roles. Drawing on the president's honorary title and linking it to a song from Sir Walter Scott's *Lady of the Lake,* James Sanderson produced a tune that has been officially linked to the presidency since James Polk used it for his inaugural in 1845. Albert Gamse provided the anthem's (seldom sung) lyrics:

Hail to the Chief we have chosen for the nation,
Hail to the Chief! We salute him, one and all.
Hail to the Chief, as we pledge cooperation
In proud fulfillment of a great, noble call.

Yours is the aim to make this grand country grander,
This you will do, that's our strong, firm belief.
Hail to the one we selected as commander,
Hail to the President! Hail to the Chief!

What began as a respectful civility in the eighteenth century soon drummed up far more powerful associations. Presidents have actively labored to expand executive branch powers by appealing to their war powers, and in the twentieth century they discovered that they could command higher approval ratings from the nation when they ordered troops into combat. U.S. voters haven't elected an active-service war veteran since George H. W. Bush, but we continue to link our respect for the presidency with the authority of the military, encouraged in no small part by the actions and gestures of presidents.

This chapter reviews the founders' reasons for conferring on the president the title of commander in chief. After a quick look at Abraham Lincoln's wartime actions, the chapter examines a series of key twentieth-century executive wartime expansions—along with judicial and legislative rebukes, and support. Finally it studies the institutional, political, and cultural consequences of how many have come to think of the nation's executive as *our* "commander in chief."

War Powers and the Constitution

As I showed in chapter 1, the framers of the Constitution borrowed the term *commander in chief* from King Charles, who began a tradition of granting that title to colonial governors in the seventeenth century. Aside from that borrowing, the framers explicitly and clearly rejected influential theories of European legal and political philosophers like William Blackstone, Montesquieu, and John Locke, who for example insisted that war powers were always an executive privilege that should be hindered neither by legislative bodies nor by law. Quite differently, the men who built the U.S. Constitution were in solid agreement about and clearly designated numerous powers of war exclusively for the law-making branch: the power to declare (that is, to announce and authorize) and to fund wars, along with other associated powers. Article 1 (the article that spells out the powers of the legislative branch) specifies in section 8 that

The Congress shall have the power . . .

To define and punish Piracies and Felonies committed on the high Seas, and Offenses against the Law of Nations;

To declare War, grant Letters of Marque and Reprisal, and make Rules concerning Captures on Land and Water;

To raise and support Armies, but no Appropriation of Money to that Use shall be for a longer Term than two Years;

To provide and maintain a Navy;

To make Rules for the Government and Regulation of the land and naval Forces;

To provide for the calling forth the Militia to execute the Laws of the Union, suppress Insurrections and repel Invasions;

To provide for organizing, arming, and disciplining, the Militia, and for governing such Part of them as may be employed in the Service of the United States, reserving to the States respectively, the Appointment of the Officers, and the Authority of training the Militia according to the discipline prescribed by Congress.

As notes from the Constitutional Convention record, only one participant, Pierce Butler of South Carolina, spoke in favor of giving these powers to the president. Sharply rebuked by Elbridge Gerry of Massachusetts ("I never expected to hear in a republic a motion to empower the Executive alone to declare war"), Butler saw his motion wither without a second. George Mason of Virginia summarized the prevailing sentiment, declaring himself against giving such powers to an executive whose personal ambition for glory, fame, or power might lead the United States into danger. In Madison's summary of Mason's words, "He was for clogging rather than facilitating war, but for facilitating peace." In ratification debates at the state level, proponents of the Constitution celebrated how its system of checks and balances would, in the words of the Pennsylvanian James Wilson, "not hurry us into war. . . . It will not be in the power of a single man, or a single body of men, to involve us in such distress; for the power of declaring war is vested in the legislature at large." As Supreme Court justice Joseph Story would later elaborate in his commentaries on the Constitution, "War . . . is sometimes fatal to public liberty itself, by introducing a spirit of military glory, which is ready to follow, wherever a successful commander will lead."

The delegates did agree to leave the executive branch the power to "repel sudden attacks." They wanted the president to have the ability, in the Connecticut delegate Roger Sherman's words, to "repel and not to commence" war. They deliberately divided the power of command from the power (in Madison's summary) to decide "whether a war ought to be commenced, continued or concluded." And they designated him, in Article 2, section 2, "Commander in Chief of the Army and Navy of the United States and of the Militia of the several States, when called into the actual Service of the United States," to ensure that the nation's forming military would be under *civilian* control. Thus when Washington came to the presidency, his status as commander in chief was not a military but a civilian title.

The Presidential Expansion of War Powers

For the most part during the nineteenth century, advances in presidential war powers were limited. In the most egregious case, Polk stampeded Congress into declaring war on Mexico by maneuvering to provoke an attack, but despite this unconstitutional prewar maneuvering, he still deferred to the notion that he needed a congressional declaration of war in order to prosecute his aims. And so it was not until the Civil War—an event unparalleled before and since in U.S. history—that the actions of President Lincoln loosed a force that would, over time, vastly aggrandize executive power, reorient the structure of government in both wartime and "peace," and redirect the structure of accountability between citizens and their "sole elected representative." The historian Geoffrey Perret claims that before Lincoln's presidency, it wasn't clear if presidents in the role of commander in chief could determine military policy. By his analysis, Lincoln's response to civil war created the role of commander in chief as we have come to know it today.

Lincoln's initial interest in political leadership emerged (like Harry Truman's later) while he was in military service. Lincoln served three months during the Black Hawk War in 1832, where he didn't see any action unless we count the skirmish he got into with officers in the Regular Army over distributing rations. Elected captain by his Illinois militia, the young Lincoln relished his experiences in leadership and made up his mind that when he returned home, he would become a candidate for legislature. He was elected to the state legislature in 1834, when he was twenty-five. After four terms there, he began serving in the U.S. Congress in 1846. In his first term, Lincoln distinguished himself by attacking Polk's claim to presidential war powers to justify his decision to send U.S. troops into Texas and Mexico, thereby provoking a war. Lincoln's opposition was so attention grabbing that his law partner in Illinois, W. H. Herndon, wrote him a cautionary letter. Herndon spelled out his own support for allowing the president to "invade the territory of another country" if it preempted that country from invading the United States. Lincoln rebutted his business partner and friend as confidently as he'd been challenging President Polk:

> Allow the President to invade a neighboring nation, whenever *he* shall deem it necessary to repel an invasion, and you allow him to do so, *whenever he may choose to say* he deems it necessary for such purpose—and you allow him to make war at pleasure. Study to see if you can fix *any* limit to his power in this respect, after you have given him so much as you propose. If, to-day, he should choose to say he thinks it necessary to invade Canada, to prevent the British from invading us, how could you stop him? You may say to him, "I see no probability of the British invading us" but he will say to you "be silent; I see it, if you dont [sic]."

Representative Lincoln concluded the letter by reflecting on the rectitude of the framers in granting war powers to Congress. The power of kings to involve their countries in endless, expensive wars constituted their tyranny, and the framers "resolved to so frame the Constitution that *no one man* should hold the power of bringing this oppression on us." He closed by chiding Herndon for placing "our President where kings have always stood."

As president, he would come to feel differently. Of course, the putatively "defensive" war on Mexico and the Civil War were two vastly different things. But the legacy and constitutionality of Lincoln's executive decisions during the early months of his presidency continue to be debated among historians and invoked as precedent by presidents. Congress was in recess when Lincoln arrived in Washington in March 1861. The new president, clearly facing war, delayed convening that democratic body for several months in order to operate unilaterally. He claimed as authorization the notion of a presidential "mandate" that he and everyone knew was nothing more than executive fiction in such a fractious and divided nation. As historian Arthur Schlesinger pithily summarizes:

> In his twelve weeks of executive grace, Lincoln ignored one law and constitutional provision after another. He assembled the militia, enlarged the Army and the Navy beyond their authorized strength, called out volunteers for three years' service, spent public money without congressional appropriation, suspended *habeus corpus*, arrested people "represented" as involved in "disloyal" practices and instituted a naval blockade of the Confederacy—measures which, he later told Congress, "whether strictly legal or not, were ventured upon under what appeared to be a popular demand and a public necessity; trusting then as now that Congress would readily ratify them."

Despite Lincoln's appeal to a popular demand for presidential leadership, many of his contemporaries in the North described him as a "despot" and derided his grab for power as monarchical. He described his actions as constitutionally mandated. While war powers had previously been invoked as extraconstitutional, Lincoln argued that these emergency powers, under the circumstances of Civil War, were constitutionally implied, and that these implied powers belonged to the executive (his logic forms the basis of George W. Bush's defense of the wiretapping program of the National Security Agency and its domestic telephone data collection in 2006).

Lincoln, whose deference to the founders seems elsewhere quite pronounced, seemingly dumped their cautions about checks and balances wholesale during the run-up to Civil War. He claimed constitutional authority for an array of executive usurpations, including declarations of martial law, seizure of property, arrests without warrant, the trying of civilians in military courts, and suppression of newspapers and mails. In defending his unilateral suspension of habeas corpus, calling up the militia, exercising blockades, and expanding army and navy forces, powers specifically granted to Congress, Lincoln initiated a new branch of interpretation (one that has culminated most recently in the work of legal scholar John Yoo, who as part of the executive branch's Office of Legal Counsel during the formative years of the so-called war on terror is widely credited for helping formulate policy regarding both George W. Bush's war powers and techniques for prisoner interrogation). This mode of interpretation distorts the nation's founding documents and history, taking passages out of historical and textual context to offer "proof" that the framers intended for the president to have powers that the historical record shows they factually located elsewhere. Justifying his suspension of habeas corpus, Lincoln explained:

> It was not believed that any law was violated. The provision of the Constitution that "the privilege of the writ of habeas corpus shall not be suspended unless when, in cases of rebellion or invasion, the public safety may require it" as equivalent to a provision—is a provision—that such privilege may be suspended when, in cases of rebellion or invasion, the public safety does require it. It was decided that we have a case of rebellion and that public safety does require the qualified suspension of the privilege of the writ which was authorized to be made. Now it is insisted that Congress, and not the Executive, is vested with this power; but the Constitution itself is silent as to which or who is to exercise the power; and as the provision was plainly made for a dangerous emergency, it cannot be believed that the framers of the instrument intended that in every case the danger should run its course until Congress could be called together, the very assembling of which might be prevented, as was intended in this case, by the rebellion.

Lincoln was right that the wording of this sentence does not specify which branch is to exercise the power to suspend habeas corpus. But it's simply wrong to assert that the Constitution offers no clue as to which branch will exercise this power: the authority to suspend habeas corpus is spelled out in Article 1, which delineates *congressional* powers.

As his decontextualizing maneuver evidences, Lincoln knew that his executive decrees stood on shaky constitutional ground. In the same July 4 message to Congress, Lincoln asserted that these "measures, whether strictly legal or not, were ventured upon under what appeared to be a popular demand and a public necessity, trusting then, as now, that Congress would readily ratify them. It is believed that nothing has been done beyond the constitutional competency of Congress." In his appeal to Congress to ratify retrospectively the actions he'd taken under his claimed inherent presidential war powers, Lincoln offers a sotto voce admission that he had indeed maneuvered extralegally by exercising powers constitutionally designated not to the executive but to Congress. If Jackson's innovation was the "mandate," Lincoln's contribution to the presidential power grab was his insistence that in the case of war, the president's war powers superseded those of Congress in his capacity as the nation's "commander in chief." The Taney Supreme Court, in a narrow decision and without the support of its chief justice (who had tried and failed to prevent Lincoln's suspension of habeas corpus), upheld Lincoln's innovations on presidential powers as constitutional. As Schlesinger summarizes, this redefinition of presidential powers "marked the beginning of a fateful evolution," redefining crisis government as *presidential* government.

No one finally faults Lincoln, who is lauded, even by critical political scientists and historians, for his role as a national protector. They highlight how judiciously he balanced his power grabbing with personal humility and political restraint: "He stretched the Constitution but preserved the Union," as presidential scholar Michael Genovese familiarly summarizes. Acknowledging national debts of gratitude should not, however, prevent us from thinking critically about what President Lincoln set in motion, a process he had in fact presciently predicted in his criticisms of Polk: "Study to see if you can fix *any* limit to his power in this respect, after you have given him so much as you propose. If, to-day, he should choose to say he thinks it necessary to invade Canada, to prevent the British from invading us, how could you stop him? You may say to him, 'I see no probability of the British invading us' but he will say to you 'be silent; I see it.'" Indeed, under the reigning logic of the Bush Doctrine (published as the *National Security Strategy of the United States,* September 20, 2002), the founders' delegation to the president of the power "to repel sudden attacks" has become the power of preemptive war, determined by the commander in chief's perception of threats to national security, not just when threats are imminent but even where those threats are "emerging" or "if uncertainty remains."

The Sole Organ

By the turn of the century, unilateral exercise of military force became an important strategy for building on the executive's constitutional strong suit: foreign policy. With the imperialistic territorial expansions led by William McKinley and Teddy Roosevelt (who once declared that "no triumph of peace is quite so great as the supreme triumph of war"), U.S. presidents elaborated on a nineteenth-century practice of initiating military actions against other countries to "protect lives and property"—in fact to expand U.S. economic interests. In Cuba, Nicaragua, Guam, Puerto Rico, Mexico, Haiti, the Dominican Republic, Panama, and the Philippines, presidents initiated military action without declaring war as a form of expansionist foreign policy aimed at benefiting U.S. business interests. As political scientist Peter Irons comments, "Every president from Taft through Herbert Hoover sent troops or warships to Nicaragua, with the purpose of affecting the outcome of that country's presidential elections. Between 1909 and 1933, there was hardly a year during which U.S. troops did not patrol the streets of Managua, the capital. During these years, the Roosevelt Corollary to the Monroe Doctrine turned the Caribbean and Central America into a gigantic American colony, in fact if not in name." Irons credits the conservative, probusiness makeup of the early-twentieth-century's federal judiciary for the fact that there were no challenges to such presidential action during this period.

The conservative Court did push back against the presidency's *domestic* powers. In 1935 alone, the Hughes Court handed FDR four major decisions that voided New Deal programs in agriculture, labor, and industry. But in 1936, the same court handed the presidency an enormous grant of power in its decision on *United States v. Curtiss-Wright.* Justice George Sutherland, writing for the Court, made a sweeping finding for executive authority in foreign affairs, describing the "plenary and exclusive power of the President as the sole organ of the federal government in the field of international relations—a power which does not require as a basis for its exercise an act of Congress." In a decision that called for examining legislative, not executive, powers, Sutherland went far beyond the facts and demands of the case. His decision not only argued for broad executive foreign powers in the *absence* of legislation on an issue but also outlined a novel theory of executive sovereignty, one widely disputed by legal scholars and historians ever since.

As Fisher explains in "The 'Sole Organ' Doctrine," the decision roughly follows Sutherland's previous publications on the subject of executive power during his term as a senator from Utah and after. In those works, Sutherland had argued for a model of executive agency that could not be checked by other branches in the area of foreign (or "external") relations. In his controversial *Curtiss-Wright* decision, Sutherland attempted to legitimate his novel theory with an equally new theory of executive sovereignty. Here, Sutherland suggested that power comes to the president not as a delegation of the U.S. people but through the British *monarch* (he argues that in the act of declaring independence and eventually negotiating a peace treaty with England, the king's sovereignty transferred directly to the Union as a whole and to the president, who stands at the head of that union). Thus in Sutherland's account, the president's power *preexists* the U.S. Constitution and comes to him not through the formation of government authorized by the citizenry in that legal document but as a mystical transfer of power from the rejected British sovereign, a transfer initiated and confirmed by the War of Independence. Here we can see Sutherland wielding the full power of the judiciary branch as he succumbs to the allure of presidential glory, much as his predecessor, Justice Story, had warned against more than a century before.

The problem is, of course, that this argument has no legitimate historical or legal foundation, as countless scholars have since argued. The presidency is a creation of the Constitution and thus presidential powers cannot possibly, legally or historically, preexist that document. Sutherland plays as fast and loose with fact as with history in his citation of Representative, and later Chief Justice of the Supreme Court, John Marshall as the authority for his declaring the president the "sole organ" of foreign relations, implying that Marshall, in an 1800 congressional debate, had supported independent presidential powers to *formulate* foreign policy. But as

Louis Fisher carefully documents, that is not at all what Marshall meant—then or in his later Supreme Court decisions. Nor did Marshall's many contemporaries understand him to have asserted such unilateral powers for the president. Rather, Marshall, his contemporaries, and subsequent commentators understood "sole organ" to reference the president's responsibility to *implement* foreign policy as decided between the executive and legislative branches. Even the promonarchical Alexander Hamilton, often invoked by unitary executive proponents today in support of the "sole organ" theory, argued in *Federalist* number 75 that it would be "utterly unsafe and improper" to give the executive complete power over foreign policy.

If scholars have long disputed Sutherland's ruling and its grant of "implied," extraconstitutional, and unilateral powers for the presidency, judges and presidential administrators have repeatedly invoked it to make a case for upholding and widening executive powers. FDR's attorney general, Robert Jackson, would soon cite it to legitimate FDR's executive agreement with Britain to exchange fifty U.S. destroyers for the right to use military bases on British islands in the Atlantic and Caribbean, creating what was in effect a treaty with neither the advice nor the consent of the Senate as mandated by the Constitution. Similarly, the Supreme Court would reference *Curtiss-Wright* in upholding FDR's authority to detain Japanese Americans during World War II, as well as his right to create secret military tribunals to try German spies. As Fisher summarizes, despite its factual inaccuracies and historical, legal, and analytic distortions, the decision has supported presidential appeals and numerous federal and Supreme Court findings in the years since.

Crisis Presidentialism

FDR's presidential greatness and the new centrality of the executive to national government were forged through two crises, the Great Depression and World War II, and soon the appeal to "crisis" became a standard strategy for presidents trying to command support. As Fisher outlines in his book *Presidential War Powers,* FDR began declaring executive emergency and war provisions as early as 1939 (when Germany invaded

Poland), and he, and then Truman, would continue operating under those provisions for more than twelve years, even though the United States was involved in actual hostilities for only four. If FDR maneuvered the country into World War II, the constitutionality of his strategizing was mooted by the Japanese attack on Pearl Harbor and the swift congressional declaration of war. Truman, who scrupulously avoided using the word "war" to describe what he preferred to call the "police action" in Korea, actually flirted with a third world war as he elaborated on the powers a president could draw on in the name of crisis. There has been no end to the *rhetoric* of crisis in the years since, which tends to invoke the moniker "war": war on poverty, war on drugs, war on terror. The communications scholar Jeffrey Tullis observes that the "continual or routine use of the 'crisis tool' was meant to make the president more effective in normal times. . . . If crisis politics are now routine, we may be losing the ability as a people to distinguish genuine from spurious crisis." But as long as invocation of crisis and war—spurious or not—functions to mobilize voter support for the sitting president, these appeals will continue maintaining executive power.

Truman presided over a nation newly strengthened by victory in World War II, and by the fact of nuclear weaponry, which he swiftly used to bomb a defiant Japan into submission. Of course, the Soviet Union was poised as the check to U.S. dominance in world affairs: the Soviets believed their share of the victory over the Nazis had ratified their economic policies and political system. They saw U.S. capitalism and imperialism as an ongoing threat to their existence; the United States increasingly felt the same about the USSR. After the conclusion of World War II, as Stalin descended into paranoia, accumulated his own nuclear stockpile, and moved deeper into Eastern Europe, Truman held a hard line, in contrast to FDR's willingness to negotiate mutually recognized spheres of influence and his hopes at cultivating the USSR as a reliable partner in maintaining world peace. And Truman recognized that the American electorate would respond to tough talk from the commander in chief. By 1946 he had announced to his staff that "we are going to have a war with Russia"—a war that could emerge anywhere from Eastern Europe to East Asia—and his administration began formulating policies for military containment

Truman, here at the Army–Navy game, presided over a nation newly strengthened by victory in World War II. To win support for his Cold War policies, he took back one of FDR's famous freedoms: freedom from fear. U.S. Navy; courtesy of the Harry S. Truman Library and Museum.

of the "communist threat." Soon the two powers were maneuvering to something like a standoff over military bases in Turkey and popular uprisings in Greece.

With his declaration of what would come to be called the Truman Doctrine, our thirty-third president launched the Cold War and the ballooning of the national security bureaucracy. This speech was a sweeping call for the United States to provide economic and strategic support to nations resisting communist advances. Speaking before a joint session of Congress in March 1947, less than two years after the end of World War II, Truman urged that we must be

> willing to help free peoples to maintain their free institutions and their national integrity against aggressive movements that seek to impose upon them totalitarian regimes. This is no more than a frank recognition that totalitarian regimes imposed on free peoples, by direct or indirect aggression, undermine the foundations

of international peace and hence the security of the United States. . . . The free peoples of the world look to us for support in maintaining their freedoms. If we falter in our leadership, we may endanger the peace of the world—and we shall surely endanger the welfare of our own nation.

Truman's immediate aim was to gain congressional approval for aid to Greece and Turkey. He had been advised that in the immediate aftermath of World War II, a war-weary nation would consent to an open-ended military commitment that could lead into armed conflict with the USSR only if Truman made as alarming a case as possible. Truman and his advisers crafted a speech that invoked a looming communist threat and backtracked on FDR's famous first freedom: instead of promising Americans freedom from fear, he asked them to be very afraid. And so, even though it seems Truman only meant to establish policy for the very limited cases at hand, his formulation of Cold War crisis, following in the wake of Winston Churchill's famous "Iron Curtain" speech the year before, launched a governing ethos for a new age and simultaneously redefined the nation's mission. As Schlesinger notes, the indiscriminate rhetoric of threat endured and carried forward, "as did the technique of scaring the hell out of the country." Although the congressional debate was lengthy and probing, both houses passed the administration's bill by sound margins. Truman's job approval ratings, which had sunk to the low 30s at the midterm election in 1946, took an impressive boost back up into the 60s, a boost good enough to carry him through reelection against Thomas Dewey.

The next big spike in his job approval ratings came in 1950, when Truman sent U.S. troops into Korea (from the mid-30s to near 70 percent). The communist forces of North Korea invading South Korea seemed to confirm the exact menace Truman had outlined in his appeal for funding for Turkey and Greece. Neither citizens nor government officials seemed much inclined to question the constitutionality of Truman's commitment of U.S. troops to the conflict. As David McCullough says, "Editors praised Truman for his 'bold course,' his 'momentous and courageous act.' . . . White House mail ran strongly in favor of the President's action. . . . the entire mood in the capital had suddenly, dramatically changed. 'I have lived and worked in and out of Washington for twenty years,' wrote Joseph Harsch of the *Christian Science Monitor.* 'Never before in that time have I felt such a sense of relief and unity pass through the city.'"

In this extraordinary reaction to the president ordering U.S. troops into an overseas conflict that in no way involved or endangered Americans, we can see how citizens had begun learning to feel their power not as their grant of representative sovereignty to the president but as a reflection of presidential wartime powers—as his grant to *us.* Truman's extra-constitutional action inspired "relief and unity." Through "crisis" government, the president is able to capture democratic power—our power—as though it emanates from him, as though we need his power to protect and unify us. At a deeply emotional and subconscious level, it effects a fantastic, crucial reversal of sovereignty. From this moment forward, crisis presidentialism worked to consolidate acceptance of the notion that the president, as commander in chief, commands the military *and* the loyalty and support of U.S. citizens.

When Truman announced that he was sending forces into Korea on June 27, 1950, he suggested that the Soviet Union was behind the invasion (thereby deflecting the idea that what the world was witnessing was a civil war), and he signaled that he was acting under United Nations authority. He promised the nation that the United States would defend South Koreans and "uphold the rule of law." But as Irons summarizes, Truman broke constitutional law in three ways: "First, the president committed military forces to combat, in what constituted an act of war, without prior congressional approval or a formal declaration of war. Second, he violated the provisions of the UN Charter—and thus, a U.S. treaty obligation—by taking unilateral military action even before the Security Council had called on member nations for their assistance. And third, Truman violated the U.N. Participation Act by ignoring its requirement for prior congressional approval of any special agreement with the United Nations for the commitment of U.S. forces." Indeed, the major sticking point against passage of the United Nations Participation Act had been this very scenario: that the UN Charter could authorize the president to commit U.S. troops to war without congressional approval. Truman had seemed attuned to his former fellow congressmen's reservations on this score. He assured senators as they negotiated in 1945 that when "any such agreement or agreements are negotiated it will be my purpose to ask Congress for appropriate legislation to approve them." The final bill enacted by Congress and signed by Truman indicated, as Irons notes, that "the White House could not deploy U.S. troops for UN military actions on its own initiative."

During negotiations over U.S. participation in the UN charter, at least, Congress was extremely protective of its war powers. When Truman sent troops into Korea, though, there were few hints of protest. Senator Robert Taft from Ohio declared that Truman had "no legal authority" for his actions but assured the president that he would vote to support a joint resolution authorizing U.S. intervention, an action that Senator H. Alexander Smith from New Jersey suggested the administration request. Truman, advised by Secretary of State Dean Acheson, declined to request such congressional authorization. Instead, he insisted that his constitutional powers as president and commander in chief were sufficient authority for him to proceed, relying on a State Department memo that asserted that there was a "traditional power of the President to use the armed forces of the United States without consulting Congress" and cited eighty-seven instances of presidents sending U.S. forces into combat without congressional authorization. As Schlesinger notes, these precedents offered dubious license. They were examples of "limited action to suppress pirates or to protect American citizens in conditions of local disorder. They were not precedents for sustained and major war against a sovereign state." Not until the war began to go badly, with China's entry into the conflict, would congressmen begin voicing their regret over the precedent their initial silence had set. And it's been a heckuva precedent. As Irons summarizes (and who is counting so-called actions and conflicts in his total), "Not a single president since FDR has gone before Congress to seek a declaration of war, while the nation has been engaged in wars— big and small—in every decade since the end of World War II."

With China's entry into the Korean police action, the war's popularity began plummeting and with it Truman's job approval ratings. But even though he lost popularity, he racked up important new powers for the presidency—powers that only once were constitutionally checked. In 1952, as the nation's steelworkers threatened to strike to force a resolution to long-standing conflicts between the United Steelworkers Union and the nation's steel companies, Truman issued an executive order that mandated a Department of Commerce takeover of the plants to keep them open and running. His action was fully in line with his prior decision in 1946 to break a rail-worker strike by calling out the army *and* by drafting all the striking rail workers into army service. Then, Truman announced his decision to a wildly enthusiastic crowd in the House chamber, only to be interrupted by the announcement that the strike had been settled.

In this instance, with the takeover in effect, steel giant Youngstown Sheet and Tube Company fought back. It sued, arguing that the order exceeded the constitutional powers of the executive branch. In reply, administration lawyers insisted that Truman had inherent authority as commander in chief to protect the "well-being and safety" of the nation. In a 6–3 decision, the Vinson Court (with Chief Justice Fred Vinson dissenting), found against Secretary of Commerce Charles Sawyer, and Truman's action. Writing for the Court, Justice Hugo Black found,

> The contention is that presidential power should be implied from the aggregate of his powers under the Constitution. Particular reliance is placed on provisions in Article II which say that "The executive Power shall be vested in a President . . ."; that "he shall take Care that the Laws be faithfully executed"; and that he "shall be Commander in Chief of the Army and Navy of the United States."
>
> The order cannot properly be sustained as an exercise of the President's military power as Commander in Chief of the Armed Forces. The Government attempts to do so by citing a number of cases upholding broad powers in military commanders engaged in day-to-day fighting in a theater of war. Such cases need not concern us here. Even though "theater of war" be an expanding concept, we cannot with faithfulness to our constitutional system hold that the Commander in Chief of the Armed Forces has the ultimate power as such to take possession of private property in order to keep labor disputes from stopping production. This is a job for the Nation's lawmakers, not for its military authorities.
>
> Nor can the seizure order be sustained because of the several constitutional provisions that grant executive power to the President. In the framework of our Constitution, the President's power to see that the laws are faithfully executed refutes the idea that he is to be a lawmaker.

Justice Robert Jackson's concurrence is pithier in rebutting Truman's presumptions on the title of commander in chief: "The clause on which the Government next relies is that 'The President shall be Commander in Chief of the Army and Navy of the United States. . . .' These cryptic words have given rise to some of the most persistent controversies in our constitutional history. . . . There are indications that the Constitution did not contemplate that the title Commander in Chief *of the Army and Navy* will constitute him also Commander in Chief of the country, its industries and its inhabitants. He has no monopoly of 'war powers,' whatever they are. While Congress cannot deprive the President of the command of the army and navy, only Congress can provide him an army or navy to command." Despite this decision, as political scientists Matthew Crenson and Benjamin Ginsberg note in their book *Presidential Power,* the "clear trend of case law since at least World War II and most markedly since the Vietnam War has been to support the president's use of emergency and war powers."

As I show in more detail below, it's rare in the extreme for either Congress or the Supreme Court to effectively check a president's power—momentum is nearly always in favor of the president keeping the powers he seizes. And so, for the most part, Truman's power grabs were allowed to stand. War powers have always accrued powers for the presidency—powers that recede when peace is restored. But in indefinite wars, such as the Cold War and the so-called war on terror, the president remains commander in chief into an unforseeable future. The Cold War served effectively to fortify the doctrine of executive supremacy, and the increasing militarization of the period lent further civil gravity to the title commander in chief. From Truman's Korean police action to Dwight D. Eisenhower's extension of presidential privilege to *everyone* in the executive branch, to John F. Kennedy's missile crisis, Congress, the Court, the media, and the people all have become more and more comfortable with the notion that the president could and should act unilaterally with regard to foreign policy, and even domestically, to protect the nation's "well-being." More and more during the twentieth century, the United States looked to the White House—and to the single person of the president—for leadership, government, responsibility, and command.

Chosen by the People to Decide

When Lyndon Johnson assumed power, he brought his own imposing assumptions about presidential prerogative before a national government and a public that was inclined to treat the officeholder with full deference in war matters. As he would announce in 1966, he saw the president as the nationally designated "decider" (to use a turn of phrase popularized by George W. Bush): "There are many, many, who can recommend, advise and sometimes a few of them consent. But there is only one that has been chosen by the American people to decide." Johnson, notoriously raunchy, relished his decision-making role to an even self-parodying extent. Mocking—perhaps unintentionally—the "sole organ" theory, he once reportedly brandished his penis (which, as Robert Caro recounts, Johnson affectionately called "Jumbo") at cabinet members who questioned why the United States was in Vietnam, barking, "This is why!"

Vulgar and bullying, Johnson was nevertheless an undeniably deft politician. In the tragic aftermath of Kennedy's assassination, the elevated vice president, who came into the office with near 80 percent job approval ratings, moved quickly on issues dear to his own political heart, launching the war on poverty and his Great Society that featured voter and civil rights reform, as well as Medicaid and Medicare. The most activist presidential lawmaker of the twentieth century, Johnson, who had served both in the House of Representatives and as minority and majority leader in the Senate, worked with, and just plain *worked* Congress to accomplish the passage of his highly controversial and undoubtedly high-minded domestic reforms. He aimed, as he liked to say, to finish the job Lincoln had begun.

At least in part because of the ambition of his domestic reforms—he was asking the white middle-class majority for sacrifices that would benefit not them but the poor, the elderly, and the socially excluded—Johnson had to contend against regular charges that he was soft on communism, charges political foes like Richard Nixon, who was busy rebuilding his Republican base after his own failed presidential and gubernatorial bids, kept active. At least in part to demonstrate that he could hold a hard line against communism, and facing election, Johnson seized an opportunity

Known as a bully, Johnson was both a formidable and effective politician. Here, Associate Supreme Court Justice Abe Fortas gets the famous "Johnson treatment." LBJ Library photograph by Yoichi R. Okamoto; courtesy of Lyndon B. Johnson Library.

to prove U.S.—and his own—toughness. With little solid evidence about attacks on U.S. destroyers in the Tonkin Gulf during the summer of 1964 (and with the help of active misinformation from both the Department of Defense and the Johnson administration), the president turned to Congress in full outrage, asking for their "opinion." Congress handed Johnson—notably using the precise language Johnson's administration had suggested to them—the Southeast Asia (or Gulf of Tonkin) Resolution in August:

> That the Congress approves and supports the determination of the President, as Commander in Chief, to take all necessary measures to repel any armed attack against the forces of the United States and to prevent further aggression.

Section 2. The United States regards as vital to its national interest and to world peace the maintenance of international peace and security in southeast Asia. Consonant with the Constitution of the United States and the Charter of the United Nations and in accordance with its obligations under the Southeast Asia Collective Defense Treaty, the United States is, therefore, prepared, as the President determines, to take all necessary steps, including the use of armed force, to assist any member or protocol state of the Southeast Asia Collective Defense Treaty requesting assistance in defense of its freedom.

Section 3. This resolution shall expire when the President shall determine that the peace and security of the area is reasonably assured by international conditions created by action of the United Nations or otherwise, except that it may be terminated earlier by concurrent resolution of the Congress.

This vaguely worded document granted the president extraordinarily wide latitude for action, although escalation of the conflict was exactly what the president, currently campaigning against Barry Goldwater, had promised voters he would *not* do ("we are not about to send American boys some 9 or 10,000 miles away from home to do what Asian boys ought to be doing for themselves").

But securely in the presidency after his 1964 election, Johnson felt he had full authority to make whatever decisions necessary—even if they contradicted earlier promises—and that it was Congress's job to support him. Immediately after the election, Johnson began preparing for a massive intervention, beginning bombing in February and increasing the number of troops. Later, when members of Congress began protesting everescalating U.S. involvement, Johnson would brandish the resolution as proof of their consent to all of Johnson's subsequent actions. And, as he liked to insist, he had never asked for anything more than their "opinion"— he did not consider it constitutionally necessary to obtain congressional authorization for his war actions.

When Johnson "Americanized" the war early in 1965, he exercised presidential prerogative and privilege for a historically unprecedented war effort. Unlike the Korean police action, there was no UN resolution to sanction U.S. military intervention. There was no invasion by which to justify U.S. troop involvement. There was no emergency threat to the United States. And Johnson did his best to keep the U.S. public from realizing the fact of the escalation, ordering that the "actions themselves should be taken as rapidly as practicable, but in ways that would minimize any appearance of sudden changes in policy." If Justice Jackson admonished President Truman in the 1952 ruling on *Youngstown Sheet and Tube Co. v. Sawyer* against overinterpreting the "commander in chief" clause, it was a caveat against preemptive presidential power that American citizens have been much slower to register.

As the public gradually began to process the fact of U.S. involvement in offensive operations (Johnson announced a doubling of the draft in July of 1965), there was a newfound willingness to question presidential prerogative inspired, in part, by the memory of Johnson's own widely televised campaign promises that if elected, he would not do what he was now, precisely, doing. Thanks to the innovation of television evening news programs in 1963, Americans were able for the first time to access regular war coverage as the Vietnam War developed and U.S. troop involvement escalated. The Vietnam War would indeed be the most censorship-free war in U.S. history. With casualties mounting, antiwar protests beginning in 1965, and the brutal Tet Offensive of 1968, newscasters broadened and intensified their war coverage. Media stories about the Selma bombing, civil rights marches, developing urban riots throughout the mid-sixties, and the assassination of Martin Luther King Jr. on April 4, 1968, similarly worked to fuel debate about Johnson's domestic policies. His job approval ratings continued on a near-steady slide into the low forties.

It wasn't just the president, his administration, and government and military leadership that came in for questioning in this emerging national debate, characterized by the historian Vaughn Davis Bornet as being "like no other since the War between the States." The role of the media was also hotly debated, with President Johnson indicating that he took any negative media coverage as an attack on his presidential leadership. His bungling arrogance with the media and his crude behavior was no small part of his problem here. This negative coverage caused the Johnson administration to rethink its previous acceptance of media presence, especially abroad: critical television coverage was shattering the mystique that had attached itself to the "imperial presidency" as it developed from FDR through JFK.

Because of steadily critical coverage, the escalation of political debate, and what was increasingly evident as an unwinnable war, Johnson decided not to run for reelection. Thus it was his successor in office, Nixon, and his accelerating claims to unlimited presidential prerogative, who would lead Congress and the American public to call for a cooling-off in the love affair with the office of "the most powerful man in the Free World."

War Powers Act: Cui Bono?

By the late 1960s, Congress had begun fighting back against executive war powers. Criticizing its own passivity, the Senate Foreign Relations committee reexamined the Gulf of Tonkin Resolution and argued—with an excuse that will sound familiar in our own historical moment—that they had not meant to acquiesce to a war in passing the resolution but had only agreed to such stern language to provide the president with negotiating authority in order to *prevent* a war. Still, the report placed blame on Congress, for "the error of making a *personal* judgment as to how President Johnson would implement the resolution when it had a responsibility to make an *institutional* judgment, first, as to what *any* President would do with so great an acknowledgment of power, and, second, as to whether, under the Constitution, Congress had a right to grant or concede the authority in question." In response to the report, the Senate passed the nonbinding National Commitments Resolution, which reasserted the importance of legislative branch involvement in war decisions, with a decent bipartisan showing, thereby signaling to Nixon their intent to retake their constitutionally allocated role in war powers decisions.

Nixon early signaled his disinterest in sharing war powers with Congress, let alone in honoring his deliberately ambiguous campaign promises to end the war. Relying on the constitutional interpretations of Assistant Attorney General William Rehnquist, who argued that the Constitution's commander in chief clause provided "a grant of substantial authority" to the president, Nixon didn't even start preparing legal arguments to explain his war actions against Cambodia to Congress until days after the invasion had begun. Rehnquist's arguments suggested that authority as commander in chief provided the executive prerogative to invade even neutral countries posing no direct threat to U.S. security, if the president suspected they contained agents hostile to U.S. forces. This rationale worked, loosely speaking, until the peace treaty in 1973, and subsequent withdrawal of U.S. forces from Vietnam, past which Nixon still showed no inclination to cease hostilities against Cambodia. Moreover, he began maneuvering to end military conscription and create a professional army, calculating that "for pay" armed forces would be less tied to ideals of citizenship, and the men—as well as their families back home—more pliable for the purposes of the commander in chief.

Congress all the while was trying to withdraw its passive acquiescence to the expanding war. In 1969 and 1970, it voted to deny funding for U.S. ground troops in Laos, Thailand, and Cambodia. In 1971, it added the Defense Procurement Authorization Act, which declared as U.S. policy the intention "to terminate at the earliest practicable date all military operations of the United States in Indochina." Nixon signed the bills into laws with signing statements that declared their antiwar provisions "without binding force or effect," elaborating that "my signing of the bill . . . will not change the policies I have pursued and that I shall continue to pursue toward this end." And so the war—and the president's war powers—continued.

Finally, after much deliberation, deal making, and wrangling, Congress passed the War Powers Resolution of 1973, which Nixon promptly vetoed and both Houses immediately overrode. This bill, the self-congratulatory Congress assured the U.S. public, would command presidential accountability to Congress in war matters. But as the record shows, it has been completely ineffectual. Irons summarizes: "The measure was badly drafted, replete with loopholes, and has been simply ignored by every president—seven in number, from Richard Nixon to George W. Bush—since its enactment." It has in fact delivered more power than ever to the president as commander in chief. Because the bill grants the president authority to use armed forces for up to ninety days without seeking or gaining authorization from Congress, and because the ninety-day count does not even begin until the president reports his action to Congress, the bill gives the president a far wider latitude for unilateral action than granted by the Constitution. Most presidents don't, in fact, bother reporting to Congress under the Section 4 (a) (1) provision that starts the ninety-day clock, and so dodge that legal restraint. In fact, only one president has even reported an action to Congress under this provision of the bill: President Ford reported his May 1975 retaliation for the Khmer Rouge's capture of the U.S. merchant ship *Mayaguez* (whose crew had been released by the Khmer Rouge before the retaliatory attack began). By the time he reported, the military action was already over.

The Mystique of the Commander in Chief

When Ronald Reagan took office in 1981, he quickly moved to remedy Carter's homespun dressing down of presidential authority. One of Reagan's key innovations for restoring pomp and circumstance to presidential drama was to begin returning the courtesy salute to the Marines standing guard for a president disembarking from Air Force or Marine One. As leader of the nation's military, President Reagan's memorably snappy salute may have impressed photographers and citizens with its bracing formality. But that seeming formality actually undercuts constitutional form: since civilians traditionally do not return military salutes, the presidential salute erodes the careful distinction the framers built between civilian and military leadership. Reagan did of course serve in the Army Enlisted Reserves during World War II, a service that the military symbolism of his funeral richly commemorated. (Because of his bad eyesight, he was not eligible for overseas service and combat. For the most part, his duties had him working close to home, in Army Air Force public relations and the First Motion Picture Unit in Culver City, California.) But his status as a veteran is, quite simply, irrelevant to his civilian responsibility as president, something veteran-presidents from Washington to Ford have symbolically honored. Here, though, Reagan's sense of dramatic timing, subtly positioning himself as the nation's commander in chief, was spot-on for his ambitions to expand executive branch powers.

What is the mystique of the commander in chief? As I showed in the last two chapters, during the twentieth century, with the combined expansion of media and the advent of opinion polling, presidents increasingly worked to enhance their symbolic image as head of state to leverage

Reagan's dramatic instincts helped him present himself as the nation's commander in chief and expand executive branch powers. Courtesy of Ronald Reagan Library.

their specific political agendas with Congress. Scholars call this "campaigning over the heads of Congress," and as approval ratings consistently show, nowhere is this more effective than in their symbolic manifestation as commander in chief. The symbolic commander in chief is the United States' superhero incarnate, and as such he provides the most satisfying embodiment of the United States' international preeminence. In this vestige (or salute, or costume) the president invokes the classical terms of heroic action, which Joseph Campbell so memorably summarized:

> A hero ventures forth from the world of common day into a region of supernatural wonder: fabulous forces are there encountered and a decisive victory is won: the hero comes back from this mysterious adventure with the power to bestow a boon on his fellow man.

Reassured by the strength of the superheroic commander who makes the world safe for democracy, ordinary Americans can get along with the business of daily life—exactly the appeal made by President Bush in the aftermath of 9/11, as he launched a war effort, what he termed a "new kind of war" that had no definable end point (as Secretary of Defense Donald Rumsfeld elaborated on September 27, 2001: "Forget about 'exit strategies'; we're looking at a sustained engagement that carries no deadlines"). As we find our way into an indefinite war, all we have to do is conduct life as though all were normal—and "go shopping more." The commander in chief will take care of the dangerous business and make the necessary sacrifices, all for us. We didn't need to worry, he suggested, or even think about it.

The mystique of the commander in chief encourages citizens to feel secure in "regular" life as it exacts their ever-less-questioning loyalty. Insofar as we subscribe to the idea that the president is *our* commander in chief, we reimagine American democracy through the lens of the military: not equalitarian but hierarchical, a command where accountability flows only upward, not downward to the citizens now reconceived as "rank and file." President George W. Bush relied on this logic when he explained to Bob Woodward: "I'm the commander—see, I don't need to explain. . . . That's the interesting thing about being president. Maybe somebody needs to explain to me why they say something, but I don't feel like I owe anybody an explanation." This is a philosophy that has informed Bush administration policy across the board. We could see its ramifications clearly in the National Security Agency's warrantless surveillance controversy, where Bush enacted his assertion that he does not owe citizens explanations, but feels free to listen in for theirs. This program violates the Foreign Intelligence Surveillance Act (FISA) of 1978, which was designed to protect citizens from precisely this type of governmental surveillance by repudiating executive powers to use electronic surveillance domestically without statutory authority. But citizens literally cannot succeed in appealing this maneuver, precisely because of the logic framed by President Bush. On July 6, 2007, the Sixth Circuit Court of Appeals in Cincinnati threw out an ACLU challenge, arguing that the plaintiffs did not have standing: they could not prove that they'd been personally targeted by the NSA secret wiretapping program. And of course they will never be able to discover, let alone provide, such proof so long as the program's status is protected by executive-mandated secrecy.

Yet many profess themselves comfortable with such measures as warrantless wiretapping and the president's newly claimed ability to designate U.S. citizens "enemy combatants" (stripping them of their constitutionally guaranteed rights), as long as the commander in chief deems such measures necessary. President Bush's declaration of commanding power over us can only seem democratically commonsensical to him and to citizens insofar as citizenship has been overtaken by the antidemocratic symbolics of the military presidency. This is the precise accomplishment of the mystique of the commander in chief. In a 2007 editorial, the historian Garry Wills highlights the susceptibility of citizens to these symbolics in recounting the infamous Saturday Night Massacre firings during Watergate, when President Nixon ordered Al Haig, his chief of staff, to have Special Prosecutor Archibald Cox fired. Haig's first choice for the job, Attorney General Elliott Richardson, refused and resigned. His second choice, William Ruckelshaus, similarly balked. Haig admonished him: "You know what it means when an order comes down from the commander in chief and a member of his team cannot execute it." Ruckelshaus took the hint and resigned. Finally the third in line, Robert Bork, took care of the job. In Wills's rejoinder: "President Nixon was not Mr. Ruckelshaus's commander in chief. The president is not commander in chief of civilians." But the ease with which we have come to consider the U.S. president our commander in chief, whose decisions command our unthinking loyalty or our willingness to stand down, signals, in Wills's phrasing, the "militarization of our politics."

This militarization has layers of consequences: institutional, cultural, and political. Let's start with institutional. As I've shown, the framers created the Congress to be, as governmental scholars Thomas E. Mann and Norman J. Ornstein put it, "first among equals." The theory of checks and balances solicited interbranch competition as a healthy feature of U.S. government. What the framers did not imagine was that the president would be able to consolidate powers that would make Congress—symbolically and factually—the weaker branch. Seemingly in coordination with the rising mystique of the commander in chief, presidents' recourse to and expanding repertoire of unilateral powers has grown over the twentieth century. As their unilateral powers rise, congressional powers and Congress's standing in the public's eyes decline.

One important reason for this change is a radical imbalance in each branch's incentives for and ability to protect institutional interests. Scholars and analysts have typically imagined the executive and legislative branches to be structurally on a level playing field, but recently, some have hazarded the observation that they're actually not. As a single actor, the president represents the whole of the U.S. electorate; representatives and senators are accountable to states and districts. When presidents, in presidential scholar Terry Moe's words, "want to shift the status quo by taking unilateral action on their own, whether or not that authority is clearly established in law, they can simply do it—quickly, forcefully, and (if they like) with no advance notice." Congress has no such ability, and, moreover, it is *disinclined* to react in a way that protects its own institutional interests. Instead, legislators work to advantage their state and district interests. And so they would, as a consequence, usually be divided on any unilateral action made by the president. Protecting the interests of their individual constituencies, Congress has collectively let its institutional power slip away.

Another important reason for Congress's diminishing standing concerns "transaction costs"—what it takes for each branch to arrive at decisions. The president has a whole bureaucracy at his command to advise him on matters of budget and policy. Because of the principle of executive privilege—especially in the realm of foreign policy—he can decide how much of this information to share with Congress. When he doesn't share fully, congressional members are forced to try to accumulate this information on their own, with staffs far less ample and with access to far less information than that of the executive branch. And if an imbalance of information can make it harder for Congress to react to the president in terms of foreign policy, the routine work of Congress makes it more laborious for that branch to accomplish business than in the executive branch. In political scientist William G. Howell's summary: "Members expend vast resources, in terms of both time and staff allocations, to design policy, build and sustain coalitions, and to monitor a proposal's progress through the legislative process. In the end, the number of laws Congress is capable of enacting in any given session is substantially limited. Such uncertainties generally do not encumber the president."

Imbalances in incentives to protect institutional interest and transaction costs make it hard for Congress to do much more than divide over presidential assertions of unilateral power. But in fact, Congress is seldom divided over presidential unilateralism. Tracking such showdowns over a nearly thirty-year period, Howell documents that "Congress appears nothing short of eager to back up the president when he exercises his unilateral powers." As the mystique of the commander in chief has accumulated, Congress has tended to support presidential unilateralism. And it is often penalized in public opinion for its failure to do so (there are some exceptions to this—for instance, in the aftermath of Oliver North's congressional testimony on the Iran–Contra scandal, polls showed that citizens for the moment at least had more confidence in the trustworthiness of Congress than the president). Since Woodrow Wilson's sustained (and failed) attack on Congress for its unwillingness to ratify the League of Nations (precisely because they feared it would deliver unilateral war powers to the president), presidents have more and more directed their public to view Congress as either an obstacle to righteous presidential ambitions or a weak foil to them. And the public trust in and approval for Congress has steadily declined. While voters tend to see the president as making noble sacrifices on behalf of the nation, as political scientists John Hibbing and Elizabeth Theiss-Morse have found, they tend to see members of Congress as merely greedy, self-interested, and deceptive. As political scientist Mark Rozell highlights in his book *In Contempt of Congress,* although the public tends to know little about what is actually going on in Congress, they steadily contrast the president's "decisiveness" to Congress's partisan "squabbling."

Thus the more power Congress gives to the president, the harder it is to get it back, and the weaker and sillier they look for trying (and that's especially true when they try and *fail* in these competitions). Consider the interbranch impasse over withdrawal from Iraq and the rejoinder of current and former members of the Bush administration: cut off the funding, they taunted Congress, and if you don't have the nerve to do that, then stay out of the commander in chief's way. As former Office of Legal Council staff member and current Berkeley law professor John Yoo evocatively summarized their point, "It would be Congress's power of the purse that would control the executive sword." As a machtpolitik maneuver, this "option" delivers Congress into a perfect catch-22. If they cut off funding, exercising the little bit of power they have remaining, they come off as being unsupportive of the troops and thus look weaker than ever to the public. And so their bitter pill: the more power Congress gives over to the president, the more symbolically "macho" he looks as commander in chief (with his "executive sword"), and the more feminine (power of the purse?)—and even childlike—Congress looks when members try to oppose him in the name of constitutional balance.

Machtpolitik

The subject of machtpolitik brings us to the second layer of consequences in the militarization of our politics. A popular if controversial book in the early twenty-first century, *The Art of Political War, and Other Radical Pursuits,* provides an economical outline of this view of politics. Its author, David Horowitz, reflecting on Clinton-era political strategy, redescribes democratic politics not as deliberation and persuasion but as raw power maneuvers in a zero-sum game, reversing—to arresting effect—the truism that "war is politics by other means." He argues that "politics is war conducted by other means. In political warfare you do not fight just to prevail in an argument, but to destroy the enemy's fighting ability." Horowitz elaborates that politics "is a war of position. In war there are two sides: friends and enemies. Your task is to define yourself as the friend of as large a constituency as possible compatible with your principles, while defining your opponent as the enemy whenever you can. The act of defining combatants is analogous to the military concept of choosing the terrain of battle. Choose the terrain that makes the fight as easy for you as possible." He urges that "in political wars, the aggressor usually prevails." One side will know that it's won when the other side no longer has power.

The militarization of our politics redefines democratic practice in aggressively antidemocratic ways. Democracy is a system that thrives on and

George W. Bush in a flight suit after landing on the aircraft carrier USS *Abraham Lincoln*. Bush's dramatic entry in military flight gear flourished his administration's machtpolitik as he warmed up the audience for his "Mission Accomplished" speech on May 1, 2003. Photograph by Pablo Martinez Monsivais; courtesy of AP Photo.

benefits from disagreement: it encourages a government where citizens, working together, can find plus-sum solutions out of their ongoing disagreements to the benefit of political, social, and economic community. While you can't say that everybody's always a winner in democracy, you stay in the game assuming your interests will be represented frequently enough. At its best, then, democracy works at providing incentives for keeping everyone in the game. Quite differently, machtpolitik assumes that there are only two positions in the game: winners and losers. It imagines a limited supply of democratic good that should not be evenly distributed but instead monopolized for the victors. In such a climate, no wonder senators threaten each other with the "nuclear option." (This is what Trent Lott, in 2005, renamed the Senate's "constitutional option," a strategy that ends a Senate filibuster by majority vote, in response to Democratic filibustering of Bush judicial nominees.)

The militarization of our democratic politics fosters a Manichaean worldview. You're either with us or against us, on the side of the good or the axis of evil. It's easy to attribute these politically reductive and vicious characterizations to the "other" side, but thinkers on both the right and the left have become infected with the knee-jerk habits of political demonization. It is on such habits that "shouting head" television and radio have thrived, as well as a book industry that produces such titles as *If Democrats Had Any Brains, They'd Be Republicans,* and *Rush Limbaugh Is a Big Fat Idiot.* These political actors (in the fullest sense) scorn reasoned deliberation and compromise. Instead, with an evangelical fervor, they denounce their opponents (the losers) in the shrillest and most aggressive terms possible. They maximize and overdraw political difference in order to vilify it. Demonology demands that your hero is my villain (which helps explain opinion polls that, for instance, in 2007 showed 75 percent of Republicans approving Bush's performance, as opposed to 8 percent of Democrats). With such opponents, compromise is demeaning when it's not unthinkable. With such opponents, no one can deliberate. If you don't agree with the president, this demonology teaches (and both Democrats and Republicans have made this claim in the past twenty years), you should leave the country.

The macho mystique of the commander in chief feeds the civil war atmosphere of U.S. democratic culture. The exaggerated and irremediable differences painted by its Manichaean pundits work to create a climate of political and social fear, activating and feeding what political scientists have described as an "authoritarian dynamic" or "situation-sensitive" authoritarianism. Recent research shows "that the effect of an authoritarian disposition on partisanship has . . . increased markedly between 1992 and 2004." Marc Hetherington and Jonathan Weiler's study draws on four questions introduced in the 1992 National Election Study, which probe for two of three key authoritarian attitudes, submission and conventionalism (the third is aggression). Hetherington and Weiler, like fellow political scientist Bob Altemeyer, are interested in showing authoritarianism's effect on current expressions of conservative partisanship. Others, like Karen Stenner, caution that it's important to distinguish between the authoritarianism that is situationally manifested by those predisposed, for whatever reason, toward authoritarianism, and the apparent authoritarianism of some kinds of conservatism. But there is a growing consensus that normative threats and fears about bad leadership summon authoritarian behaviors into our political scene—exactly the kinds of threats cultivated and kept alive by our politics-as-war culture, and that cultivate the habit of mistaking the president as "our" commander in chief, whose policies we must honor, whether or not we like them.

As touted Senate strategies like the "nuclear option" suggest, and as analysts like Mann and Ornstein, and Crenson and Ginsberg, demonstrate, key democratic political skills for consociation and deliberation are declining in government. Shouting-head culture has encouraged citizens who do want to talk politics—face-to-face or online—to seek these conversations only among those with whom they believe they'll find agreement. But this reassuring habit only feeds the cycle of war culture. Groups of like-minded people are highly susceptible to the phenomenon of group polarization, something legal scholar Cass Sunstein has recently described at length in *Why Societies Need Dissent.* In settings where a group shares basic leanings or opinions, deliberation tends to radicalize the opinion of the group and individuals within it, polarizing rather than moderating opinion. Democratic deliberation *needs* civil injections of diverse opinion, different expertises, and diverging institutions that support civil dissent. Politics-as-war kills this possibility as it strangles citizens' ability to imagine a richer, more active, and productively dissensual democratic community. We can't say that the mystique of the commander in chief *causes* all these ills, but we can say his macho symbolic presence certainly encourages them.

Finally, politics-as-war spills over into our daily lives. The post-1965 trend toward social enclaving and gated communities crucially reinforces tendencies toward political enclaving, as Bill Bishop so richly documents in his book, *The Big Sort.* Politics-as-war has spawned culture wars and what the sociolinguist Deborah Tannen has described as "argument culture," an agonistic, warlike stance that assumes all differences must be seen in oppositional terms and all decisions must be produced by adversarialist means. This attitude permeates our most mundane interactions. As Tannen notes, it's become habitual to conceptualize joining a conversation as "leaping into the fray" rather than as "sharing ideas." Argument culture encourages Americans to approach every subject as though it were war, a proclivity that feeds aggressive debate, "slash-and-burn" argumentative styles, and a winner-take-all attitude toward discussion that can inspire irrelevance and even dishonesty in routine interactions, all in the name of "coming out on top." Some people, clearly, are good at argument culture and even thrive on it, but for the rest, the energy required for routine defensiveness in argument culture is drawn away from more creative, generative enterprises. And those who have intelligent qualifications to contribute to debates, but fear being slaughtered in the war of words, withdraw. With them go vital, enriching insights.

These layers of consequences—institutional, political, and social—to the militarization of our politics are mutually reinforcing. Their downward spiral pulls us farther away from being able to revitalize, or even to imagine, a functioning process of democratic self-governance. The deeper we go, the harder it becomes to pull ourselves out, the farther away we are from being able to remember that democratic power is *our* power: it's what we delegate to the president, not the other way around.

Chapter 4
Going Corporate with the Unitary Executive

THE MASSIVE AURA OF POWER THAT ACCRUES TO THE COMMANDER
in chief does not seem to secure the power, efficacy, and legacy of individual presidents. Despite their successes at building powers for the presidency, both Harry Truman and Lyndon Johnson left the office in a thick haze of disapproval over wars to which they'd unilaterally committed U.S. forces. And as George W. Bush moved toward the final phase of his second term, his job approval ratings took a worse dive than any president since Richard Nixon, which doesn't bode well for his presidential legacy. Political scientists like Richard Pious call this kind of presidential failure in the face of increased executive powers a "performance paradox," suggesting that the seemingly endless ramping up of presidential dominance presents simply a kind of intellectual puzzle, a structural conundrum that functions contrary to expectations and hamstrings presidents. If anything, as this perspective implies, we should be worried that for all their ability to dominate the national and international agendas, presidents still don't have the right kind of powers, since those they do have seemingly only work to jeopardize their legacy. But the model of the executive power touted by Bush pushes against the limits of such common sense spouted by presidential analysts who keep insisting that we needn't worry that the accumulation of powers around the presidency could ever be a threat to democracy.

This chapter studies the extension and refinement of unilateral presidential powers (what scholars call the president's "power tools") from Nixon to Bush. It pays particular attention to the political and economic implications of a theory of executive power first proposed during Ronald

Reagan's administration, the "unitary executive," tracing its institutional development from Reagan, through Bill Clinton, and into the Bush presidency. It examines the looming threat of the unitary executive to democratic government, and to U.S. democracy more generally. While executive branch power is something that, constitutionally at least, has been dependent on the consent of Congress, the new theory of the unitary executive, should it gain judicial approval, will tip governing power decisively and permanently toward the executive branch, mooting many of the questions about democratic sovereignty and formal citizen agency I've been raising in this book. This chapter maps the stakes of this battle, identifying the winners and the losers in a democracy led by a unitary executive.

Presidential Power Tools

As Johnson left office, he told his successor that if "it hadn't been for Edgar Hoover, I couldn't have carried out my responsibilities as Commander in Chief. Period. Dick, you will come to depend on Edgar. . . . He's the only one you can put your complete trust in." It wasn't Nixon's style to put his complete trust in anyone. But he did tap into the resources that the longtime head of the FBI could offer his presidency, specifically in the form of intelligence files and wiretaps on various "enemies"—journalists, political opponents, and even National Security Council officials.

Years after his resignation, Nixon would sit for what turned into an electrifying interview with the British journalist David Frost. There he detailed his position on the many controversial aspects of his presidency, including his views on presidential power. In response to a question Frost framed about the "Huston Plan"—a proposed committee on interagency intelligence to be led by a young White House lawyer, Tim Huston, that would indirectly route presidential authorization for illegal wiretapping and information gathering to the various agencies in order to make such activities more efficient and productive—Nixon, a mere three years past his impeachment hearings and resignation, outlined his radical views on presidential supremacy with breathtaking candor:

FROST: So what in a sense, you're saying is that there are certain situations, and the Huston Plan or that part of it was one of them, where the president can decide that it's in the best interests of the nation or something, and do something illegal.

NIXON: Well, when the president does it that means that it is not illegal.

FROST: By definition.

NIXON: Exactly. Exactly. If the president, for example, approves something because of the national security, or in this case because of a threat to internal peace and order of significant magnitude, then the president's decision in that instance is one that enables those who carry it out, to carry it out without violating a law. Otherwise they're in an impossible position.

The nation was (at least temporarily) shocked by this bald assertion of inherent powers that could claim its precedent only in kingly prerogative. Frost's focusing of public outrage, combined with Congress's (not entirely effective, as we've seen) attempts to reign in the executive, and the nation's recent selection of the folksy and unassuming Jimmy Carter worked to reassure the public that Nixon's ideas about presidential powers had been firmly repudiated.

In fact, Nixon's exercise of the presidency's unilateral powers had *expanded* the presidential arsenal with tools that his successors—including Carter—were careful to protect and develop. At the height of the Watergate scandal in 1974, in *U.S. v. Nixon,* the Burger Court found against Nixon's claim of executive privilege in withholding Watergate tapes from congressional investigators. But, as political scientists Matthew Crenson and Benjamin Ginsberg recount with palpable impatience in *Presidential Power,* "instead of leaving matters there, the Court proceeded to recognize, for the first time, the validity of the principle of executive privilege. . . . The justices granted judicial recognition to a previously questionable principle" and thus enabled subsequent presidents to lay claim to the privilege of withholding materials from the public and Congress "with the Court's apparent blessing."

One of the twentieth century's most influential theories of presidential power, Richard Neustadt's *Presidential Power and the Modern Presidents,* memorably argues that the president's power lies largely in his ability to persuade. By Neustadt's description, the Constitution's separated powers in fact make presidents "chief" of very little, and so their authority of necessity depends on their ability to convince others. Guided by Neustadt, generations of presidential observers focused on presidential personality and registered the ways presidents were able to cooperate with or were blocked by Congress. But more recent presidential scholars and analysts have begun analyzing the use of presidential powers that do *not* depend on persuasion and have discovered an impressive and growing arsenal. Presidents since George Washington have deployed orders and proclamations, most usually to clarify the means by which they intend to carry out congressional intent. But since Franklin D. Roosevelt, presidents have increasingly used such authority to bypass Congress altogether, in effect legislating unilaterally. As government scholar William G. Howell observes, many "of the most important policy changes in the modern era came at the hands of presidents going it alone: Roosevelt's orders to implement the National Industrial Recovery Act, Truman's order to compel loyalty oaths from federal employees, Kennedy's efforts to control racial violence in Alabama, and Johnson's subsequent establishment for the first affirmative action policy."

The ability of presidents to exert their will without the support of other branches or even the U.S. public comes through what political scientists have denominated the president's "power tools"—an array of resources like proclamations, executive orders, decrees, memoranda, national security directives, and legislative signing statements—that allow the president to enact both foreign and domestic policy directly, without aid, interference, or consent from the legislative branch. For instance, presidents can bypass the Senate's constitutionally mandated "advise and consent" on treaties with foreign nations by declaring the agreement to be not a treaty but an executive order. Theoretically, Congress can countermand an executive order with legislation, but such legislation is always subject to presidential veto, and so it must be prepared to marshal a supermajority in order to face down such unilateral actions from what West Virginia senator Robert Byrd disparagingly terms the "superlegislator."

This ability to legislate by decree is not always well understood by those who work in government and policy. It's also not well known to the general public. While Congress created a classificatory scheme for recording and publishing executive orders during FDR's presidency, presidents soon realized they could bypass these requirements simply by naming their policy something else: memo, determination, finding, directive, or proclamation (and we're talking here only about actions that are supposedly public, different from those unilateral powers that fall into the category of national security, which are not required to be made public). The categories for the public actions are baffling, even to government experts, and some scholars argue that the perplexities they cause government and academic analysts can in fact be strategic for the exercise of presidential power. Howell argues that the president's power tools "are often used together in combinations that can be confusing, to be charitable, and just plain deceptive in a number of instances." Even those who study these tools can't agree on a complete catalog. For instance, one government scholar, Harold Relyea, has identified twenty-four types of presidential directives, a list that a Heritage Foundation fellow, Todd Gaziano, characterizes as "incomplete." Presidents themselves don't keep these categories straight. For instance, Clinton more than once announced to the public that he had just signed an executive order (which has to be federally recorded and published) when what he had actually signed was an executive memorandum (which doesn't). Presidents have created this ever-changing arsenal by drawing on an expansive reading of Article 2. They invariably cite congressional logjamming or national security as their reason for seeking recourse to such powers. As Howell summarizes, these unilateral strategies "represent one of the most striking and underappreciated aspects of presidential power in the modern era."

Nixon famously used executive orders to mandate that federal contractors establish specific goals for minority hires, to institute wage and price controls, and to establish the Environmental Protection Agency. The EPA joined a set of new congressionally created independent regulatory agencies established between 1970 and 1974, including the National Highway Traffic Safety Administration, the Occupational Safety and Health Administration, and the Consumer Product Safety Commission. Nixon acted in response to public pressure and congressional legislation (the National Environmental Policy Act of 1969). His order for the creation of the EPA came with a reorganization order (No. 3) that outlined his intention to build this new regulatory agency from an assembly of already existing programs in the Departments of Interior, Health, Education, and Welfare, and Agriculture, as well as in numerous bureaus, administrations, and commissions. Nixon may have acted unilaterally to preempt a more sweeping congressional initiative to create such an agency, but his orders won the approval of Congress. Environmentalists were supportive as well, at least until Nixon's Executive Order 11523, which, as political scientist Graham Dodds summarizes, "established the Department of Commerce's National Industrial Pollution Control Council, a group composed entirely of industry executives that had the ability to press for changes formally in proposed environmental regulations."

Nixon's most influential executive branch reorganization was also accomplished by executive order. Reorganization Plan No. 2 restructured the Bureau of Budget, an office created in the Department of Treasury by the Budget and Accounting Act of 1921, which was moved into the executive office in 1939, when it became responsible for organizing the federal budget. Despite significant resistance, Congress approved Nixon's proposal for reorganization in 1970, whereupon Nixon issued an executive order that re-created the bureau as the new Office of Management and Budget (OMB) and directed that, in addition to its duties in preparing the federal budget, it would now monitor independent (that is, non–executive branch) agency programs and budgets. Nixon's initiative effectively created the OMB as a powerful policymaking tool for the executive.

The OMB's new director, George Shultz, promptly declared that it had the authority not just to review but also to "clear" proposed regulations from independent agencies—agencies like the Consumer Product Safety Commission or the U.S. Trade and Development Agency—that were not under executive control. Nixon's administration herein launched a new and significant round of battles between the separate branches over mixed powers. Since in most cases, Congress had delegated legislative authority specifically to the heads of these agencies, decreeing that experts and not elected officials should lead regulatory and administrative processes, Shultz's declaration that the president would be making final decisions on policy signaled a serious interbranch turf war. Because of an

Power tools for presidents: Nixon's exercise of the presidency's unilateral powers expanded the presidential arsenal with tools that his successors were careful to protect and develop. Courtesy of the Nixon Library and Museum and of the U.S. National Archives and Records Administration.

immediate welter of legal objections and political outcry, Shultz backed off this claim. Instead, the OMB contented itself with subjecting regulatory agencies (the freshly created EPA in particular) to new—and, critics claimed, burdensome—layers of bureaucratic review before their regulations could be recorded and implemented.

Nixon's insight here was profound. As Crenson and Ginsberg put it in *Presidential Power,* unilateral powers like executive orders look wimpy when compared with the auxiliary legislative powers presidents wield through regulatory review: "By appropriating the rule-making powers of the federal bureaucracy, presidents can legislate without consulting the legislative branch." In retrospect, it's clear that Nixon's administration, which seemingly represented the culmination of citizen demands for industry, economic, and environmental regulation, also paved the way toward the great era of deregulation, much to the benefit of the corporations protesting such oversight. As much for big corporations, then, Nixon's maneuver was a significant turning point in the accumulation of presidential power, in the executive's receptiveness to business concerns, and in the diminishing responsiveness of federal government to citizen interest.

Reagan's Unitary Executive

Carter's appeal for the electorate came in his presidential antiheroism, and his perdurable image as a "soft" president can obscure how hard he worked to fortify presidential powers during his term in office. One story has it that when his team transitioned the Reagan team into the White House after the 1980 election, Carter's people touted the importance of exploring and pushing the constitutional boundaries of presidential power as a key strategy for a successful administration. Carter's specific contribution to the project of securing regulatory agency for the president came in multiple executive orders. Executive Order 12044 required federal agencies submitting regulations that would have an economic impact in excess of $100 million to file statements with the White House that detailed the aims of the regulation and alternatives to the regulation, as well as how the particular regulatory recourse had been arrived at and its economic impact. He created two agencies to provide oversight on compliance with that order: the Regulatory Analysis Review Group and the Regulatory Council. (He apparently contemplated creating a third that would extend these reviews into independent agencies, but was advised against such a confrontational overreaching of executive power.) As Dodds summarizes, "Carter instituted an important shift in presidential control of the bureaucracy." Instead of focusing, as Ford had, on the inflationary impact of a regulation, Carter asked that federal agencies publicly justify the benefits and cost of a rule beyond its immediate aims.

Carter also created the Office of Information and Regulatory Affairs (OIRA) within the OMB. Under Carter, the office simply screened the independent agencies' requests for compliance with the Paperwork Reduction Act. But OIRA would provide Reagan's administration with the exact vehicle it needed to mobilize deregulation, a counterattack on costly consumer/citizens protections and a cornerstone of the neoliberal economic policies that have guided every presidency that followed. For Reagan, OIRA was the ideal platform for launching a decisive, probusiness pushback against the New Deal philosophy that had aimed to provide crucial supports and protections for all citizens and had led to the big government that Reagan and his supporters despised.

Reagan had come into office promising to set the private sector free and get big government off the backs of people. He effected his tax cuts in collaboration with Congress. But industrial, corporate, and economic deregulation was an agenda he aimed to accomplish unilaterally. One of Reagan's early acts as president was to issue Executive Order 12291, which in political scientist Phillip J. Cooper's summary "transformed the OIRA into the lead agency for deregulation by delegating sweeping authority to the OMB to interdict agency rulemaking efforts and to maintain ongoing control over their operations." EO 12291 implemented stringent new procedures for regulatory review and added an approval process to the reporting that Carter had innovated. Under Reagan's new order, agencies could no longer federally record rules without OIRA—that is, executive—clearance. Reagan also reserved the right for OIRA to revise the rules as part of the review process, as well as the ability to block altogether any rule it disapproved of. In 1985 Reagan pushed again, issuing a new executive order requiring all federal regulatory agencies to submit an annual agenda for their planned activities. In this new order, Reagan aimed to control the regulatory process *before* agencies started making rules, ensuring that they would be limited to working within the president's political agenda.

Reagan also wielded his unilateral powers to deepen executive and governmental secrecy. Beyond authorizing arms shipments to Iran against an official U.S. embargo, Reagan used executive orders to give new life to the covert activities of the U.S. domestic and foreign intelligence community. He countermanded Carter's order on classification that security interests be weighed against the public's need to know and instead ordered that such questions *always* be resolved in favor of secrecy, thereby vastly expanding the amount of information that became subject to classification.

He ended a long-standing CIA practice of providing background information intelligence briefings to reporters and nullified a legislative amendment mandating that the CIA inspector general provide reports to congressional intelligence committees. He promoted and signed legislation that closed CIA files to public scrutiny under the Freedom of Information Act. He worked to clamp down on classified information leaks by limiting access to such documents within the executive branch and by promising to pursue "by all legal methods" any future leaks (a promise he had to back off from in the face of public outrage). He made it illegal to reveal intentionally the identities of covert agents (a policy it seems Dick Cheney, then working in Congress to uphold and rebuild executive powers, would later deliberately flout as vice president, tasking Scooter Libby with the job of outing Valerie Plame as a CIA operative). Reagan issued a directive that mandated lifetime secrecy pledges and lie detector tests for all government employees with access to classified information. Not even the ultrasecretive Nixon fought to have such high levels of secrecy.

Reagan's efforts toward concealment thus made his response to the congressional investigation of the Iran–Contra scandal—Reagan's own lively application of his secret powers—a surprise for close observers of his administration. He waived all executive privilege and went so far, when Congress demanded, as to agree to turn over his own personal diaries. Those who support expanded executive powers denounced his "weakness" on this score, his refusal to fight for the presidential right to secrecy, given how sure they were that Reagan could easily have won a battle over something that was arguably not an official record. But other observers commend his caginess, noting that his willingness to waive executive privilege in the wake of Watergate in all likelihood saved him from impeachment, considering that Reagan had not only broken numerous laws but had blatantly defied the clear will of Congress both in funding the Contra rebels in Nicaragua and in selling arms to Iran.

Despite the controversy over his refusal to defend executive privilege in this instance, analysts credit Reagan with creating an actual revolution in constitutional understandings of executive-branch administration. In ways that were simply unprecedented, Reagan moved, from the very first days of his term in office, to take wide-reaching control of the executive branch. In addition to the unilateral maneuvers described above, Reagan's administration famously practiced counterstaffing—a strategy of filling noncareer positions with inexpert staffers to slow agency work (and create more rank loyalty to the president than to their agency's objectives); using civil service positions as political appointments; and offering training for his incoming political appointees in dealing with bureaucracy.

Hand in glove with these initiatives, Reagan administration officials and soon Federalist Society lawyers (a network of societies that began forming in the early 1980s for politically conservative students at law schools across the United States) began elaborating a broad new model of presidential power, what they called the "unitary executive." This was in fact a project Reagan supporters began fleshing out before he entered office, for instance, in the Heritage Foundation project "Mandate for Leadership," published in 1980. The original aims of this new model were, according to Terry Eastland, publisher of the *Weekly Standard,* to get control of the regulatory state and entitlement spending, lower taxes, and to win the Cold War by boosting defense spending. The idea was that only a strong president could accomplish the project of limiting big government. Drawing on a model for "unitary" *corporate* leadership that gained particular prominence in the United States, where the CEO also served the company as the chair of the board (advocates insist that unitary corporations outperform those with divided board and company leadership), the unitary executive offered an aggressive brief for strong and undivided presidential control of the executive branch, expanded unilateral powers, and avowedly adversarial relations with Congress. Counselor to the president, and later attorney general, Edmund Meese began voicing publicly—always to great outrage—some basic tenets of this new theory. He insisted, for instance, that the president had the power of "nonacquiescence" to Supreme Court decisions; that the president had a right, coequal with the other three branches, to interpret and decide on constitutionality; and that, as he argued in a letter to the *New York Times* in May 1985, the administration had the right to disregard laws.

There were many and strong reactions against particular actions that Reagan's administration took on behalf of this new model for executive power, but there was little formal register of the unitary executive theory per se during Reagan's presidency (and in fact, although all presidents since have built on its strategies, George W. Bush was the first president to use the phrase officially). Behind the scenes, former members of Reagan's administration and conservative legal professionals began working throughout the 1990s to provide this theory with the cover of a constitutional basis and history. Drawing somewhat deceptively on Constitutional Convention debates about whether the presidency should be limited to one person (as I showed in chapter 1, the framers' term for this option was "unitary") or should involve three people (one from each national region—they termed this a "plural" executive), Federalist Society legal scholars like Steven Calabresi and Christopher Yoo have insisted that the framers intended the adoption of their newly conceived corporate model of hierarchical executive power from the nation's very beginning. Rejecting what is known as the "Madisonian" concept of constitutional collaboration, scholars and policymakers supporting the "Unitarian" ideal resurrected ideas rejected during the debates of promonarchical Alexander Hamilton. They foregrounded his advocacy for giving kingly powers like prerogative to the executive to suggest (again deceptively) that all the framers *intended* for the president to have prerogative powers as a way to ensure executive "energy." Calabresi and Yoo have published hundreds of pages in law journals attempting to prove the unitary executive as both the model the framers intended and the principle of executive power subscribed to by every president in U.S. history. Law professor Martin Flaherty has dismissed their historicist work as "History 'Lite,'" asserting that "history should matter in separation of powers analysis but only if credibly pursued." Citing the work of law professor Abner Greene, Flaherty observes that other historicist analyses consulting the same (and more) material come "to nearly opposite conclusions" about the framers' intentions for executive power and the balancing of powers between the branches.

As Pious recently summarized, the Hamiltonian argument about prerogative power that undergirds the unitary executive theory "is the antithesis of Madisonian principles: it involves governance by *fait accompli*." This preemptive model of presidential powers aims to counteract the difficulties presidents face in the era of politically divided government. At

the same time it highlights a growing contempt from the business, industrial, and corporate communities for Congress's supposed "inefficiency"
and for the way it roadblocks "leadership"—what had formerly been considered "checks and balances." Repudiating the constitutional system of
separated branches with shared powers, Unitarians argue that Congress
had no right to create independent administrative agencies, because they
exercise executive powers outside the control of the president.

This model not only seeks executive branch control over agencies that
Congress thought should come under congressional oversight, it also looks
for ways to end-run the Congress, whose weakness and so-called legislative
imperialism it scorns. Advocates for the unitary executive theory like to
recall that the framers termed Congress the "most dangerous branch,"
ignoring the fact that they did so because Congress was *popularly* elected
and thus more subject to the passions of the electorate—a feature that
the executive, then elected solely by the electoral college and *not* the
People, could then check. Exemplifying the cowboy sensibility of this
model, Michael Horowitz, who served as the chief legal officer in the
OMB under Reagan, defensively and dramatically complained that "Congress is a very potent institution and can do in the presidency. . . . congressional power is real, and it shoots real bullets." Other Reagan officials
framed the new "shoot-'em-up" quality of the interbranch relationship.
As Meese would later recall, "We were up against the 'establishment,'"
including "a Congress whose senior members ranged from skeptical to
overtly hostile"—this at a time when, as political scientist Philip Cooper
points out, Republicans were in control of the Senate. The new Reagan
administration planned to block what it termed congressional "oppor-
tunism" by disavowing collaboration and strategic relations in favor of
unilateralism.

Operating on the theory's principle that presidents usually get to keep
the powers they seize (a maneuver political scientist Ryan Barilleaux calls
"venture constitutionalism"), Reagan used executive orders to create policy on family, intergovernmental review of programs, and eminent do-
main, all policies that he couldn't successfully move through Congress.
And as subsequent congressional hearings would reveal, Reagan secretly
used national security directives—ostensibly aimed at foreign relations—

to accomplish *domestic* aims. As Cooper summarizes from a General Accounting Office study of the directives issued during the Reagan years, the GAO found "there were as many Reagan orders that had domestic impact as there were with military impact and more than that number with a foreign policy impact"—including National Security Decision Directive (NSDD) 189, which constrained the sharing of scientific research.

As important, Reagan aggressively expanded the use and aims of presidential signing statements. While the issuing of these statements with signed legislation had traditionally been ceremonial, and although these documents do not themselves have the weight of law, presidents from Monroe forward have used them on occasion to flag parts of the legislation that they object to as an incursion on the Constitution or on executive powers. In these cases, as political scientist Christopher Kelley summarizes in his article on signing statements, the president will "cite the section as erroneous and may urge Congress to pass corrective legislation or may more drastically refuse to execute the law or defend it if it is challenged." Sometimes, presidents have used signing statements to exploit a weakness or loophole in the legislation, delivering an interpretation or instructions to the agency assigned to implement the law that directs the interpretation of the law away from Congress's and toward the president's intent. Finally, presidents have used these statements rhetorically, to signal either their approval or their disapproval of specific aspects of a bill, hoping to influence either the media and the public, or the Supreme Court's interpretation, should the law be challenged.

As many observers have noticed, the use of signing statements has escalated radically since the Nixon era. Kelley's numbers document a total of 994 signing statements from Washington to LBJ, and 1,103 from Nixon to Clinton. This trend seems to be exponential: President George W. Bush issued signing statements challenging over 1,100 provisions of federal law in seven years of his presidency. Under the theory of the unitary executive, presidents have begun acting as if these statements do have the force of law, in effect nullifying key provisions of laws and taking in practice what the Supreme Court (in *Clinton v. City of New York,* 1998) has explicitly disallowed, a line-item veto. This practice has become controversial enough that in July 2006, the American Bar Association formally denounced the practice as presenting "grave harm to the separation of powers doctrine, and the system of checks and balances, that have sustained our democracy for more than two centuries."

Under Meese's guidance, the Reagan administration refined the signing statement for the purposes of the unitary executive. As Cooper explains, they "worked to make it a systematic weapon to trump congressional action and to influence not only the implementation of law but also its legal interpretation." Reagan's statements moved beyond offering warnings and alternative legal interpretations to making unilateral determinations about the validity of the provisions of particular statutes. Attorney General Meese announced in 1986 that West Publishing Company had agreed to publish the president's signing statements with the legislative history section of the *United States Code Congressional and Administrative News,* one of the two print sources for public law. In the same year, Reagan would pick up a significant victory with regard to a signing statement that had objected to the comptroller general provisions of the Gramm–Rudman–Hollings Act (the Balanced Budget and Emergency Deficit Control Act). In April, the Supreme Court would rule on *Bowsher v. Synar,* a challenge to the Gramm–Rudman–Hollings bill, upholding Reagan's objections and relying on his signing statement for their decision. And in the 1991 ruling on *Freytag v. Commissioner,* Justice Antonin Scalia's concurring opinion would support Meese's controversial assertion that the president had a right to "disregard" laws altogether "when they are unconstitutional."

Reagan's presidency profoundly reoriented theories about presidential power and famously revitalized the Republican Party. Significantly, it also served as a platform for applying neoliberal principles in U.S. government and society. Reagan's administration and fiscal policies supported the economic theories elaborated in corporate-funded conservative think tanks that had been formed in the 1970s to promote the principles of economists like Milton Friedman, Michael Jensen, and Friedrich Hayek. Neoliberalism (alternately termed "neoclassical liberalism," "neoconservatism," or "market fundamentalism"), forwards itself as an apolitical philosophy for government and categorically rejects the idea that government's job is to guarantee the general welfare. As economist Noreena Hertz summarizes, these theories "harked back to ideas that had shaped economic policy from the Victorian era through the Wall Street crash, that 'the role of the state was to enforce contracts, to supply sound money . . . to ensure that market forces were not distorted,' and, essentially, to provide the best environment for business to flourish, evoking memories of President Calvin Coolidge's dictum, 'The business of America is business.'" A network of think tanks, societies, foundations, and journals did the work of selling neoliberalism's new political economy not just to government but to the public, producing editorials; magazine, newspaper, and television pieces; media releases; and a phalanx of talk show political commentators. Their various efforts all aimed to uphold, as political commentator Kevin Phillips chronicles, "corporations, profits, consumption, wealth, and upper-bracket tax reduction and [cuts in] government and regulation."

The Reagan administration was able to start claiming success for the practices of market fundamentalism—through tax cuts, union crushing, and reluctance to enforce antitrust legislation, combined with cancellation of oil price controls and loosened restrictions on railroad transportation, oil and gas industries, and broadcasting—as early as 1982, when an economic recovery began. The upturn seemingly validated their formula for the economy: a strong commitment to military and defense spending, deregulation, debt financing, and the "supply-side" theory that insisted that top-tier tax cuts would spur investment and industry, resulting in a "trickle-down" effect on unemployment and rising income for the lower classes. Reagan's 1981 tax cut bill famously introduced myriad corporate loopholes, setting off a boom enterprise in tax sheltering and allowing many large U.S. corporations to evade paying taxes altogether. The stock market more than tripled in value between 1982—when *Forbes* magazine published its first list of the four hundred wealthiest people in the United States—and 1992. Supply-side economists argued that the Reagan era's economic policies produced tens of thousands of merger and acquisition deals that Harvard economist Michael Jensen assessed at a total value of more than $3 trillion. George Gilder, in an influential *Forbes* article praising the career of junk-bond trader Michael Milken and lauding the economy that sponsored his rise, cited $899 billion in shareholder gains during the Reagan era. During the 1980s the Forbes 400 would see their collective wealth double and even triple. Those not on Forbes's list saw rougher water in the waves of downsizing or "right-sizing" that dominated corporate agendas during the 1980s. White-collar unemployment rates more than doubled as the middle class's effective tax rate edged *up*.

From the Athenian 500 to the Forbes 400

By the time New Democrat Bill Clinton took office, FDR's New Deal social policies had been definitively rejected. Now, the nation-state was seen as a conduit for private sector growth rather than as an engine for growth itself. Although he rode into office promising to remedy problems created by the economic policies of the Reagan and George H. W. Bush eras, Clinton was committed to the same basic principles of market fundamentalism as he was to the theory of the unitary executive.

Throughout the 1990s, the unitary executive model gained appeal for government officials, policymakers, and scholars. It did so not because of the historical *léger de main* of scholars like Calabresi and Yoo but because of its appeal to promarket models of business efficiency, competitiveness, accountability, and strong, top-down leadership. For instance, in 1994, University of Chicago law professors Cass Sunstein and Lawrence Lessig made their own (arguably New Democrat) case for the unitary executive. Rejecting out of hand as "just plain myth" the historical arguments of Calabresi and Yoo, Lessig and Sunstein offer a brief for the theory "not relying on false history but on the best reading of the framers' structure translated into the current, and radically transformed, context." They deliver a nuanced corrective reading of the historical terms of the debate while making the case that the move to bureaucratic administration since the New Deal, and the increasing politicization of regulation, necessitates clearer lines of administrative accountability, which, they argue, can most profitably be realized in a strongly unitary executive.

Of course, it made perfect sense that the Democrats wanted to keep unitary executive powers now that they controlled the presidency. The theory offered tangible appeal to a Clinton administration facing a federal bureaucracy filled with Republican appointees. The New Democrats' version featured a tempered unilateralism, one that was not just accountable but responsive to citizens, or "customers" as Vice President Al Gore would redesignate those who utilized the services of the "U. S. Postal Service, Social Security, Department of Veterans Affairs, the National Park Service and scores of other federal organizations." "From Red Tape to Results" was Gore's 1993 plan to remake U.S. government by using the formulas for downsizing and "reinvention" that the nation's corporations had employed in the 1980s. Promising to turn national government from "complacency and entitlement" toward "initiative and empowerment," Gore drew on neoliberalism's keywords to imagine federal agencies that would rely on computer and Internet resources as well as the innovative structure of successful corporations like Saturn and Intel, marketing their resources to individual *and* corporate customers alike. The problem Gore identified was a lack of leadership, poor management, and overstaffing. As a corrective, he proposed a massive and thorough overhauling of all federal agencies, with the "president's vision of a quality federal government" as the force animating these changes. The best and most efficient route for achieving this massive project in waste reduction and entrepreneurial reinvention, Gore promised, was to give the president *more power.*

From the first, Clinton had moved to put the presidential agenda—and presidential power—front and center in government. Within his first week in office, along with numerous other executive orders, Clinton signed Executive Order 12835, creating the National Economic Council and thereby centralizing control over U.S. economic policy. The following year, he issued Executive Order 12866, which addressed the OMB and OIRA. Here, while redirecting some of the antiregulatory aims of the Reagan administration toward improving public health and safety and adding environmental protections, Clinton added an important new feature to Reagan's innovation: his order brought independent agencies, like the Social Security Administration, under regulatory review for the first time. While he did not require them to submit proposed regulations for executive review, the order did require them to submit their annual agendas to the OIRA, which brought their programs under scrutiny for consistency with presidential priorities. Additionally, as Crenson and Ginsberg recount in *Presidential Power,* at least 107 times "Clinton ordered regulatory agencies to publish in the *Federal Register* rules that originated in the White House."

Clinton issued a flurry of executive orders at the start of his term in office, many of which reversed or modified orders issued by his Republican predecessors (several of which were subsequently reversed in the face of negative public opinion, military resistance, and court findings). Some of his most controversial orders came after the Democrats lost congressional control in the 1994 midterm elections to Republicans. Here Clinton began deploying a strategy White House aides referred to as "Project Podesta," after Chief of Staff John Podesta. Project Podesta combined various unilateral executive powers with other strategies like White House–backed lawsuits and regulations selectively aimed at targeted corporations to impose policies opposed by Congress and even by the U.S. electorate. Clinton initiated maneuvers against tobacco and gun manufacturers, launched military action against Yugoslavia, and refused to honor congressional provisions for a semi-autonomous director for the new National Nuclear Security Administration (NNSA). When Secretary of Energy Bill Richardson was called onto the congressional carpet to answer questions about how Clinton's refusal, according to a GAO report, compromised national security, Richardson simply dismissed the opinion of Congress's investigative arm: "I have yet to find the GAO to say something positive about anything." (For this he then endured lectures from both Robert Byrd and Joe Lieberman about White House arrogance and its evident, Constitution-defying scorn for the legislative branch.)

Clinton eventually did appoint a director for the NNSA in 2000, but he never did acquiesce to the independence for the position that Congress had demanded. When Congress tried to hedge him in with laws outlining the conditions under which the new officer could be removed from office, Clinton simply noted in his October 2000 signing statement that these conditions would include a failure to comply with the president's directives. Kelley summarizes: "He used the signing statement in a fit of presidential power at the very moment when many presidential scholars suggest a president's power should be at its weakest." It's important to note that this brinksmanship with Congress occurred late in his putative "lame duck" period. Refusing to be hobbled during the final weeks of his presidency, Clinton issued twenty-one executive orders, expedited a bevy of new regulations, and in his last day in office, created seven national monuments.

Clinton's powers should have been compromised at the end of his presidency according to the lame-duck theory, but they were not. Nor were they during the Monica Lewinsky scandal or during his impeachment. The taint of Whitewater and a host of other simmering controversies substantially marred Clinton's presidential standing while in office, as they threatened to compromise his legacy. These credibility deficits, counterbalanced as they were by his enormous charisma, nevertheless cramped his ability to persuade government officials and citizens alike. But public disapproval and congressional opposition never at any point impeded Clinton's ability to act unilaterally.

Clearly, the powers presidents accumulate for the *presidency* don't do any more to protect their legacy than their stature and actions as commander in chief. With regard to how successfully presidents deal with Congress and how well they hold up under public opinion, the rate of presidential "failure" is so pronounced that many, like Pious, "take as a given the political weakness of the post–World War II presidency." He regards this weakness in the face of the presidency's growing powers as a paradox: "With greater institutional resources, with more delegated powers from Congress, and with (presumably) more accumulated experience from presidency scholarship, one might expect the institutionalized presidency to perform at a higher level." Many scholars, both those who support the unitary executive and those who oppose it—have begun speculating that presidential unilateralism might in fact be *causing* this problem. For instance, Michael Fitts, a unitary executive proponent, argues that the very accountability that Lessig and Sunstein herald as the key reason for supporting the unitary executive is in fact its Achilles' heel. The president becomes *overly* accountable: his ability to act unilaterally and to dominate the agenda makes the public see him as more responsible than he might actually be for what happens in government, complains Fitts. Thus while presidents frequently can force actions past Congress and judicial review, they can't evade the condemnation of the American public.

Whether the practices of the unitary executive consolidate or hobble the legacies of individual presidents, it's misleading in the extreme to conclude from their failures that presidents are "weak," as my analysis of Clinton's presidency indicates. These powers may not consistently seal the stature of presidents, but they are working, without doubt, for a variety of aims and agendas, and are in fact accomplishing a great deal. And in general, what seems most evident is that the unitary executive has worked from its inception in the 1980s to advance and consolidate market fundamentalism. It has retooled presidentialism for the globalizing aims of the "liberalized" economy, serving the needs not so much of U.S. citizens but of financial markets, international corporations, and the wealthiest of U.S. citizens. It has worked to turn citizen democracy into shareholder democracy, moving the United States definitively away from the ideal of self-governance enshrined in the ancient Greek agora, where a majority of active citizens were poor, toward the ideal of corporate governance, supervised by and for the people heralded by the annual Forbes 400 list of the richest Americans. (Awareness of this key transition may well be another reason why so many regular citizens have stopped bothering to vote—which is to say they are not apathetic so much as they are aware of their disenfranchisement from our current political system.)

By the early 1990s, when Clinton took office, neoliberal corporatism was going global. Countries worldwide were suffering from the inflation kicked off in the early 1970s by the collapse of the Bretton Woods Agreement (the post–World War II international agreement on commercial and financial rules and money management that led to the creation of the World Bank and the International Monetary Fund), the formation of OPEC (Organization of the Petroleum Exporting Countries) and the end of the Cold War in the 1980s, which lowered U.S. priorities for providing aid to poorer countries to keep them from coming under the influence of the Soviet Union. This reduction of aid was exacerbated as the United States and Great Britain retooled their economies in the early 1980s for neoliberal priorities, which emphatically denied the benefits of such aid as leading inevitably to dependency, not innovation. But as corporations began eyeing such countries for the promise of cheap labor, it became equally necessary for their governments and economies to have some stability for the deals to endure. Loans, not aid, were the new carrot, and they came attached to the stick of neoliberal economic reform—a package of policies that became known as the "Washington Consensus." Countries from Argentina to Zimbabwe received such loan packages under the condition that they implement a variety of policies—reduction of public spending; privatization of state enterprises; strict property protections; industrial, labor, and economic deregulation; competitive international exchange rates; trade liberalization and tax reforms—that would stabilize their economy for foreign corporate investment.

These policies were controversial in the United States (as they have been worldwide), not in the least because they enabled corporations to play hardball with U.S. labor, leaving the court altogether if they didn't get concessions they wanted. George H. W. Bush began the press for the U.S.–Mexican–Canadian Free Trade Proposal in the late 1980s, paving the way to a welter of free-trade agreements, forums, and organizations that during the 1990s, shepherded by Clinton, would come to include

- APEC (Asia Pacific Economic Cooperation), including most countries with Pacific Ocean coastline, passed in 1993;
- GATT (General Agreement on Tariffs and Trade), which aims to reduce tariffs on international trade, passed in 1994;
- NAFTA (North American Free Trade Agreement), also passed in 1994;
- WTO (World Trade Organization), which took over the functions of the newly expanded GATT agreement and went beyond traded goods to include trade within the service sector and intellectual property rights, passed in 1995.

These various trade agreements would, it was promised, benefit Americans with wealth creation and greater choice in cheaper foreign goods, while U.S. companies would gain in foreign markets. Detractors heralded not only massive losses in U.S. jobs but reduced labor bargaining lever-

President Clinton bows before an approving audience after signing NAFTA. Of the agreement, he had this to say: "This is our opportunity to provide an impetus to freedom and democracy in Latin America and create new jobs for America as well." Courtesy of Reuters.

age, predicting a "race to the bottom" for labor interests. While GATT, NAFTA, and APEC may certainly be credited with job creation, questions about where the jobs are located and what their working conditions entail have become familiar background noise in the news, with stories about gothic working conditions both at home and abroad, and forced and child labor in "developing" countries becoming daily fare.

Less noticed was how these trade agreements undermined local and national democratic self-governance. In the words of Hank Brown, a former Republican senator who opposed its passage, the WTO "creates a form of world government limited to trade matters without fair representation for the U.S., and an international court system without due process." WTO proceedings are shielded by secrecy, and this organization, like NAFTA, has the ability to use secret proceedings (dispute resolution panels) to overturn consumer, industrial, and trade protections that have been ratified by state and federal democratic processes. For instance, under NAFTA rules, a corporation can sue a government, forcing that nation (i.e., its taxpayers) to reimburse the corporation for any profits it might have lost because of the passage of laws detrimental to its free-trade interests. The threat of such a suit was enough to persuade the Supreme Court to strike down state laws banning the import of products manufactured with child labor.

Clinton used the persuasive powers of his presidency to facilitate the signing of NAFTA and other agreements. He used unilateral powers to benefit U.S. corporations and wealthy Democratic supporters through national security directives that authorized a global electronic surveillance network that operated under the code name ECHELON (created during the Cold War era to spy on the Soviets) to procure industrial and trade negotiation secrets from U.S. competitors. Reportedly capable, by the 1990s, of picking up electronic communications relayed by satellite anywhere in the world, ECHELON was apparently authorized by Clinton early in his presidency to tap into routine commercial and corporate communications in Europe, Asia, and the Middle East, as revealed by declassified American Defense Department documents in 2000 and supported by a European Parliament report released soon after. The NSA funnels information to the Office of Intelligence Liaison, in the Department of Commerce. According to these documents, during the late 1980s and 1990s, ECHELON had for example helped

- AT&T win business in Indonesia that intelligence intercepts indicated would go to Japan;
- Raytheon win a $1.5 billion contract from Brazil to create a satellite surveillance system for the Brazilian rainforest;
- Big Three U.S. automakers procure information about Japanese-designed zero-emission cars;
- Boeing and McDonnell Douglas gain a $5 billion Saudi Arabian contract the Saudis had been negotiating with the European consortium Airbus; and
- Kenetech steal wind-power technology from German manufacturer Enercon.

The conservative current events magazine *Insight* reported in a series of 1997 articles that Clinton had authorized ECHELON to put participants at the 1993 APEC conference under surveillance. Intelligence gathering on oil and hydroelectric deals pending in Vietnam was delivered to Democratic Party contributors bidding for the contracts.

Clinton promised individual citizens that he could "feel their pain." He used his unilateral powers (not always successfully) to address some of the labor concerns generated by NAFTA and consumer concerns generated by two decades of deregulation. But he also resolutely kept business and free market interests at the forefront of his agenda. The slogan from his first campaign, "It's the economy, stupid," was capacious and ambiguous enough to reassure both individual citizens being dinged, even hammered by neoliberal economic policies, *and* corporate interests reaping their benefits. Clinton's reversal on China at the start of his presidency made clear how the ambiguity would resolve. During the 1992 election, he had criticized George H. W. Bush's willingness to grant China most favored trading nation status, given its record on human rights—especially in the aftermath of the Tiananmen Square massacre. This was perfectly within keeping of his promise to feel peoples' pain. But once president, he quickly reversed himself, ensuring China's admission as a full partner in the WTO, arguing quite differently that "trade encourages democracy," the mantra of market fundamentalism.

That mantra is entirely misleading. Liberalization makes markets *efficient,* but seldom fair—something neoliberal boosters will also happily acknowledge. And so, while average worker pay stagnated during the years of Clinton's presidency, CEO compensation would rise by more than 400 percent, as average corporate profits rose by more than 100 percent. By the year 2000, according to the Global Policy Forum's Corporate Watch, international corporations would for the first time dominate the rankings of the worldwide largest economies: there were fifty-one corporations and forty-nine countries on the list.

With a steady boost from Clinton's executive leadership, the 1990s cemented neoliberal economics as the new politics. Rational choice theory, neoliberalism's academic fellow-traveler, which models human decision making across an array of social contexts as though it all functions exactly like individualistic marketplace choice, gained sway across a range of disciplines, including political science, anthropology, law, cultural geography, sociology, and environmental sciences. Suddenly, market behavior became the "best" explanation. Proponents used it to account for and predict everything from voting behavior to dating rituals, land use, and wildlife management, proposing policies in accordance with its dog-eat-dog maxims. Rational choice theory offers an emphatically desocialized view of human behavior, insisting that our primary concerns are always essentially about our own financial advancement and not about the other people whom we live among. Operating more successfully as theory than empirical science, it remains cynical in the extreme (despite its problems with predictive success) about peoples' ability to engage in democratic self-government in its projections and prescriptions. It insists—often against solid evidence to the contrary—that individual selfishness will always and inevitably undermine any commonwealth. In market liberalism's "rational" understanding, even so politically fundamental a document as the nation's Constitution should be understood solely as a "cost transaction model" and not at all about democracy, as one of my colleagues recently explained to me with no discernible irony.

The MBA President, or The Unitary Executive on Steroids

In the run-up to the 2000 election, the corporate community widely heralded the Republican Party nominee for president, George W. Bush, as the "Nation's First MBA President." With one of the most prestigious business school degrees in the United States (Harvard), Bush and his educational, family, and career pedigree promised to continue the project of transitioning the political state into the corporate state. His cabinet appointments added reassurance for the Fortune 500: it was dominated like no other in U.S. history by people who had extensive personal financial and professional ties to giant U.S. and multinational corporations. Their connections to oil, energy, defense, electronic data, and communications companies were especially deep. Of course the Bush family is historically and complexly involved not just in oil but in what Dwight D. Eisenhower termed the military–industrial complex—armaments, ammunition and ordinance, war contracts, war production, and intelligence technology—and also in finance, as Phillips has detailed in *American Dy-*

nasty. Vice President Dick Cheney was famously the former CEO of Halliburton, the world's largest oil field services company, whose European subsidiaries sold spare parts to Iraq's oil industry despite UN sanctions. Condoleezza Rice had a Chevron oil tanker named after her—until 2001, when Chevron quietly renamed the ship the Altair Voyager to tamp down controversy surrounding her corporate involvements. Bush cabinet members and council appointments had corporate ties to food and agriculture (Kraft, Kellogg's ConAgra, Tyson, Archer Daniels Midland, Brinker), to chemicals (Cabot, Clorox), to finance (Fidelity, Charles Swab, Transamerica, Goldman Sachs, Bank of America), to engineering and construction (Bechtel; Kellogg, Brown, and Root; Shaw Group), and more. Corporate America was optimistic for continuing support—nor would it be disappointed. As the *New Republic*'s senior editor Jonathan Chait notes, the Bush administration began routinely to "appoint lobbyists to oversee their former employers," installing a regulatory philosophy that made it "increasingly difficult to distinguish between business and government."

Executive unitarians were similarly hopeful that the president's CEO style would translate into ongoing strengthening for executive powers. Still, given Bush's platform as a "compassionate conservative" and the tumultuous circumstances of the 2000 election, observers and analysts predicted his early presidential demeanor would be conciliatory. They figured he would need to build credibility on the job and govern from the middle. They were famously wrong. From his first days in office, Bush demonstrated his commitment to the strongest possible version of the unitary executive theory. He began with a salvo of executive orders that included the creation of a White House Office of Faith-Based and Community Initiatives; the reclassification of presidential materials that had previously been made publicly accessible (altering scholars' as well as the public's access to presidential records and thereby deepening the realm of executive privilege beyond the immediacy of a president's years in office); and reversals of Clinton policies on the environment, labor, and health policy. Given the new president's stated disdain for his predecessor's actions, many observers were surprised by the Bush administration's *defense* of Clinton's late-term executive orders that set aside thousands of acres for national monuments. But Solicitor General Theodore Olson's arguments before the Supreme Court, suggesting that the Court had no standing whatsoever to question Clinton's orders, clearly signaled the Bush administration's commitment to defending not just unilateral executive powers but a beefed-up theory of the unitary executive.

The attack of Islamic radical terrorists on the World Trade Center and Pentagon in September 2001 authorized President Bush to take on the mantle of commander in chief. Creating the Department of Homeland Security by executive order, Bush began pushing both in public and in secret for vast expansions of presidential powers, through the USA PATRIOT Act, national security directives, and military orders. As early comments by UN ambassador John Negroponte suggested and the National Security Strategy of 2002 would confirm, the Bush Doctrine depended heavily not just on U.S. unilateralist preemption in the war on terror but on specifically presidential unilateralism. As the political scientist Michael Cairo details,

> Its [i.e., the Bush Doctrine's] proactive stance is the basis for expanded presidential power. The strategy suggests that due to the nature of the threat a president may act alone to start a war against a perceived aggressor. The strategy presents an incontestable moral claim that in certain situations preemption is preferable to doing nothing. . . . In fact, the entire strategy is based on the presumption that a president can and must act to prevent future attacks on the United States or U.S. interests. . . . it denies the necessity for congressional action of any kind in the use of force.

Other unitarians proved willing to go farther in support of this model of power. The Harvard law professor Harvey Mansfield argued in a May 2007 *Wall Street Journal* editorial that not only should the president not be subordinate in any way to Congress, he should also be above the rule of law. Making the president follow the law unnecessarily weakens the executive, and, Mansfield dramatically insisted, weakening the executive leads inevitably to a weakened United States. Indeed, as the NSA warrantless wiretapping controversy revealed, President Bush had not considered himself bound by the rule of U.S. law, any more than had his advisers found him to be bound by federal law, international war rules, treaties, or the Geneva Conventions in deciding how to deal with foreign combatants or U.S. citizens captured in the war on terror.

Bush's decisions—guided by John Yoo, Alberto Gonzales, David Addington, Timothy Flanigan, and others—to defy national and international law in his administration's policies on torture exemplify his administration's position on presidential power, its claim to supremacy over Congress, the Supreme Court, the American people, and the world's peoples and laws, indeed, the conditions of human life. In the view of the conservative lawyers who provided the legal reasoning for these new policies, the president's powers as commander in chief should be unchecked and uncheckable. They created numerous opinions and documents—for instance, the infamous August 2002 Office of Legal Council memo drafted by Yoo and later nicknamed the "torture memo" when it was leaked two years later—that argued for the president's inherent right to redefine legal methods for interrogating and trying "unlawful enemy combatants" at will. Indeed, from the earliest moments of the so-called war on terror, Yoo, the midlevel attorney in the Office of Legal Counsel who was central to many of the Bush administration's early decisions on presidential war powers, enemy combatants, and torture, decreed in a September 2001 memorandum opinion that Congress had no legal basis for checking the president when it came to "any terrorist threat, the amount of military force to be used in response, or method, timing, and nature of the response." Based on these principles, Bush proceeded to defy every congressional attempt to thwart his illegal policies by threatening a veto. Or, he simply added signing statements to laws that attempted to put constraints on the treatment of prisoners, such as the one backed by John McCain in 2006, asserting when he signed the bill in December that, as commander in chief, he would not consider himself bound by such laws.

The Bush administration, it was evident, was pushing the theory of the unitary executive to new levels. Earlier debates about the theory relied on an at least apparently democracy-friendly theory of branch equality—each branch has its separate and "equal" powers; the president has an "equal" right to interpret the Constitution with the other two branches. Thus unitarians could claim that they were simply working to make interbranch relations more fairly competitive. But these claims to democratic "equality" for the president's power could hardly restrain the unitary executive theory's realpolitik aim for supremacy. The "hierarchy" that

Reagan unitarians touted for organizing the executive branch would, in the new Bush–Cheney vision, extend beyond the executive branch to the entire federal government, and indeed, the world.

In retrospect, it is clear that Vice President Cheney (who began his Washington career as an intern in the Nixon administration) made public his commitment to this more extreme version of the unitary executive as early as 1987, in the minority response to the congressional report on the Iran–Contra hearings. Dissenting from the report's condemnation of the Reagan administration's "pervasive dishonesty and inordinate secrecy," Cheney, then a U.S. representative from Wyoming, issued a blistering counterattack. He excoriated Congress for legislative imperialism, arguing in essence that "the long-accepted notion that the Constitution's structure was intended to check government power" was a "fallacy." In historian Sean Wilentz's summary, not only did the minority report "defend lawbreaking by White House officials, it condemned Congress for having passed the laws in the first place."

Cheney's withering hostility toward the "ill-equipped" legislative branch seemed to inform the Bush administration's summer 2007 suggestion that it would counter congressional contempt citations for White House officials refusing to turn over key evidence in the Justice Department attorney-purging scandal simply by declining to allow the Justice Department to pursue congressional charges. To legitimate that position, Bush administration officials invoked internal OLC memorandums from both Republican and Democrat administrations that conclude congressional contempt charges apply neither to the president nor to those whom he covers with executive privilege. It was a moment that confirmed the *Onion*'s August 2006 spoofing headline "Bush Grants Permission to Grant More Power to Self" as a realistic prediction. In late July 2007, political analysts, while admitting there was no precedent for this claim of executive immunity from congressional contempt charges, were predicting that Bush's bid would likely prevail. Such a precedent would mean that Congress can't check the president when the president doesn't want to cooperate.

The Bush administration currently seems to hold the position that *everything* it does, with regard both to foreign policy and to domestic policy, is covered by the mantle of Bush's uncheckable privilege as commander in chief, powers that come to him, he and his counsel assert, both through the Constitution's Article 2 and through the 2001 Congressional Authorization for Use of Military Force ("That the President is authorized to use all necessary and appropriate force against those nations, organizations, or persons . . . "). Yoo, now a professor in Berkeley's law school, has energetically advocated for the legality as well as the necessity of these unchecked powers, in government documents, in scholarly articles, and in popular press books. In a 2002 article published in the *University of Chicago Law Review,* Yoo mapped an explicitly monarchical genealogy for presidential war powers. Drawing on Lockean theories of a *king's* "executive" powers, Yoo insists that while the framers may have "altered other plenary powers of the King, such as treaties and appointments," they nevertheless meant to give "all other unenumerated executive powers to the President." In other words, the very fact that they did not say they were giving monarchical powers to the president in the text of the Constitution is for Yoo good enough evidence that they intended for him to have them.

It's not hard at all to rebut this argument, and many have in detail, including constitutional scholar Louis Fisher and Georgetown law professor David Cole. Cooper neatly trashes Yoo's originalist argument for granting the president kingly prerogative:

> Prerogative is both misunderstood and misapplied by presidents and their supporters as a formal constitutional claim to authority. . . . First, the assumptions about the prerogative powers of the British monarch are often incorrectly stated. Second, after independence, the newly formed states reacted against assertions of prerogative powers by creating weak executives. Third, at the time the Constitution was drafted and the campaign for its ratification was waged great pains were taken to deny that the new presidency would have the broad powers that had been understood to lie at the heart of the prerogative power of the king.

Identifying these claims as (laughably) bad history is simple enough. But we need to ask why unitarians would even be willing to go public with an argument on behalf of a democratic president having a king's powers. It seems plausible to wonder if the market excess of the 1990s, its corporate and shareholder fascination with "charismatic" leadership, has not made it for the first time culturally attractive to vest our most central democratic leader with the "mystery" of kingly executive charisma. Or to approach this from another angle, it's not necessarily that the unitarians are depending on the idea that Americans want a king. They could just be counting on the idea that we've become so enamored of the idea that leaders—especially our president—should have "enough" power that we might be willing passively to acquiesce to the idea that "the most powerful man in the world" should, really, get to have the *powers* of a king.

King George and the Supremes

Whether or not the U.S. public will sign off on the idea that our Revolution was only for a different kind of monarchy (this would be what the legal commentator Glenn Greenwald terms a "devolution"), the promotion of this argument has, for some commentators, exposed a grand presumption behind this administration's pressure on the theory of the unitary executive. Many, from journalists and commentators like Greenwald, Jacob Weisberg, and Stuart Taylor, to legal scholars and analysts like Frederick A. O. Schwarz and Aziz Z. Huq, began denouncing Bush's "monarchical" pretensions. That's actually an easy sport, especially when his campaign issued bumper stickers that feature his middle initial looking like nothing so much as a crown, or when Bush himself speaks earnestly to *New York Times* reporter Elizabeth Bumiller about his "presidential DNA," or when his administration feudally farms out no-bid contracts to the very U.S. corporations or their subsidiaries to which Bush's family and cabinet members have such deep ties (e.g., by 2007, Halliburton and its subsidiaries had earned more $20 billion from the U.S. military in war-related contracts in Iraq since the March 2003 invasion, according to CorpWatch). However satisfying such charges may be for Bush's detractors, though, labeling his monarchical pretensions can't account for the democratic optimism that has fueled Bush policy statements.

Others, like social theorist Andrew Arato, have begun using terms like "dictatorship" or (only less scary for the larger mouthful) "plebiscitary presidency." The latter notion is one that historian and Kennedy adviser

Arthur Schlesinger Jr. warned against as early as 1973, in his Nixon-era study, *The Imperial President*. There he recounted Nixon's unprecedented attempt to accomplish these powers for his own presidency: "If this transformation were carried through, the President, instead of being accountable every day to Congress and to public opinion, would be accountable every four years to the electorate. Between elections, the President would be accountable only through impeachment and would govern, as much as he could, by decree." More recently, Massachusetts congressman Barney Frank delivered a thoughtful analysis of "Bush's plebiscitary presidency" on the House floor. Frank credits Bush's commitment to democracy, observing that in the sixth year of Bush's presidency, the United States is still "a very free country." But he finds that Bush's conception of democracy is strikingly different from the one he feels pledged to uphold: "Thanks to the acquiescence of a Republican majority in this Congress, driven in part by ideological sympathy, he has been allowed to be the decider. So we have a very different kind of American Government. We have had an American Government in which the President gets elected and exercises an extraordinary amount of power. It is democracy, but it is closer to plebiscitary democracy than it is to the traditional democracy of America."

This plebiscitary democracy, as Frank indicates, serves citizen interests once every four years, when they are asked to sign off on elite decision making by choosing between two presidential candidates, both thoroughly corporate sponsored, thanks to the astronomical and ever-growing costs of presidential campaigns. In the meanwhile, this form of democracy serves market, corporate, and shareholder interests full time. We could think of the "very different kind of American government" that Frank identifies as a new feudalism, a condition where thanks to two decades of deregulation, tax cuts, and now an apparently endless war, state power has ebbed and local power brokers have taken over, forming relationships of reciprocity between military and economic powers. As former CEO, business and marketing consultant, and commentator Thom Hartmann says, feudalism coincides with the weakening of a nation-state's protective capacity: "When the wealthiest in a society take over government and then weaken it so much it can no longer represent the interests of the people, the transition has begun into a new era of feudalism." And it's fair to be clear here: such critiques (mine included) are not being mounted by people hostile to capitalism but simply opposed to the model of capitalism that has gained ascendancy in this era of market fundamentalism. As the cofounder and editor of *Business Ethics* Marjorie Kelly explains, neoliberalism has created a "corporate aristocracy." She urges that the democratic ideals of the American Revolution can lead us to an alternative ideal, a democratic capitalism that would "create an economy where all can accumulate capital, and where the living capital of the commons is preserved for all to enjoy." That would be an economy and a political system more than a little different from the one we witness now, where by 2006, the Forbes 400 were *all* billionaires, and where the conservative op-ed columnist David Brooks defends the current administration's economic policies by touting "sharp" rises in wages: "Real average wages rose by 2% in 2006, the second fastest rise in 30 years." (For contrast, let's just recall: in 1978 the average CEO made 78 times what a minimum-wage worker made. We can legitimately use the word "sharp" for the rise that occurred in that percentage through the next two decades. It peaked at *815* times the average worker salary in 2000 before falling to 416 in 2002, in response to the Enron scandal. And so much for corrections: in 2005, it was already back past the 815 crest, hitting an all-time high of 821 times the average worker salary, according to the Economic Policy Institute.)

Still others, while conceding that the Bush administration is overreaching on its claim to executive powers, reject the alarmism of terms like *king* or *dictator,* arguing that this very overreaching will work to *limit* the presidency and set back the march of the unitary executive in ways that might be regrettable for future presidents. Journalist Jeffrey Rosen takes this position, citing Supreme Court rulings handed down by the Rehnquist Court in 2004 and 2006 that checked many of Bush's operating assumptions with regard to military prisoners. Concludes Rosen: "Bush's extremism may have ultimately weakened executive power in the same way Clinton did when the Supreme Court rejected his sweeping assertions of executive privilege in the Monica Lewinsky investigation. By taking implausibly aggressive positions before the Supreme Court, both presidents precipitated a judicial backlash."

But Rosen's conclusion ignores his own cogent framing of the potential differences between the Rehnquist and Roberts courts. The Court's older members came of age in an era that was skeptical of New Deal presidential excesses. Rehnquist *scoffed* at the notion that the Constitution meant to give the president the kind of "plenary and exclusive power" that would equate with kingly prerogative in *Dames and Moore v. Regan* in 1981. But its new conservative jurists, like John Roberts and Samuel Alito, were educated in a period when conservatives began to see the executive as the only force that could wrest their ideals from the machinations of big-government Democrats, liberal courts, and a sprawling federal bureaucracy. Unlike the older members who rarely served in the executive branch before entering the Court, *all* of the unitary executive proponents on the court served in the administrations of Ford or Reagan.

The Most Dangerous Branch

This generation of conservative jurists takes the executive branch's hostility toward Congress as a credo. Cooper in fact credits the unitary executive model with the breakdown of the Washington Rules—a code of civility that governs day-to-day dealings within Congress and between the legislative and executive branches. (This breakdown might have been best exemplified when Vice President Dick Cheney told senior Democratic senator Patrick Leahy to "go f— yourself!" on the Senate floor in June of 2005.) It is this ingrained hostility to democratic governance that leads Justice Department lawyers advising the president to argue that the president has the same powers as the British monarch to suspend laws passed by Congress. This team of legal advocates has grafted on to the right granted to presidents since *Youngstown Sheet and Tube Co. v. Sawyer* (discussed in chapter 3) to act unilaterally in the face of congressional *silence* on an issue, a new level of entitlement altogether, concluding that presidents have the right to act unilaterally even when clearly opposed by Congress and law. This new arrogant assertion of executive supremacy is what Mansfield offers in his "Case for the Strong Executive." There, he redescribes our three-branch constitutional government in altogether new terms, insisting that the essential checking contest lies not between the three governmental branches but between "the strong executive and its adversary, the rule of law." Our Constitution, according to Mansfield, actually provides for "one man rule" insofar as its federalist proponents designated the president as government's "source of energy." The fact that this language is not in the legal document of the Constitution does not give Mansfield reason to pause. The prominent journalist Anthony Lewis says of such "logic" on the part of our nation's most influential jurists: "There is a French phrase for betrayal of standards by intellectuals: *la trahison des clercs.* I think this is a lawyer's version: *la trahison des avocats.*" Lewis's comments, directed at the gymnastic contortions of logic in Yoo's torture memos, are equally suitable for describing Mansfield's efforts. Cavalierly denying the antimonarchical and democratic legacy of the American Revolution as well as the clear historical record, this influential law professor, like other Bush-era unitarians, insists that the framers actually intended for the president to stand above the laws that govern us all.

Thus those who imagine that the Bush administration's presidential power grab has been definitively set back by such Rehnquist Court rulings as *Hamdan v. Rumsfeld* (2006) should pay attention to the new Roberts Court and its impressively low regard for legal precedent. With four unitary executive proponents already in place (Clarence Thomas, Alito, Scalia, and Roberts), the Roberts Court plus just one more pro–unitary executive appointment will have the power constitutionally to validate Mansfield's scheme for presidential supremacy, potentially turning it from theory into constitutional fact.

Once we're there, it's hard to see how we might take a more robust democracy—the kind of democracy where citizens have and can exercise self-governing power—back from the unchecked and uncheckable president imagined by Mansfield, Cheney, Bush, and other hard-line unitary executive proponents. When I began working on this book in the late 1990s, I imagined I was offering a provocative argument directed simply toward reorienting the ideas and democratic habits of people who were unhappy with the offerings of current presidents and presidential candidates. I wanted to argue that we might have a political system we could find more satisfaction in if we became more invested in local democracy, in the art—the messy, often time-consuming work and not always clearly rewarding work—of face-to-face self-governance. It was a puckish

The nation's leading proponent of the unitary executive. Mission accomplished? Photograph by J. Scott Applewhite; courtesy of AP Photo.

endeavor asking my fellow U.S. citizens to think about the democratic project as something wider, deeper, and more athletic than voting for the president every four years and complaining all the years in between.

I still mean to ask for all that (in the next chapter, in fact, where I outline what we can do about the problems that have flourished under presidentialism). But this is no longer a mere thought experiment about a way that citizens might revitalize U.S. democracy at home. The clear tendencies of the unitary executive model for the presidency—its aims to remodel and redistribute all the powers of our Constitution to the executive office—have added a different, unhappy, and necessarily alarmist aspect to my appeal. Now, it's not so much a matter of perhaps revitalizing democracy as it is of losing its possibility altogether from formal government, and soon.

Rosen notes that "with Bush's excesses, conservatives are reaping the consequences of the Leviathan state that they once warned against: Once executive power is viewed as absolute, centralized, and indivisible, it tends inevitably to grow." He points to conservatives as the origin of this current phenomenon, but the problems he identifies and that I've been outlining in this book will most certainly not be remedied by electing a Democrat. No president has consented or will ever consent to giving up the powers accumulated under the theory of the unitary executive. Every president believes he needs such powers—and more—to accomplish his mandate and protect his legacy. This threat to U.S. democratic government—we could without being overly dramatic think of it as a final threat to formal democracy within U.S. government—will not likely be remedied by any person we elect to the Oval Office.

Conclusion
Reclaiming Democratic Power for Ourselves

IF THERE IS A REMEDY FOR THE THREAT I'VE DESCRIBED IN chapter 4, of the president overtaking democracy, it will have to come from all of us. As I've argued, we can't just trust in the separated and balanced powers of our constitutional government to remedy this threat mechanically—like the swinging of a clock pendulum—for us. The Supreme Court is now only one vote short of a unitary executive majority, and Congress institutionally does not have a strong incentive to unite against presidential unilateralism unless the constituents of individual representatives are demanding it.

Why should we work to see that the president has *less* power? Throughout this book, I've argued that it has been a mistake to let the presidency have so much symbolic force in our democracy and so much actual sway over federal government. This is a mistake that threatens not just democratic government but democratic spirit—our ability to imagine what it means as well as what it takes to engage in the project of self-governing together. The sway of presidentialism reduces our democratic skill-set and reinforces a dangerous trend of social, economic, and political enclaving that has emerged over the past forty years, a trend that has polarized U.S. politics and has made it all the harder to imagine not only how to make democratic community together but even how to picture why we would want to.

In this conclusion, I'm calling on readers to reimagine democracy as an open system, a group project, something larger than federal and local government and definitely more expansive than presidential leadership.

I'm asking us to rethink politics not as poison but, differently conducted, as the lifeblood of a democratic system, as an exercise that draws at least periodically on the civic energy and commitment of each of us. I'm appealing for us to check our own intolerance for political disagreement. I'm insisting that we must work at cultivating a better patience: for those who differ from us; for the never-ending work of negotiating democratic disagreement; for a certain level of political disunity that is absolutely fundamental to the vitality and well-being of a democratic polity; and for the unpredictability that lives hand in glove with increased creativity. Over the past political generation, we've isolated ourselves among those with whom we agree politically and have come to regard those with whom we disagree as utter strangers, even aliens to the polity we envision for ourselves. We've let go of democratic creativity and let reactive snarkiness and political demonization fill the void. If the concept of democracy is something we still treasure, I'm urging us to figure out together how to remake a democratic project, precisely with those who have become strangers to us.

I don't want to be misunderstood here. I'm not talking about changing attitudes so we can have that magical kumbaya community where we all hold hands, sing a song, just get along. I'm talking about developing skills that help us keep engaging in a democratic polity without the necessity of overly strong unity and agreement, skills that allow us creatively to problem solve in plus-sum ways across experiential, attitudinal, affiliational, identity, political, and ideological differences that will always exist among us. I'm talking about developing an adult comfort with and a creativity about disagreement that I think many of us are actually longing to imagine and build as we turn away, disgusted, from shouting-head TV, radio, and Internet blogs. There's something in between the romance of community and the warring talking points that pass for political coverage these days, and it's that in-between that I'm suggesting we can explore and utilize if we free ourselves from the polarization that our love affair with the presidency feeds.

In short, I'm arguing that we imagine democracy as something we, the people, lead together, amid our differences. I'm not suggesting that fed-

Iraq war protesters, Chicago. Imagine democracy as something we, the people, lead together—
not the president. Photograph copyright Marc Manley.

eral government doesn't need an executive branch (though I'm surely convinced we would be better served by getting constitutional balance back between the three branches). Instead, I've been urging us to realize that democracy is not served by the president. Rather it's served by us, the people, working together for its present and its future. It's time we stop looking for the next president to deliver changes and wake up to the possibility that *we* might change our course, starting now. This is a project for all of us, not just those of us with economic means or those of us with lots of spare time. This project is already underway: there are many worthwhile models, initiatives, and actions to draw from as we begin reimagining and expanding democracy as an open system, a project nourished both by our independence and by our interdependence. In this chapter, I first map some arguments on behalf of the changes I'm suggesting, then outline some possible forms we could use to implement them.

Owning the Results: Leadership's Psychic Prison

The sovereignty of the People forms the radical promise of democracy: *demos* (people) + *kratia* (power). This idea that the people, and not the king, are the locus of political power and legitimacy constituted the American Revolution—in belief and action. It is that claiming of power for the many—away from the king or the dictator, from the aristocracy or the oligarchy—that establishes democratic power: government of the people, *by* the people, for the people, in Lincoln's resonant formulation. In the notion of the American Revolution, the people lead, together. That ambition helps explain why, in the first organization of U.S. government, there was no separate office created for the president of Congress.

But over the centuries of our own democratic experiment, as I've shown in this book, U.S. citizens have come to believe, quite to the contrary of the democratic premise, that the *president* is the source and center of democratic power and political action. Although we don't, for instance, believe that peace treaties are the same thing as peace itself, we have somehow come to think that presidential leadership, or getting the right president into office, is democracy. As that belief has taken hold over decades and centuries, our nation has moved farther and farther away from its democratic revolution as well as from the more conservative vision of the framers, who made the presidency one part of their constitutional scheme for balanced and separated federal powers and representative government, and who established Congress as the "democratic branch," the branch that would represent the interests of the many, the People. Yet over the last century, as executive branch powers have increased, our obsession with the president as the center of and source for democracy has only deepened.

This problem is pervasive to our culture and not just to our hopes for the president. Business culture, especially since the 1980s, has witnessed a parallel phenomenon in its emphasis on securing charismatic corporate leadership. The Harvard professor Rakesh Khurana has described the poor practical and financial outcomes of this obsession for corporations, employees, and shareholders in his *Searching for a Corporate Savior.* Looking outside the firm for solutions to company problems and erroneously believing that the attributes of the CEO are the most important factors for firm performance, corporate boards have come to value "charisma" over demonstrable skill and company records, overpaying prized candidates at the same time that they load these charismatic saviors up with impossible expectations. Soon these expectations are disappointed, and the CEO bails (usually with a fabulous severance package) and the expensive search for the charismatic corporate savior begins anew, with ever-higher expectations for performance and lower odds for rescue.

But there are more fundamental questions to be asked than whether a leader is better equipped with insider knowledge and on-site experience or with indefinable and hope-charged "charisma"—for both corporate culture as well as democratic government. Our society believes strongly in the fundamental necessity of some kind of leader for everything—for business, for work, for politics, for knowledge building, for community, for government, for democracy. This organizational premise has become an unquestionable assumption. Seldom do we stop to analyze what *specific* problems, issues, or goals call for some kind of leadership, separating them from those that don't.

If we do question, some argue, we can think critically not just about what does and doesn't call for leadership but also about what groups actually get from leaders besides the tautological reassurance of "leadership." Organizational behavioralists Gary Gemmill and Judith Oakley describe the concept of leadership—arrestingly—as a "psychic prison" for the group. They argue that a cultural reliance on leaders actually works to induce "massive learned helplessness among members of a social system . . . characterized by an experienced inability to imagine or perceive viable options, along with accompanying feelings of despair and a resistance to initiating any form of action." In their analysis, the leader too often becomes the focus for "dependency issues," encouraging a kind of group self-infantalization. And so-called empowerment seminars and self-help books are hardly a solution to this problem, since, in encouraging individuals to take more responsibility for outcome and self-management as part of leadership, these programs seldom question the fundamental premise that we all need leadership in the first place.

Organizational development consultant Jeffrey Nielsen agrees that U.S.

culture has oversubscribed to a "myth of leadership." Shelves are crowded with books on leadership, and a quick Google search on the word turns up myriad training, education, skills and development teachers, seminars, plans, and programs. Our endless search for great or even just good leadership perpetuates and proliferates a problem. As Nielsen summarizes, most people use the words *leader* and *leadership* when trying to describe something else altogether: "A sense of vision, of greater responsibility, of ownership over results, as well as greater productivity and more cohesive teamwork. What people often don't realize is that this concept and practice of leadership actually robs many individuals in the organization of the opportunity to contribute and share in these elements of organizational success." People say leadership, in other words, when they mean coproduction. Their inability to conceptualize this difference is disempowering. And more than affecting individuals, Nielsen emphasizes, this problem undermines organizations, keeping them from living up to their own expectations and goals.

Democracy depends on the premise that people can govern themselves together; in the field of organizational theory this would be called a peer-based gestalt. Assumptions about the necessity of leadership, on the other hand, turn democracy over to rank-based thinking. And one problem with rank-based thinking is that leaders (like presidents, members of Congress, policy managers, and members of the political class that Joan Didion so memorably describes in *Political Fictions*) are seduced into believing they have everything necessary for the tasks at hand, even as followers (like citizens) are led to believe that they don't. There are psychological, behavioral, and even physiological effects to the inevitable distributions of power in rank-based culture, as social psychologists have documented. Those in power tend to live in what Dacher Keltner and other researchers summarize as "strikingly different worlds" from those they lead. People in leadership feel happier and more reward oriented. They view those below them in rank as instruments for their own purposes and goals. They are often more self-serving, they feel more self-consistent (e.g., when they smile, it's because they feel happy), and they're more uninhibited about controlling resources and exhibiting bad manners (like eating more than their share of common food and doing so with their mouths open). On the other side, findings show that those who are lower in rank are less confident in their abilities, less likely to reveal their true emotions, less attuned to reward than punishment, and even, for some, less able to perform capably because of that sensitivity to the threat of punishment or disapproval. The followers are attuned to the proper expression of manners, of the importance of minimizing their own needs and of maximizing their attention to the demands of their leaders.

In rank-based organizations, the confidence that leaders have about their own abilities often encourages them to restrict employees from participating in company goal setting and decision making. When this happens, according to Nielsen, individual employees stop trying to engage in the larger good of the company. In turn, leaders see workers' disengagement as further proof of leaders' "need to control decision-making." Fatefully, few stop to consider that perhaps the problem is not with employee narrowness, inability, and selfishness but with the dynamics that follow naturally from assumptions about the necessity of leadership. The way leaders can (mis)understand their employees as intrinsically selfish, unimaginative, and unmotivated to participate in the company's goals and vision sounds impressively similar to the way many political scientists have long depicted American voters, as they pose putatively "realistic" arguments against the possibility of expanding citizen governance or the necessity for curbing presidential power. It's not hard to see them trapped in (or perhaps committed to) the same kind of rank-based thinking that I've been describing here. The problem is, it's not democratic.

It's worth considering, I am urging, that many of our discontents with U.S. democracy—our dissatisfaction with government, our frustration with our own inability to influence its direction—might flow significantly from our unquestioned assumption that we need a president to lead it, precisely because this assumption traps us within a gestalt that is inimical to democracy. Either we believe that people can self-govern—in which case we can continue finding ways to develop our democratic project together—or we don't. If it's the latter, we need honestly to resign ourselves to a political system that is something other than the democracy we say we prize.

Leaderless Organizations, Open Systems, and the Wisdom of Crowds

Although our habitual assumptions about leadership and our unthinking commitments to a rank-based logic run deep, they are being challenged by the innovations in knowledge and organization that have accompanied the Internet's expansion. These innovations offer compelling ways to think about recapturing democratic possibility, allowing us to catalyze democracy as a group project, one we can and indeed already are building independently of presidential leadership.

Internet networking has become a powerful tool for knowledge and information at the same time that it has offered a potent conceptual analogy for a new democratic organizational theory, providing models that transition from hierarchical configurations so dependent on leadership—centralized authority and chain of command—to network designs generated from peer relations, information and communication flow, and decentralized, collaborative decision making. Proponents argue that organizations based on this model are more flexible, adaptive, responsive, competitive, and successful.

The Internet did not invent leaderless organizations; they've been around a long time. For instance, social and business entrepreneurs Ori Brafman and Rod Beckstrom explain in their analysis of the "unstoppable power of leaderless organizations" how indigenous groups in the Americas that were centralized (like the Aztecs), no matter how powerful before European contact, were far more susceptible to quick defeat than decentralized groups like the Apaches, or the Mapuches in South America, who took centuries longer to subjugate. While this organizational model is as ancient as humanity, the advent of the Internet has proliferated the phenomenon of such networks as it has amplified attention to them.

Brafman and Beckstrom's metaphor for the difference between centralized, leadership organizational models and the networked, leaderless organizations they tout is "spiders" versus "starfish." These creatures can look similar at first glance—a body with lots of legs—but there is a crucial difference. You can defeat a centralized organization by going after its leadership: if you chop off a spider's head, the whole thing dies. Decentralized networks are not susceptible in this way: because both information and ability is dispersed through the organization, there is no centralized location for an efficiency-maximizing attack. There is no head, so if you chop off a starfish's leg (as schoolchildren know), it regenerates—and some can even do this if you chop them in half! Its lack of a central brain turns out to be its key strength, and Brafman and Beckstrom offer the starfish analogy to explain the competitive benefit of leaderless networks, which don't rigidly rely on a central leader but instead on dispersed networks of people flexibly and independently acting in loose and effective coordination.

Many businesses have, over the past several decades, been adapting features of leaderless networks to competitive advantage—like Toyota in industry, eBay and Amazon on the Internet. They have changed the rules of business, forcing centralized, command-and-control business models to adapt. But more interesting for the purposes of thinking about leaderless democracy are knowledge communities—like Wikipedia and other wikis like Tax Almanac and Flu Wiki—and service communities like Craigslist or the time banks that are beginning to proliferate around the country (for a three-minute video on what time banks can do within communities, go to nqtimebank.org). These sites and their organizations have allowed individuals to pool expertise, knowledge, goods, and services for the benefit of the many. Here, the sites' innovators have served as catalysts for democratic action. That is, rather than centralize power and authority around themselves as leaders, they make it possible, by providing open infrastructure, for others to proliferate and share the power they generate together, whether that's intensely specialized knowledge about medieval Muslim psychology, tax expertise, a used dinette set for sale, carpentry skills to exchange for reading lessons, or free boxes left over from a move. These sites are run by users, for users, not as consumers but as *co-producers* of social services, social change, and knowledge production.

A wiki—a database concept invented in the mid-1990s by Ward Cunningham—is the Internet exemplar of an open system. Wikis are designed to invite and allow contributions from anyone who wants to add or edit material. As Cunningham's software development wiki (WardsWiki or the Wiki Wiki Web) explains: "'Wiki' is a composition system; it's a discussion medium; it's a repository; it's a mail system; it's a tool for collaboration."

The most famous wiki is surely Wikipedia, "the free encyclopedia anyone can edit," whose founder, Jim Wales, adopted the wiki concept to supplement his Nupedia free encyclopedia project, which was floundering in its slow, top-down editorial and peer-review processes. According to Wikipedia's history page, editors and reviewers strenuously resisted incorporating the wiki into Nupedia, so Wales set it up as a separate page. Once Wales let users in to collaborate on that site, starting January 15, 2001, its offerings exploded and quickly surpassed the now-defunct Nupedia. As Cass Sunstein notes in *Infotopia*, "Wikipedia had one thousand articles by February, ten thousand by September 7, and forty thousand by August 30, 2002." Early in 2008, there were well over two million articles in English, and millions more in dozens of other languages.

Wikipedia's policies are impressively democratic. Its introduction for visitors explains: "Visitors do not need specialised qualifications to contribute, since their primary role is to write articles that cover existing knowledge; this means that people of all ages and cultural and social backgrounds can write Wikipedia articles. With rare exceptions, articles can be edited by anyone with access to the Internet. . . . Anyone is welcome to add information, cross-references or citations, as long as they do so within Wikipedia's editing policies and to an appropriate standard." And despite loudly voiced skepticism about its potential for producing bad information and succumbing to vandalism, Wikipedia and its user-contributors have been impressively successful at accumulating good information on a breathtaking array of subjects, sponsoring open debates on controversial topics such as current politics (as you can see — and contribute to — if you click the discussion tab on any page), and keeping pages clean from both focused and random attempts to sabotage, mislead, misdirect, or shock users.

As Sunstein observes, wikis "offer distinct models for how groups, large or small, might gather information and interact. . . . They provide important supplements to, or substitutes for, ordinary deliberation. They might even be seen as central places in which deliberation is now occurring — with increasing social importance." While wikis cannot capture the full spectrum of work in a democracy, it's increasingly clear that they can provide a good resource for democratic knowledge-production, productive (as opposed to destructive, polarizing or misleading) deliberation, and problem solving in a complex society. One key feature of the wiki model's success comes in the power of numbers: wikis encourage large numbers of people to participate, and because there are so many paying attention, mistakes are usually rapidly corrected.

Another key feature that wikis share with other open-system structures is that they elicit active membership, a key feature of a healthy democracy. Brafman and Beckstrom in fact generalize active membership as a key advantage of decentralization: "Put people into an open system and they'll automatically want to contribute." There are, strikingly, no economic rewards in many open systems for sharing resources, services, and information. Rather, there's just the satisfaction of building something together that benefits everyone. All kinds of users can participate in these structures. This openness to creative user contribution is what appeals to participants in time banks. In the time bank philosophy, every person is an asset. Time banking asks people to think about what they can offer to their community in service—maybe the ability to read books or bank statements to someone who is illiterate or blind—in exchange for "time dollars" that they can then use for what other community members have to offer them, maybe rides to the grocery store or house cleaning. Time banks, like other open systems, prize unrecognized community value, engaging the elderly, the young, and the marginalized in the coproduction of commonwealth, opening the community to shared good. And in general, what is notable is how seldom these open systems run into problems. Take, for instance, Burning Man, Nevada's annual eclectic and communal art event. This "city" built once a year in the desert aims to foster radical participation, radical individualism, and civic responsibility (see "10 Principles" at its site). As Brafman and Beckstrom summarize the event that has grown from twenty participants to nearly forty thousand over the past twenty years, "When you put people into an open system, some of them will get high, dance all night long, and attack street signs. But most people will create elaborate art, share snow cones, and try as hard as they can—in their own way—to contribute to community."

Wikis, time banks, and other open systems appreciate the wildly different contributions individual users can make because they benefit the entire group, creating productive virtual communities and reinventing real ones. They reduce the customary and often counterproductive distance between experts and citizens, providers and clients, as well as between political strangers. By aggregating the efforts of individuals and creating norms for open contribution and deliberation, open systems can often produce impressively better results than the smartest and most expert single mind could working alone. They weave independence into productive and beneficial interdependence.

The rank-based leadership model, however, trains us to ignore the possibilities open systems proffer. The myth of leadership orients us to look to experts and leaders as repositories for and providers of valuable knowledge—about stocks, national defense, energy, business, government, services, and so forth. It teaches that a select group of leaders always holds the keys to solving problems or making good decisions. The success of open systems puts the test to this habitual assumption. As business analyst James Surowiecki reports in his book *The Wisdom of Crowds*, groups—in wiki pages, in predictions markets, in aggregated and averaged form—are impressively good under the right circumstances at providing correct answers to cognition problems in particular but also to problems involving coordination and cooperation. As he puts it: "With most things, the average is mediocrity. With decision making, it's often excellence. You could say it's as if we've been programmed to be collectively smart."

Not just any group is smart, however, as Sunstein cautions in *Infotopia*. Some groups, as even Surowiecki acknowledges, can be terrible at producing good decisions. He marshals data to show that groups of "experts," like-minded groups, groups that are bound by strong social ties, and individuals all tend to produce less healthy decisions than properly diversified crowds of loosely linked individuals. The expert, like-thinking, and socially connected groups do so because they tend toward an unhealthy homogeneity that biases decision making toward extremes. And study after experiment has shown that no individual is as smart or as good at problem solving as a diverse and informed group of individuals. Surowiecki highlights the work of political scientist Chandra Nemeth, who establishes that "the presence of a minority viewpoint, all by itself, makes a group's decisions more nuanced and its decision-making process more rigorous. This is true even when the minority viewpoint turns out to be ill-conceived." Groups of like-minded people are in fact highly susceptible to group polarization, a phenomenon Sunstein has described at length in *Why Societies Need Dissent*. In settings where a group shares basic leanings or opinions, deliberation tends to radicalize the opinion of the group and individuals within it, polarizing rather than moderating opinion. Thus the fundamental importance of diverse opinion, differing expertises, and norms that support dissent. In general, as Surowiecki and Sunstein summarize, groups need only satisfy a few basic conditions—of diversity, equality, independence, and decentralization—to be smart and effective.

Democracy as Public Disagreement

These conditions—diversity, equality, independence, and decentralization—can comfortably stand as democratic ideals. Why not try finding ways to use our collective intelligence on behalf of the democratic system we say we love and want to share with the rest of the world? Political scientists and pundits often denounce schemes for democratic renewal that appeal to citizen input as so much romantic fantasy. But so, too, as I've shown, is looking to be rescued by a heroic president. Given what we're learning from open systems like time banks and other forms of social and economic coproduction, as well as wikis, prediction markets (using real or virtual money), and other forms of information aggregation, it seems as if it might be better to bet on the people, not the president, when it comes to the task of finding innovative routes for reformulating and revitalizing our democracy.

But political scientists, theorists, and policy advocates have long argued that we can't implement a strong democratic system—where citizens take on more of the work of self-governing—because people inevitably disagree: our disagreement would gum up the works, keeping innovative projects and solutions from ever happening. Thus the only way to have a good and efficient government is, as much as possible, to leave citizens out of the process, letting them vote for their representatives and then leaving the bulk of the decision making and policy design to those

---

delegated "deciders." The above models put that wisdom to test as well—clearly we could make what people have been learning from open systems start working for effective democratic deliberation and input into decision making about laws and policies, and to organize networks for achieving social supports and change.

Open-system models will still clash, however, with a more generalized cultural wisdom about politics in the United States. Their emphasis on the value of productive dissent to producing good decisions runs headlong against the emphasis that spans our culture on consensus and its ally in political culture, "bipartisanship." Consensus and bipartisanship promise the means to end the unpleasantness of disagreement. Voters frequently voice the opinion that disagreement is bad for government and select bipartisanship as their preferred way to see Congress or local government do business. Minority-party politicians who use procedural rules to slow things down in order to gain a hearing for their objections are thus often seen as not playing "fair." As Sunstein explains in *Why Societies Need Dissent,* "Conformists are often thought to be protective of social interests, keeping quiet for the sake of the group. By contrast, dissenters tend to be seen as selfish individualists, embarking on projects of their own." But he suggests we could benefit from a paradigm shift on this subject: "In an important sense, the opposite is closer to the truth. Much of the time, dissenters benefit others, while conformists benefit themselves." In other words, conformists don't risk their social standing by bucking the group, whereas dissenters sacrifice theirs in order to point the way toward alternatives that benefit the group.

Consensus and conformity, while much admired in our political culture, turn out to be bad for the knowledge building and decision making of the systems and organizations described above. We typically take agreement as a sign everything is going well, but according to people working in open systems, it can be a sign of big problems that may hurt the group; for instance, people are succumbing to social pressures for status or acceptance and failing to offer crucial knowledge, because it might disrupt the consensus and contradict the group's leaders or bosses. Open systems proponents observe three minefields in deliberative processes—conformity, cascades (where one person or group copies another in an escalating trend: an example would be when a state passes a law, like "motor voter" or "three strikes," that toughens or loosens up on something, and then suddenly such initiatives appear on fifteen more state agendas without much investigation into the actual effects of such legislation on the perceived problems), and group polarization. All these problems, they insist, can be forestalled with healthy group supports, even rewards, for disagreement and dissent.

But disagreement is not an easy subject in U.S. democracy today. One reason people long for more consensus is that disagreement feels so damaging to the fabric of our political culture—and arguably, it is, at least as we currently practice it. I argued in chapter 3 that our majoritarian political system combines with presidentialism to cement U.S. democracy in a winner-take-all form. This system leads participants to conceptualize politics as civil war. Within war culture, politics threatens *all* players: kill or be killed. Losers are not continuing interlocutors: they're enemies, to be exiled from the goods of the system: "If you don't like it, leave the country," winners habitually suggest to the losers. This conceptualization of politics-as-war has been reflected in and has exacerbated the trend toward political and social enclaving in U.S. culture. Because our political field looks like nothing *but* a terrain of dangerous disagreement, we insulate ourselves from it as much as possible. Even politically minded and engaged citizens turn largely to news and information sources—on television and radio, in print and electronically—that report in ways we find friendly to our preexisting beliefs. In this entirely well-meaning way, we all contribute to ideological polarization, which reduces common ground for the political compromise so fundamental to a well-functioning democracy.

Thus our civil war political culture, in its very zeal for ideological battle, actually produces a surprising result: it *lowers* our tolerance for disagreement, as well as our capacity to imagine alternatives. Accepting that politics can produce only winners and losers, we lose the will, the skills, and the imagination to seek out plus-sum solutions within our public political disagreements. We draw back from the ugliness of civil war politics to circles of like-minded thinkers, those whom we feel to be like us in lifestyle, economic class, religious and social belief. But this comes at a cost:

from inside our cozy social bubbles and comforting political cocoons, we oversimplify issues and processes, as well as the lives and concerns of our fellow citizens. When everyone we talk with and listen to shares our specific concerns, it's easy to imagine that the issues we care about are the only issues that matter and, more problematically, that other voters must share the priorities by which we rank our concerns. From inside our enclaves, it's hard to understand how people might disagree on something that seems so obvious to everyone we talk to. When politicians or fellow citizens take a stand that disagrees with ours, we can castigate them as being "out of touch," since none of the people we talk with would agree. So it's far easier to dismiss the debates in Congress as so much smoke and mirrors for corruption and private interests: as ridiculous tactics for vicious politics rather than as representing legitimate alternative positions; as unnecessary to good government rather than as the heart of good government. Our political cocooning trains us to see politics as *creating* conflict. We denigrate conflict and politics as the same undesirable problem, rather than regard conflict as the fundamental condition of a diverse community, and politics as a creative means by which we can find ways to transform conflict into good solutions.

I'm not saying all government battles are good battles—they surely are not—but I am insisting that we separate those bad battles from the disagreement and conflict that are essential to good democratic self-governance. Disagreement lives at the heart of good decision making and democracy simply because both processes depend on diversity—they draw power from diverse experiences, identities, vantages, knowledge sets, perspectives, political positions, feelings. From this vantage, we could say disagreement is a *good* word for democracy. Where there is diversity, there is bound to be conflict, and there's no reason to abjure that necessity—in fact, open systems embrace that necessity by creating norms to make conflict and disagreement productive for the group instead of as a way to divide dissenters from the group. Research on open systems shows that when members feel free to disagree, the group as a whole wins. So a paradigm shift may be our best move. If we swing our understanding of democracy away from presidentialism's politics-as-war, winner-take-all model, toward something more cooperative and civil, a system that prizes rather than punishes disagreement in a zero-sum formula, we might begin to imagine a mode for dissent that does not threaten but *builds* democratic possibility. It does so because it's good for the group—a group that should never treasure easy consensus and bipartisanship because they so often lead to bad decisions, bad outcomes, less knowledge, less vitality, less transformation, less progress, less democracy. Here, the recently touted concept of "postpartisanship" might be interesting, not as a promise to do away with conflict but in its suggestion that conflict could be reconceptualized as seeking creative and cooperative resolutions, making synergy out of differences, rather than mapping out a new field of war for a new round of exclusions.

That paradigm shift, though, will take real attention and practice on our part. As social scientists Nina Eliasoph, and John Hibbing and Elizabeth Thiess-Morse have richly documented, American citizens have come to vilify and avoid practices I'm describing as fundamentally democratic: politics, political talk, disagreement, and compromise. We can't revitalize democracy unless we can get over our phobias about democracy's most elementary building blocks. But it's just a lot *easier* to be mad at the president and government than it is to work creatively at taking more responsibility for democracy ourselves. Our easy and habitual negative reaction to talking politics, tolerating disagreement, and seeking compromise collaborates with our presidentially trained habit of handing democracy over to leaders and experts. We know politics affects us—we regularly complain about its impact on our lives among our families and friends. Just as regularly, we insist that we can't stand having anything to do with politics. Thus most citizens take politics *personally* (feeling angry, complaining about effects, and perhaps giving personal money to interest groups that represent our concerns) without taking it *publicly* (acting in public with others to initiate further deliberation, collaboration, and change). Avoiding the public exercise of politics, we diminish democracy.

Only by developing some comfort with the work of making disagreement productive beyond the safety of our enclaves will we be able to do what citizens of a self-governing democracy fundamentally need to do: disagree productively in public. We can't do democracy in the privacy of our own heads and homes, any more than we can do it only with like-minded people (although we can to some extent practice its skills in those places). Democracy is the power of collective self-governance. The public realm is the only place where we can create that power. Democracy happens when people deliberate and act on the world we share together. Just as exercise benefits the individual but doesn't always feel good—especially at first—the public talking, disagreement, listening, and fruitful compromising that produces democratic knowledge and power may feel uncomfortable for a while, but it leads to a healthier and stronger democratic polity.

A Habitat for Democracy

A fundamental—and perhaps the hardest—part of self-governance has to do with creating the norms by which we live together. That's what we've been wanting every next president to do for us. We appeal to the future president with the same hopes that informed our childhood pleading with parents to intervene when our siblings were getting on our nerves. But how many times did we hear, and have we said to our own children, "Work it out yourselves!" No candidate ever proffers such wisdom. Instead, each promises to solve our disagreements and "unify the country." But the president *never* satisfies on this score. The trick will come in accepting that this is work we have to do ourselves, in the public realm that we keep building together.

But arguing publicly about politics, as wisdom has it, will threaten national community. I observed in the introduction as well as in chapter 3 that another cost of presidentialism and the practice of politics as civil war is that it trains citizens to overvalue political unity and to overlook how a decently functioning disunity might perhaps be a better working principle for a healthy democratic process. We hold tightly to the ideal of compatibility and accord in our communities—this is why we've been enclaving. Our ability to create better and more productive models for doing the work of democracy may well come in loosening our notion of political community so that we can become more comfortable with *less* unity and accord. Which is to say: the transformations I've been describing will not end disagreement and create a peaceful unity—nor should they. So how do we conceptualize for democratic practice what open systems cultivate, something like what political theorist William Corlett calls "community without unity"?

Most democracy theory swings between models that prioritize either strong individualism or strong community. These two models seem inversely related, and it's hard to decide which is best. So we whipsaw between the two. What we treasure about each other is our individual uniqueness (which communitarianism threatens to absorb and blot out for the good of the group), yet we long for an at least occasional, warming sense of community (which seems all but unthinkable in our self-interested, civil-war culture). People who lean toward community accuse libertarians of overlooking the importance of interpersonal connection and mutual responsibility in their emphasis on individual liberties; people who treasure not being pinned by group norms accuse communitarians of a false nostalgia for a kind of harmonious community that never has nor ever could exist because people don't and can't get along that seamlessly.

What if we stopped thinking we have to choose one or the other, and looked for something in between these two extremes? After all, in between is where so many of us feel stuck: what happens if we stop the familiar battle and look for some creative synergy? Political theorist Sam Fleischacker proposes just that. Rather than construct our possibilities as though only strong individualism or strong community were possible, he suggests we might investigate the possibility of what he calls "particle" or "insignificant community," a model based on a "thin web of communal bonds" that could "enable a resolution of the tensions between our individual freedom or independence and our need to interact with and learn from each other." Fleischacker argues that communities tend historically to fall apart when they're driven by goals demanding strong agreement or consensus. But—counterintuitively—communities often thrive "when the possibility for such falling apart is allowed for"—that is, when the community does not require a sense of unity but can allow "room for each individual to make his or her own place." This is, for instance, something time banks allow for. The tree-trimming hour you might trade in for an hour's tax help doesn't require that you spend much time with your neighbors or identify political common ground, but it does build a richer sense of coproduced community.

Corlett gains a related insight by breaking down the Latin roots of the word *community*. As he explains, people commonly understand the etymology of "community" as *com* (with) + *unis* (unity). In this understanding, community means "with unity." But an alternative etymology would hinge on registering the second "m" in its spelling: *com* (with) +*munis* (gifts, or service). In this sense, community's meaning shifts substantively. For Corlett as for the time bank model I just mentioned, it's not about unity, uniformity, agreement, consensus, or sameness; instead it's about mutuality and service across differences. It references not identity but *action*, aiming not to change who you are but how you contribute to and receive from the democratic commonwealth.

The model for democratic community that Fleischacker and Corlett gesture toward is loosely interpersonal—individual *and* relational. In this model, we're not successful because at heart we're alike or because we can find something we all agree on. We're successful because we remain more often than not committed to the process of making what we're in together work, for the good of all of us, despite our differences and disagreements. A Habitat for Democracy, it's an exercise in construction that expands our common floor plan as it builds our civic muscles. In this model, democracy is not regularly loveable, but participating can nevertheless often be satisfying. The open-system model is vital for imagining such political possibility. Of particular value is that open systems like wikis, Burning Man, and time banks don't appeal to sameness or even strong social ties and indeed value the contribution of the individual who protects her individualism. They don't monitor membership: it's easy to check out of the work for a while, and it's easy to check back in later when you want to. Yet at the same time these models create a sense of community out of the activity of building things—knowledge, public art, mutual service, social value, social change—together. They do not depend on knowing, agreeing with, or even liking your neighbor (which is what the current trend toward political and social enclaving evokes), but on figuring out how to make a common good *among strangers*. This model for democratic community has a robust appreciation for complex networks, for the interpersonal circulation of knowledge, for the building of a commonwealth out of mutual acts of service among strangers acting as if they might be neighbors.

This open-system model for democracy asks that citizens engage the political project differently, not with the expectation that it will triumphantly end when we have the right president or when we're all agreeing on the same issues. In this looser understanding of democratic community-without-unity, we accept that politics will never go away or end as a *good* thing, because making politics go away will leave us in a totalitarian state. The project, then, is not to end politics but to transform their practice: to wed our capacity for thinking differently with an ability to act together effectively, toward the purpose of creating an active commonwealth, the source and resource for a more robust and creative democracy.

Producers, not Consumers: Citizenship as More Than Voting and Volunteering

This conception of democracy falls in line with what Supreme Court justice Stephen Breyer terms "active liberty," and what Benjamin Barber terms "strong democracy," where politics is something "done by, not to, citizens." In this understanding, democratic politics is the creative process of ongoing transformation, the constant work of creating a community of reciprocal service out of our many, often enriching and often admittedly intractable, differences. Democracy understood this way is not measured by the successes of our leaders but by the citizens' commonwealth—what we both work out of and contribute to as we publicly strive together to make a better polity. In this conception of democracy we can remember daily, and not just in awful moments of dire national emergency like 9/11, that the people—all of us—are the wisdom, the power, the wealth, and the agents of democracy.

This all sounds fine in theory. (Maybe.) Yet, you might be thinking, it seems that there's precious little for citizens to *do* in U.S. democracy besides vote—and grumble. Democratic realists, for instance influential economist and political scientist Joseph Schumpeter, insist that this is of necessity: democracy can't reasonably be ruled by citizens who, he argued, behave like "infants" in the political field. The thing Schumpeter admired about his politically ignorant and economically self-interested democratic citizen is that she's roughly aware of her own political imbecility. Thus she embraces the necessity of being ruled by leaders, making at least one adult political decision: to give up on the idea that democracy could be either a direct form of citizen self-rule or the process of determining a common good that delegated leaders then carry out. According to democratic realists (or we could call them democratic minimalists), the only sensible conception of democracy is as an open competition for political leadership, where ordinary citizens have only the power to check their leaders: the power to let them into office and, if necessary, the power to "evict" them by not reelecting them. In this minimalist theory, the history for which I outlined in chapter 2, democracy *is* voting for the president.

This idea about citizen inability and the fundamental necessity of strong leadership has powerfully informed mainstream democratic theory, teaching, practice, and development. It is the motivating logic for the theory of the unitary executive I described in chapter 4, a theory that shares and expands democratic realists' contempt for the political abilities of citizens into an equal contempt for the rule of law that citizens cherish insofar as it promises to govern the behavior of citizens and leaders alike. The contempt for citizen power is a long and accelerating historical trend that political scientists Matthew Crenson and Benjamin Ginsberg describe in *Downsizing Democracy*. This study charts the rise and fall of citizenship, which they describe as reaching the height of its powers in the revolutions of the 1700s, achieving a momentum that carried its influence well into the next century. But that energy began dissipating by the end of the nineteenth century, they argue, and since then, businesslike Western governments have sought and increasingly found ways to function without relying on the unpredictable democratic involvement of regular citizens.

By their reading, today's political elites of both parties have little reason to mobilize popular constituencies when they can accomplish their goals through courts and "'the new patronage'—grants, contracts, tax benefits and programs that employ or finance allies." Government now prefers for citizens to feel powerless so they won't try to get involved and interrupt business as usual. Envisioning us as consumers, government wants us passively to buy what it offers. Crenson and Ginsberg wryly reference as evidence the fact that neither Gore nor Bush seemed particularly interested in popular support in the aftermath of the 2000 election. Instead both candidates mobilized troops of *lawyers,* and turned to the courts, not the people, to resolve the election. Democratic minimalists pointed to the absence of voter unrest in the election's aftermath as evidence of the "maturity" of U.S. democracy, but Crenson and Ginsberg think it signals an end: "Perhaps, instead, Americans failed to become agitated because most knew the political struggle they were witnessing did not involve them." Their book concludes by direly predicting the obsolescence both of "the public and the citizens who make it up" in what they project as a "downward spiral" of civic demobilization that will culminate in "politics without a public."

In the terms of such a history, it seems less surprising that citizens of the world's leading democracy feel powerless and increasingly apathetic, offered by their "democratic" government only an ability to vote for candidates vetted not so much by party engines as by corporate backers, and to consume increasingly limited domestic government services. But not everyone has given up on citizen agency. There has been a significant resurgence in volunteerism over the past generation. President Reagan established a council on volunteering during his years in office, which his successor highlighted and elaborated on. When George H. W. Bush campaigned for president in 1988, he spoke movingly of citizens mobilizing in volunteer networks, as "a thousand points of light." Bush's administration aimed to give civic revitalization a boost, calling on people to "get involved in their communities and help to make them better places to live," and presidential administrations since have continued developing that initiative in a variety of ways.

The call for volunteering resonated with the public. In the years since, high schools and colleges have encouraged and supported student volunteerism, developing service-learning models and "alternative spring breaks" that send students into communities both local and international to do humanitarian and service projects. And notably, these programs have made a significant impact on levels of youth volunteerism. In *A New Engagement? Political Participation, Civic Life, and the Changing American Citizen,* a team of political scientists at Rutgers, DePaul, and the Pew and Annenberg Centers summarizes an extensive multigenerational study.

George H. W. Bush's call for "a thousand points of light" volunteerism has resonated with the public, but the increase in volunteering has not correlated with formal political awareness, participation, or activism. Courtesy of Maryland Food Bank.

Comparing the Dutiful (57 and older), the Boomer (38–56), the GenX (26–37), and the Dotnet (15–25) generations, they find that "today's 15–25 year olds actually post the highest rates of at least occasional volunteering. Fully 40 percent say they have given time to a group in the past year, compared to one-third of X-ers and Boomers (32 percent each) and just 22 percent of Dutifuls. Among high school students . . . 54 percent have volunteered for a nonelectoral group . . . 41 percent [of college students] have done so." Those are impressive numbers and seemingly hold out real hope for civic revitalization and agency.

Significantly, though, the study shows that this increase in volunteering is not translating into formal political awareness, participation, or activism: quite the opposite. The authors find that views of politics among the Dotnet generation "are only weakly related to membership in voluntary organizations." It's not that their volunteerism has somehow caused youth to drop out of the political process, but that the youth have never tuned in, seeing it as irrelevant to the world they live in, whether that's because they lack in political socialization or because they regard (and they do) big business as more powerful and efficacious than big government.

We might assume that their elders in the volunteer world are more engaged with politics, more expert in translating volunteerism from civic service into civic power in ways that support our commonsense image of the volunteer as the ideal citizen. But this assumption turns out to be wrong too. While participatory democracy advocates have long looked toward local volunteer groups as schools that foster and develop wider political involvement, this doesn't seem to be happening on the ground. Eliasoph, drawing on years of participant-observer research, shows how volunteer groups tend to stifle their members' impulses toward political engagement. In their emphasis on action and members' ability to make a quickly tangible difference in the world, the volunteer organizations Eliasoph studied tended actually to discourage broader critical discussions of the issues surrounding the volunteer work: "Members sounded less publicly minded and less politically creative in groups than they sounded individually," avoiding both the articulation and analysis of connections between their volunteer activity and public issues. The volunteer groups evaded discussing troubling social issues like root causes or troubling power relations, and actively suppressed from group consideration aspects of programming or examples that did *not* document success or suggested the necessity of other kinds of response than volunteer action could accommodate. (We might think of the way generous volunteers staff food banks, while the root cause of hunger, which is more properly understood as income insecurity, goes unaddressed.)

Like most of us, volunteers avoid dissent. In this way, volunteer groups function like enclaves, too, susceptible to all the social pressures that silence disagreement and squelch creativity. Although many of the volunteers had political concerns, hopes, and ideas they voiced privately, they kept these thoughts to themselves, not wanting to be seen as disrupting the group's aims. Political talk was regarded as "just complaining," and Eliasoph details how by nurturing this ethic, the groups shunned thinking about "depressing" problems along with the creative solutions they might well have devised for them: "Volunteers' political etiquette systematically silenced some *types* of ideas more than others: democratic ideas, participatory ideas, ideas with long time horizons, ambiguous or ambivalent ideas, ideas that would not lead to immediate volunteer-style solution." Volunteers' avoidance of public-spirited political conversation is, Eliasoph emphasizes, entirely well intended, aimed at facilitating the group's project and encouraging members by keeping things upbeat. But, as she emphasizes, by excluding politics from group aims, volunteers keep "their enormous, overflowing reservoir of concern and empathy, compassion and altruism, out of circulation, limiting its contribution to the common good." Avoiding public politics, such volunteers unintentionally diminish—even while laboring to support—the democratic commonwealth.

It's worth noting too that since the Reagan administration, the federal government has frequently justified cuts in services by soliciting volunteer groups to make up the difference. This institutional coordination of volunteering has also fed the depoliticization of volunteers, turning their energetic goodwill, to borrow Harry Boyte's apt phrasing, into a "sentimental footnote" to the work of government. Eliasoph details how working with social workers conditions the volunteers she studied habitually to defer to agency experts: their framing of problems, their established methods and goals. These tremendously energetic, civic-minded volunteers avoided questioning the increasing necessity for their volunteering in the first place. Nor were they able to value their own growing expertise in ways that could lead them to reformulate, modify, or challenge the preestablished goals and methods for achieving them. Thus they remained trapped in the rank-based gestalt I described earlier, depending on government leaders to determine the services that followers could then provide. Eliasoph powerfully documents how volunteers end up collaborating with the government's retraction not only of services but also of their own agency as citizens: the ability to have a role in deciding what our government will and will not support, and how that support will work.

Here the Dotnets, as it turns out, offer an alternative, peer-based, co-produced political vision and practice. If they're not plugging into formal political structures, youth the world over are nevertheless pioneering a different kind of civic activism: social entrepreneurship. Some argue that this new trend is twenty-first-century youth's response to the worldwide student activism of the 1960s. They combine the skills of business and capital development with their vision for social change, pioneering revolutionary nonprofit programs in environmentalism, education, health, economic development, democratization, social justice, and human rights in the United States and abroad. The Skoll Foundation, which supports social entrepreneurship and whose site lists the many impressive projects it supports, summarizes the concept this way: "Just as entrepreneurs change the face of business, social entrepreneurs act as the change agents for society, seizing opportunities others miss and improving systems, inventing new approaches and creating sustainable solutions to change society for the better. However, unlike business entrepreneurs who are motivated by profits, social entrepreneurs are motivated to improve society."

Social entrepreneurs have far less use for formal government than previous generations of democratic actors. As the organization Ashoka, which supports social entrepreneurs and aims at the "transformation of the civic sector," puts it: "Rather than leaving societal needs to the government or business sectors, social entrepreneurs find what is not working and solve the problem by changing the system, spreading the solution, and persuading entire societies to take new leaps." Notably, Ashoka and other social entrepreneurs choose the term "civic sector" as a way to distinguish their aims from the label assigned to such movements and organizations during the 1990s: nongovernmental organizations (NGOs). Their alternative phrasing captures their sense that governments the world over are retracting key societal supports, and rather than accept a negative label ("*non*-governmental") that implicitly denigrates the work they're doing as somehow outside the proper structure, they seek to take the "civic" away from its crumbling and antipolitical government provenance and give it back to the people. In other words, as they suggest, it's the *people,* not the government, who get to define the civic sector.

Citizen Agency, Everyday Politics, and Free Spaces

Social entrepreneurship returns us to the subject of the Internet and its ability to facilitate open systems working for democratic change. As Paul Hawken notes in his book *Blessed Unrest: How the Largest Movement in the World Came into Being and Why No One Saw It Coming*, the "Internet and other communication technologies have revolutionized what is possible for small groups to accomplish and accordingly change the loci of power." Hawken describes an emerging worldwide activist movement that is intervening politically, socially, and environmentally across the globe, a movement that is leaderless, has no predetermined ideology, and is "dispersed, inchoate, and fiercely independent . . . a completely different form of social phenomenon." It links environmental, peace, health, social justice, and antipoverty activism with democratic decision making and policy. It has not had much attention from media and scholars, simply because it is so decentralized. Emerging as an open organization of movements, it defies traditional categories of understanding. Thanks to current information and communication technologies (including Hawken's impressive Natural Capital Institute's user-edited database at wiserearth.org), this leaderless, grassroots constellation of networks and organizations can take advantage of others' experiences and expertise, as well as coordinating resources, methods, and actions.

This is a movement that stakes a renewed claim for citizens as political crafters and producers. Crenson and Ginsberg may be right that so-called democratic national governments are trying to downsize the role citizens can play within them, but they're wrong to think that citizenship is simply disappearing as a result. Rather, it's staking a new claim. These efforts at transforming the civil sector are present all over the nation and offer an important avenue for revitalized citizen energies, allowing citizens to wield power electronically and in person, against, with and without, around and beyond government power.

As these open-system leaderless networks expand globally, becoming more popular and better understood, the world increasingly regards the United States' strong-man presidential system with less favor. Instead, democratic activists have begun to lobby for parliamentary systems that emphasize consociation and compromise in place of unilateralism. In this context, there are reasons both within and without the nation for U.S. citizens to rethink their habitual attachments to presidential power. It has undermined our democratic power for too long. Its unilateralist preferences are increasingly untenable in a multilateralist global community, where, with no small thanks to the overweening power of the U.S. president, balances of power and goodwill are shifting away from the United States. And while the citizen energy I've been describing can be put to excellent use outside formal U.S. government frameworks, the threat I described in chapter 4, of the U.S. Supreme Court lending constitutional validation to the unitary executive theory and handing us over to a plebiscitary presidency, is a real one. We may feel like giving up on or going around formal U.S. government, but it nevertheless wields enormous powers both domestically and globally in our name and with our tax dollars. If we object to its agendas, it's worth noting that we can combat its most powerful trends only if we're willing to put some of our citizen energy back into formal government.

This project will take energy, multiple lines of action, and determination. It will take patience, imagination, experimentation, and creativity. It will take information, research, confidence, and ongoing practice. It will take computer networks, national alliances, and local actions. It will take a reconceptualization of democratic faith: that no one person *can* stand for the whole. This reconceptualization necessitates frequent and ongoing democratic political engagement with those who differ from us. This project will be neither simple nor easy, given how government has spent the last many years building citizen power *out* of its structures; given the dominance of the corporate lobby; given the deep entrenchment of the two-party system and the parties' growing inability to influence presidential politics; given deeply inculcated citizen lassitude; given that journalists both share and sensationally reinforce citizens' impatience with politics, disagreement, and compromise.

As the Center for Democracy and Citizenship's codirector Harry Boyte observes, our current notion of politics "depoliticizes citizenship while it professionalizes politics . . . politics is defined in distributive terms associated with government, as who gets what; and the actual process of creating the what—our public wealth—disappears from view." Our public wealth is what had disappeared from the view of the volunteers Eliasoph worked with, when they bowed to the expertise of social workers instead of talking, deliberating, listening to each other, and forwarding their own ideas, insisting on something more like a partnership with government workers and agencies. How do we create a politics that will enable us decisively to beat back the myth that we need a good president to lead our democracy, a politics that will energize us to retake democracy for our own purposes and good, to regain decision-making powers?

At the most practically available level, it's clear that we need insistently to question presidential candidates about their own position on the theory of the unitary executive and the powers they deem necessary to the executive branch. We need vocally to oppose those who support expansive executive powers. We need to question congressional candidates on this score, too, and alert them that this is an issue their constituents care about and will attend to. We need to watch presidents once in office and to lobby our congressional representatives diligently and persistently (use Congress.org to find state and local representatives' e-mail addresses and phone numbers through a quick zip code search), to let them know that their constituents will *reward* their exercise of checking powers and their muscular opposition to executive branch expansions of both public and *secret* powers. (As I have already shown, congressional representatives lack incentive to do battle on these fronts, and so we must give our representatives the impetus on a regular basis). We need to oppose presidential aggressions and expansions *on principle* and not based on whether we agree with a particular aim or outcome, simply because they are undemocratic and threaten the power of the people. And while we're in contact with our senators and representatives, we would do well to begin cultivating a renewed patience with, attention to, and appreciation for the difficult and inefficient work of what our framers denominated "the democratic branch," even as we make clear to them our determination to hold them accountable for upholding the checking powers they possess. Finally, it's clear from the 2008 primary season that presidential candidates like Ron Paul or Dennis Kucinich who oppose expansions of executive branch powers are not taken seriously by the media and are largely shut out of representation in network debates. We need to use media electronic forums and editorial space to amplify our opposition to executive branch expansions, so that the media has to take this opposition seriously, and give airtime and dignified attention to the candidates that do, too, allowing these views to inform our debates as they play out publicly.

At the same time, we might also do well to remember that we are literally surrounded by representative democratic institutions. Instead of focusing all our representative desires, demands, and energies on the U.S. president and federal government, we'd do well to note that we each have *dozens* of elected officials who act regularly on our behalf. A partial list would include federal, state, county, municipal, and school board representatives, as well as senators, representatives, judges, governors, lieutenant governors, mayors, vice mayors, treasurers, commissioners, sheriffs, tax assessor-collectors, district attorneys, clerks, surveyors, and justices of the peace. We are often far more directly and immediately affected by the decisions of local judges, public utility boards, and tax assessors than we are by the actions of the president (as counterintuitive as that might seem), and we would be serving our own interests to pay some attention to these elections (where your vote might really count, given the incredibly low number of people who pay attention to and vote in these seemingly mundane races) and to the actions of these officeholders. It's not hard to find these people if you want to communicate with them post-election: most cities have easy-to-access Web pages that quickly direct constituents to electronic links and phone numbers. If we began to familiarize ourselves with our many more local representative institutions and agents, we might find we can have more impact on our day-to-day democratic life than we imagine when we vest all these hopes and needs in our quadrennial pull of the lever for the president.

More important, we need to imagine our way beyond electoral politics, into what Boyte calls "everyday politics": a politics that gives us daily agency and routes for self-governing, where democracy is far more than voting. An important starting place for such a project would be to look, lobby, and organize for what Boyte describes as "free spaces": "Places where people learn political and civic skills" that are also "culture creating spaces where people generate new ways of looking at the world." Free spaces are geographic locations for open system practice. Fleischacker offers a concrete suggestion along these lines for publicly supported "Social Houses" that

> would have rooms for bridge and chess games, lounges or a café for talking or sitting quietly, perhaps a pool room, perhaps a library and classrooms, and always a large auditorium that could be used for movies or concerts and would in any case be used for political speeches, assemblies and debates. Anyone acting violently or offensively would be thrown out. What specific activities would be available—what kinds of classes would be taught, what games arranged, what music featured—would be determined through some sort of democratic procedure, by each neighborhood for its own local Social House.

Fleischacker suggests plans by which someone from one neighborhood could join the Social House of another neighborhood, and his point is that in this way democratic community can be at once flexibly sociable, productive, relaxing, social, individualizing, purposeful, incidental—even desirable and fun. In such "free spaces" (lobby and organize for these with your neighbors, coworkers and acquaintances, mayor and city council) we begin to experience ourselves as cocreators of democratic life. Whether through models this formal or by less formal means, we begin reconstituting politics as more than occasional elections and protests. Then democracy, conceptualized as overlapping and networked open systems, becomes more continuous. It manifests as the equalitarian organizing and problem solving we can do together every day: in our homes, workplaces, and communities as well as in our nation.

In such free spaces, we can begin to cultivate the skill of democratic talk and listening that Barber outlines in *Strong Democracy: Participatory Politics for a New Age*. For Barber, politics has been reduced to speech, the unilateralist performance of politicians that we have seen plenty enough of in the presidential primary debate season: even in the so-called town hall format, we get to ask a question (in person, electronically, or, more inventively, in a YouTube video), and they get to give a speech. In contrast, democratic *talk* is about cultivating reciprocity and dialogue, and it depends on *listening*, where listening "means to the strong democrat not that I will scan my adversary's position for weaknesses and potential trade-offs, nor even . . . that I will tolerantly permit him to say whatever he chooses. It means, rather, 'I will put myself in his place, I will try to understand, I will strain to hear what makes us alike, I will listen for a common rhetoric evocative of a common purpose or a common good.'" This could be postpartisanship's working model. As Barber summarizes, "Good listeners may turn out to be bad lawyers but they make adept citizens and excellent neighbors." And it's interesting here to note that corporations and think tanks striving toward open-system models actually hire facilitator-consultants to make sure working conversations develop around the ideal of democratic talk. We need to work at developing such capacities precisely because they have withered over our lifetimes. As journalist Bill Bishop documents in *The Big Sort: Why the Clustering of Like-Minded-America Is Tearing Us Apart,* U.S. communities over the past forty years have reversed the trend of political mixing that characterized the 1950s, 1960s, and 1970s, when more Americans than not lived in communities where Democrats and Republicans were evenly mixed. Now, he warns, the opposite is true: neighborhoods have sorted into Democratic and Republican strongholds at a startling rate since the 1980s. Our own neighborhoods, then, may no longer be a good place to locate the work that free spaces call for. Only *if* we build them deliberately to mix up our habit of enclaving, then, can such free spaces become a terrain on which we begin working at redeveloping our skills for political talking and listening.

In well-designed free spaces, we can begin to explore alternatives and alterations to our current system of winner-take-all majoritarianism—such electoral alternatives as proportional representation, preferential balloting, and election by lot. Lani Guinier notes in her introduction to Richie and Hill's essay collection on proportional representation (PR) that "the vast majority of the world's longstanding democracies . . . have developed more nuanced systems, most adopting some form of proportional representation." Proponents of PR remind us that democracy is supposed to be government by *all* the people, not alternating groups of elites representing the interests of some of the people. PR models focus not on the presidency but on legislatures, boards, and councils, ensuring that representation exists there in proportion to the distribution of votes

How do we cultivate the skills of democratic talk and listening that years of enclaving have robbed from us? Citizens in post-Katrina New Orleans at a town hall meeting. Photograph by James A. Finley; courtesy of AP Photo.

in a given population: if 20 percent of the people support a particular party, then PR models ensure that 20 percent of the governing body will represent that party, and its supporters can feel assured that their principles are being injected into policy debates. This scheme works for minorities of every kind: as Guinier documents in *Tyranny of the Majority: Fundamental Fairness in Representative Democracy,* PR voting schemes aid Republicans in Democrat-dominated districts just as surely as they help poor, or libertarian, or single-issue voters gain more representation in government agenda-setting. PR also, proponents insist, cultivates stronger participation. Preferential balloting, somewhat differently, can be used for single-person offices like mayor, governor, or president, allowing voters to rank each name on the ballot in order of preference, so that as lower-percentage candidates are disqualified, each citizen's vote is moved forward to the next viable candidate on their list of preferences until a winner is determined. This system ensures that fewer votes are "wasted" and that

BAD FOR DEMOCRACY

eventual victors have stronger majorities of support. We might even consider what sounds most ridiculous: the Athenian scheme of election by lot, which has its own virtue, argues political theorist C. Douglas Lummis, since people "would be reluctant to hand over much of their power to a president or legislator chosen by lot. They (we) would be forced to the realization that the main responsibility for figuring out what to do about war, taxes, the economy, pollution, justice, national boundaries and all the rest is theirs (ours)." Such a scheme would lead to a radical reconceptualization of democratic politics and officeholding. In addition to electoral schemes, we could discuss and organize to advocate for campaign structure *and* finance reform, considering for instance, models that restrict the length of the campaign season to a handful of months and narrow candidates by national voting in two rounds.

In free spaces, we can begin organizing to develop and build citizen-government partnerships in problem solving, at the local, state, national, and even international levels. In these spaces, through overlapping partnerships, we can begin changing the pattern of democratic governance so that it becomes both more decentralized and open to participation. Insisting on partnership and on the value of our own participation and local knowledge is worth doing not just on principle but because, as political scientist Elinor Ostrom has argued, polycentric models have important advantages in terms of efficiency, sustainability, and equity. She defines polycentric as "a system where citizens are able to organize not just one but multiple governing authorities at differing scales" and argues, referencing examples of such systems in the United States as the Maine Lobster Fishery, that a healthy blending of centralized and decentralized government institutions can offset weaknesses that typically hinder each (like uniform policies that fatally ignore local conditions; like local majority or minority tyrannies). The Fishery blends harbor gangs that govern traditional territories dating back to the colonial era with formal state laws, state agencies, democratically elected zone councils, and an informal council of councils. Its overlapping scales of authority have enabled conservation coordination, planning, and enforcement such that the industry is thriving and the state has needed only "six patrol officers on the water to police the activities of 6,800 lobstermen, all the other fisheries, and coastal environmental laws." Such polycentric systems look messy, even chaotic, in practice. But as Ostrom and others conclude of polycentric systems in local metropolitan economies, they have "significantly outperformed metropolitan areas served by a limited number of large-scale, unified governments."

The People's Branch

Many have proposed distinctive models for democratic participation that are worth exploring as we expand free space, everyday politics, and citizen agency. These ideas enhance participation to support and revitalize representative institutions, allowing citizens to combine deliberation with meaningful decision making. For instance, in *The Voice of the People: Public Opinion and Democracy,* political scientist James Fishkin outlines his deliberative polling initiative, first implemented at the national level in the United States in 1996 as PBS's National Issues Convention. In this model, a representative random sample of the electorate is brought together in small groups to allow people to articulate their primary concerns, provided with materials that factually background those concerns and address them from an array of policy positions, and then assemble together for a televised, three-day process of deliberation. During this process, they can consult with experts and talk to candidates and policy-makers and to each other. In this way, citizen-viewers can get a better picture of "public opinion" from such a process than they can from spur-of-the-moment polling. Using Fishkin's model, we can watch citizens working through problems with better information, in consultation with experts and each other, developing deliberated opinions over a period of time, and we can use this format in national venues as well as local settings. Fishkin also suggests that deliberative polling has been a useful way for public utilities to make changes in policy and rates that reflect what an *informed and self-informing* electorate would want, were they given the opportunity, materials, and time to allow them to think it through together. We can lobby for this at both the local and national levels, with both government and media.

In *Strong Democracy,* Barber outlines an array of reforms including a national initiative and referendum process. Initiative and referendum processes are in wide use at the local level. We could easily harness what we've learned about open systems to check the more dangerous consequences of these voting forms—concerns include public hastiness, majority tyranny, and voter manipulation by elites. Barber suggests a multichoice format instead of the usual yes-no format, which would offer voters a range of choices, for instance: "yes in principle—strongly for the proposal; yes in principle—but not a first priority; no in principle—strongly against the proposal; no with respect to this formulation—not against the proposal in principle suggest reformulation and resubmission; and no for the time being—although not necessarily opposed in principle, suggest postponement." Such a ballot form would produce a more-nuanced picture of what voters want—why they say yes or no to a particular initiative—and would combine with another of Barber's proposals: two rounds of voting, separated by six months, so as to encourage a period of deliberation after the first stage of voting. We can lobby for such reforms with our federal congressional representatives—those currently elected and those who might want to run for election.

Barber also proposes a universal citizenship service that would include military and civic options. Barber's proposal is a stronger version of 2008 presidential candidate Barack Obama's "Plan for Universal Voluntary Public Service": Barber argues such service should be required as "a concomitant of citizenship itself." Allowing citizens (except in circumstances of congressionally declared war) to choose how they want to serve, it would require one to two years' duty and would offer options in the four military branches or in urban, rural, or international service. As he notes, such a plan would build an ethos of citizenship during times of both peace and war, allowing everyone to contribute and fostering "a sense of mutuality and national interdependence." Mandatory universal service is certainly an easier proposition to consider during peacetime than during a time of war. But perhaps especially during a time of war, when, as Bishop documents in *The Big Sort,* poor communities, especially poor *rural* communities, in the United States are suffering the bulk of military casualties (demonstrating how thoroughly volunteer military service currently correlates to economic need), a universal requirement for service promises both to make the military a better reflection of the society it serves and protects, and to give it the resources it deserves. Such service, for wartime and peace, confirms the protection and cultivation of democracy as a responsibility that all citizens share. We can lobby for this by working to mobilize public opinion in the media and on the Internet, with local and federal leaders and with military officials (where it probably wouldn't be a hard sell).

Political scientist Kevin O'Leary has developed an ambitious and interesting two-stage plan for a citizen assembly that could become, in its second stage, a fourth governmental branch: the People's Branch. His scheme permanently institutionalizes Fishkin's deliberative polling plan and stakes a middle path between direct democracy and our Constitution's traditional representative scheme. For each member of the U.S. Congress, we would create a "one hundred-person citizen assembly whose job will be to study and discuss the great issues of the day and thereby provide us with a more deliberative and thoughtful sample of public opinion than now exists." O'Leary suggests selection by lot from each congressional ward (those who wanted to opt out of the pool could) and notes that this model would create a "decentralized National Assembly" of 43,500 citizens, meeting two to three evenings per month, face-to-face locally and nationally by Internet, for a two-year term. In the first stage, these assemblies would not have formal power, but their deliberations and votes could inform Congress and the president. While chances are slim that people know their congressional representative, their chances of knowing an assembly delegate would be far greater. This might, argues O'Leary, not only increase participation but give us a "two-tier system of public opinion": mass opinion survey and the (deliberative) National Assembly.

Stage two adds formal muscle to the assembly by giving it branch power. Here, rather than have federal law determined by 535 elite members of the United States, we would add O'Leary's 43,500 strong National Assembly. In his proposal, the People's Branch would have specific, limited power: the power to approve or reject laws passed by the House or Senate, and the power to help set the legislative agenda. Here, the decentralized local assemblies would be coordinated by a national steering committee of delegates selected by lot from a pool of the local delegates who have had a year's experience. O'Leary argues that three important advantages flow from this scheme. First, it gives "the public back to itself by creating opportunities for intelligent participation." Second, it curbs "excessive influence of special interests that have gained strength in an era of consultants and weak local parties." Third, it "provides the public with a mechanism to break legislative gridlock." In other words, contrary to those who argue that more participation will lead inevitably to less efficiency, O'Leary insists that the People's Branch will deliver more of both: more participation *and* more efficiency. We can lobby for this by working to create powerful public opinion for it, in democratic free spaces, by using referenda and by pressuring Congress to help us build it.

By the People, For the People

Politics, as Hannah Pitkin evocatively puts it, is "the art of the possible." In this book, I've been holding out for a different conceptual framework from the one we currently operate under. I offer mine in hopes that it can change the way we understand our relationship not just to the president but to the project of democracy. Democracy is not a set of institutions or a form of government, and it's definitely not the president. Rather, it is a principled commitment to action, to the work of equalitarian self-rule. We have democracy insofar as we are willing to struggle for it alongside those who are different from us. We haven't found democratic satisfaction in our ritual pursuit of the perfect president; instead we've encountered, to borrow Pitkin's words, a "fantasy of self-denigration." Like the mythical founder that Pitkin describes, who "cannot be a genuine solution to any problem in the real world," our reliance on the president to deliver the good of democracy has left us blaming him as we become more and more helpless, more and more distanced from our own political capacities, more and more deprived of a sense that democracy is working.

We won't find a "happily ever after" democracy by embracing the actions and reforms I've described here. The work I'm describing means stepping away from the childlike fantasies of complete harmony with each other and the dependencies that presidentialism fosters in us, into a clear-eyed and adult awareness of human limitations *and* human creativity. Whatever the givens of our past, our democratic present and future are open to our ideals, initiatives, and actions. Democracy does not need the president's leadership, and as I've been suggesting in this chapter, we don't have to get rid of the president to rediscover and reinvigorate it. Its energies exist and manifest all around us, in governmental forms and more especially in the civic sector, through citizen initiatives, new management models, open system organizations, as well as in people's activist projects the world over. In what Hawken terms this "blessed unrest," we can find the possibilities and develop the skills that we've been missing in our pursuit of the perfect president; we can use them to reharness our historic democratic experiment for our future, now: *by* the people and *for* the people.

Acknowledgments

A WHILE BACK I FIGURED OUT THAT WRITING ISN'T LONELY if you arm-twist a bunch of smart, nice people into listening to you talk about your book, reading and commenting on drafts, and lending their good ideas to the project. Which means, I owe a great deal to many good people.

Since arriving at Vanderbilt University, I've been lucky to work with four incredibly smart and hardworking research assistants. Three have moved on to other jobs in other cities, and I hope they will find themselves here and get back in touch: Allie J. Higgins, Dana Irwin, and April Larson. I want to single out the especially spectacular contributions of my current assistant, Nellie P. Knight, who found some of the illustrations in the book and bucked me up during the final days of writing with dependable good cheer and resourcefulness.

Thanks also to my many extraordinary graduate and undergraduate students at Vanderbilt—too many to list but you know who you are, partners in democratic planning and fun sounding-boards for these and other contrarian arguments.

I thank the institutions and programs, and all the many wonderful people working with them, that helped me try out versions of this work in public, cultivating terrific feedback for the project at various stages: Texas A&M's Melbern G. Glasscock Center for Humanities Research; University of Kentucky's Committee on Social Theory (both in its working paper series and as a visitor to its 2008 Spring Seminar on War); Vanderbilt's Out of the Lunchbox Series and its Robert Penn Warren Center for the Humanities. Thank you also to the Gertrude Conaway Vanderbilt Chair endowment, which funded some of the research on this project.

I would never have written this book but for the people who encouraged me even before its actual beginning and those who were reading chunks of it right through to the end: Ken Wissoker, Grant Farred, Colin Dayan, Tyler Curtain, Virginia Blum, Andy Doolen, Steve Weisenburger, Gordon Hutner, Russ Castronovo, and especially Monica Casper, Elsie Michie, and Chris Castiglia. I owe a special debt to Teresa Goddu and Mark Schoenfield, who challenged me to redirect the project and write the book I really wanted. I am grateful to my friend and colleague Houston Baker, with whom I'm elated to be working again, not just because of his astute readerly eye but more especially because of his sage and much-appreciated mentoring, and steadying collegial presence. Most of all, I thank my toughest, most supportive readers, Dale Bauer and my sister, Julie Hayward, both of whom read multiple drafts of many chapters, never let me get away with anything, and never let my spirits flag.

I have enjoyed every minute I've worked with the many supportive, smart people at the University of Minnesota Press. I appreciate comments from one anonymous reader and particularly from Melissa Orlie, both of whom helped me to continue thinking out problems and to push the final draft into greater clarity. Thank you to Gil Rodman and other members of the Press's board, whose comments on and observations about the book helped me refine arguments.

I owe more than I dare tally to Richard Morrison, extraordinary editor and equally extraordinary friend, who has believed in, urged on, and helped with this project and without whose encouragement I really (truly) would have quit. Getting to work with someone like Richard is the best reason to write books.

Thanks to my activist and volunteer community in Nashville—the folks at Better Decisions, Kilowatt Ours, Urban EpiCenter, and especially the Homeless Power Project. You inspire and energize me. The optimism about citizen power that informs this project comes from working with you.

Namaste to yoga teachers and friends—Amy Barnes, Tom and Daphne Larkin, Halley Walton, and others who have kindly helped me unwind from many a busy day, helping me stay centered and focused on the richness of now.

Finally, thanks to my father, Jim Nelson, from whom I learned to call "horse-puckey" at an early age and to his wife, Ann, who has always been a fun interlocutor on this project. More thanks (there's never enough) to Julie, who is as great a listener as she is a reader and always a spectacular friend. Thank you to Nancy Potter, whose quiet wisdom I hope has made it into this book. My most heartfelt gratitude belongs to my husband, friend, interlocutor, and partner in a better life, Tom Dillehay, who helps me walk the talk on disagreement and whose gifts are the greatest.

I dedicate this book to the memory of Professor Bernard Roffman, beloved teacher and mentor. Bernie (who talked me out of a political science major when I was an undergraduate) would have shaken his head and laughed his wry, silent laugh if he had been able to know about this book.

Bibliography

Altemeyer, Bob. *The Authoritarian Specter.* Cambridge, Mass.: Harvard University Press, 1996.

Altschuler, Glenn C., and Stuart M. Blumin. *Rude Republic: Americans and Their Politics in the Nineteenth Century.* Princeton, N.J.: Princeton University Press, 2000.

American Bar Association. "News Release: Blue-Ribbon Task Force Finds President Bush's Signing Statements Undermine Separation of Powers." July 24, 2006.

Arato, Andrew. "The Bush Tribunals and the Specter of Dictatorship." *Constellations* 9, no. 4 (2002): 457–76.

Barber, Benjamin. *Jihad vs. McWorld: Terrorism's Challenges to Democracy.* New York: Ballantine, 1996.

———. "Neither Leaders nor Followers: Citizenship under Strong Democracy." In Beschloss and Cronin, 117–32.

———. *Strong Democracy: Participatory Politics for a New Age.* 20th anniversary ed. Berkeley: University of California Press, 2003.

Barber, James David, ed. *Choosing the President.* Englewood Cliffs, N.J.: Prentice Hall, 1974.

Barilleaux, Ryan. "Venture Constitutionalism and the Enlargement of the Presidency." Pp. 37–52 in *Executing the Constitution: Putting the President Back into the Constitution,* ed. Christopher Kelley. Albany: State University of New York Press, 2006.

Barry, Jan. *A Citizen's Guide to Grassroots Campaigns.* New Brunswick, N.J.: Rutgers University Press, 2000.

Basler, Roy, ed. *The Collected Works of Abraham Lincoln.* Vol. 1. New Brunswick, N.J.: Rutgers University Press, 1953.

Bennett, James. "America, Inc.: The M.B.A. President." *New York Times Magazine,* January 1, 2001, 23–28, 49, 54, 57–59.

Beschloss, Michael R., and Thomas E. Cronin, eds. *Essays in Honor of James MacGregor Burns.* Englewood Cliffs, N.J.: Prentice Hall, 1989.

Bishop, Bill. *The Big Sort: Why the Clustering of Like-Minded America Is Tearing Us Apart.* New York: Houghton-Mifflin, 2008.

Bornet, Vaughn Davis. *The Presidency of Lyndon B. Johnson.* Lawrence: University Press of Kansas, 1983.

Boyte, Harry C. *Everyday Politics: Reconnecting Citizens and Public Life.* Philadelphia: University of Pennsylvania Press, 2004.

Brace, Paul, and Barbara Hinckley. *Follow the Leader: Opinion Polls and the Modern Presidency.* New York: Basic Books, 1992.

Brafman, Ori, and Rod A. Beckstrom. *The Starfish and the Spider: The Unstoppable Power of Leaderless Organizations.* New York: Portfolio (Penguin Group), 2006.

Breyer, Stephen. *Active Liberty: Interpreting Our Democratic Constitution.* New York: Knopf, 2005.

Brooks, David. "A Reality-Based Economy." *New York Times,* July 24, 2007.

Bumiller, Elisabeth. "White House Letter; Bush's Book Club Picks a New Favorite." *New York Times,* January 31, 2005.

"Bush Grants Permission to Grant More Power to Self." *Onion,* August 1, 2006.

Byrd, Robert C. *Losing America: Confronting a Reckless and Arrogant Presidency.* New York: Norton, 2004.

Cairo, Michael. "The 'Imperial Presidency' Triumphant: War Powers in the Clinton and Bush Administrations." Pp. 199–217 in *Executing the Constitution: Putting the President Back into the Constitution,* ed. Christopher Kelley. Albany: State University of New York Press, 2006.

Calabresi, Steve G. "Some Normative Arguments for the Unitary Executive." *Arkansas Law Review* 48 (1995): 23–104.

Calabresi, Steven, and Christopher S. Yoo. "The Unitary Executive during the First Half-Century." *Case Western Reserve Law Review* 47 (1996–97): 1451–561.

———. "The Unitary Executive during the Second Half-Century." *Harvard Journal of Law and Public Policy* 26, no. 3 (2003): 667–801.

Calabresi, Steven, Christopher S. Yoo, and Laurence Nee. "The Unitary Executive During the Third Half-Century," http://www.pegc.us/archive/Unitary%20Executive/unitary_exec_3rd_half_cent.pdf (accessed July 19, 2007).

Campbell, Joseph. *The Hero with a Thousand Faces.* 2nd ed. Princeton, N.J.: Princeton University Press, 1968.

Caro, Robert. *Master of the Senate: The Years of Lyndon Johnson.* New York: Vintage, 2003.

Chait, Jonathan. *The Big Con: The True Story of How Washington Got Hoodwinked and Hijacked by Crackpot Economics.* New York: Houghton Mifflin, 2007.

Cole, David. "What Bush Wants to Hear." Review of John Yoo's *Powers of War and Peace). New York Review of Books,* November 2005.

Conaway, James. "Looking at Reagan." *Atlantic,* October 1980, 32–45.

Cooper, Phillip J. *By Order of the President: The Use and Abuse of Executive Direct Action.* Lawrence: University Press of Kansas, 2002.

Corlett, William. *Community without Unity: A Politics of Derridean Extravagance.* Durham, N.C.: Duke University Press, 1989.

Crenson, Matthew, and Benjamin Ginsberg. "Downsizing Democracy, Upsizing the Presidency." *South Atlantic Quarterly* 105, no. 1 (2006): 207–16.

———. *Presidential Power: Unchecked and Unbalanced.* New York: Norton, 2007.

Croly, Herbert. *Progressive Democracy.* New York: Macmillan, 1914.

———. *The Promise of American Life.* Boston: Northeastern University Press, 1989.

Cronin, Thomas E., ed. *Rethinking the Presidency.* Boston: Little, Brown and Company, 1982.

Dahl, Richard A. "Myth of the Presidential Moderate." *Political Science Quarterly* 105, no. 3 (1990): 355–72.

Davis, Jeffrey. "Guarding the Republican Interest: The Western Pennsylvanian Democratic Societies and the Excise Tax." *Pennsylvania History* 67, no. 1 (2000): 43–62.

Dickinson, Matthew J. *Bitter Harvest: FDR, Presidential Power, and the Growth of the Presidential Branch.* New York: Cambridge University Press, 1997.

Didion, Joan. *Political Fictions.* New York: Knopf, 2001.

Disch, Lisa Jane. *The Tyranny of the Two-Party System.* New York: Columbia University Press, 2002.

Dodds, Graham G. "Executive Orders from Nixon to Now." Pp. 53–71 in *Executing the Constitution: Putting the President Back into the Constitution,* ed. Christopher S. Kelley. Albany: State University of New York Press, 2006.

Eastland, Terry. *Energy in the Executive.* New York: Free Press, 1992.

Eliasoph, Nina. *Avoiding Politics: How Americans Produce Apathy in Everyday Life.* New York: Cambridge University Press, 1998.

Emerson, Ralph Waldo. *Miscellanies.* New York: AMS, 1968.

FAIR. "Reagan: Media Myth and Reality." Media advisory, June 9, 2004. http://www .fair.org/index.php?page=1832.

Fisher, Louis. *Military Tribunals and Presidential Power: American Revolution to the War on Terrorism.* Lawrence: University Press of Kansas, 2005.

———. *The Politics of Executive Privilege.* Durham, N.C.: Carolina Academic Press, 2004.

———. *Presidential War Powers.* 2nd ed. Lawrence: University Press of Kansas, 2004.

———. "The 'Sole Organ' Doctrine." *Studies on Presidential Power in Foreign Relations.* Study no. 1. Law Library of Congress, August, 2006-03236.

Fishkin, James. *The Voice of the People: Public Opinion and Democracy.* New Haven, Conn.: Yale University Press, 1995.

Fitts, Michael A. "The Paradox of Power in the Modern State: Why a Unitary, Centralized Presidency May Not Exhibit Effective or Legitimate Leadership." *University of Pennsylvania Law Review* 144, no. 3 (1996): 827–902.

Flaherty, Martin S. "The Most Dangerous Branch." *Yale Law Journal* 105 (1995–96): 1725–839.

Fleischacker, Sam. "Insignificant Communities." Pp. 273–313 in *Freedom of Association*, ed. Amy Gutman. Princeton, N.J.: Princeton University Press, 1999.

Frank, Barney. Bush's Plebiscitary Presidency. Congressional Records, July 13, 2006 (House), H5212–H5216.

Frank, Robert H., and Philip J. Cook. *Winner-Take-All Society: How More and More Americans Compete for Ever Fewer and Bigger Prizes, Encouraging Economic Waste, Income Inequality, and an Impoverished Cultural Life*. New York: Free Press, 1995.

Frost, John. *Pictorial Life of Andrew Jackson*. Hartford, Conn.: Belknap and Hamersley, 1847.

Gaziano, Todd F. "The Use and Abuse of Executive Orders and Other Presidential Directives." Heritage Foundation Legal Memorandum Executive Summary Number 2, February 21, 2001.

Gecan, Michael. *Going Public: An Organizer's Guide to Citizen Action*. New York: Anchor Books, 2002.

Gemmill, Gary, and Judith Oakley. "Leadership: An Alienating Social Myth?" *Human Relations* 45, no. 2 (1992): 113–29.

Genovese, Michael. *The Power of the American Presidency, 1789–2000*. New York: Oxford University Press, 2001.

Ginsberg, Benjamin. *The Captive Public: How Mass Opinion Promotes State Power*. New York: Basic Books, 1986.

———. *The Consequences of Consent: Elections, Citizen Control, and Popular Acquiescence*. Reading, Mass.: Addison-Wesley, 1982.

Ginsberg, Benjamin, and Alan Stone, eds. *Do Elections Matter?* 3rd ed. Armonk, N.Y.: Sharpe, 1996.

Ginsberg, Benjamin, Theodore J. Lowi, and Margaret Weir. *We the People: An Introduction to American Politics*. New York: Norton, 2007.

Gould, Lewis L. *The Modern American Presidency*. Lawrence: University Press of Kansas, 2003.

Greene, Abner S. "Checks and Balances in an Era of Presidential Lawmaking." *University of Chicago Law Review* 61 (1994): 123–96.

Greenstein, Fred. "What the President Means to Americans: Presidential 'Choice' between Elections." In James David Barber, 121–47.

Greenwald, Glenn. *How Would a Patriot Act? Defending American Values from a President Run Amok*. San Francisco: Working Assets, 2006.

Guinier, Lani. *The Tyranny of the Majority: Fundamental Fairness in Representative Democracy.* New York: Free Press, 1994.

Hart, Roderick P. *Seducing America: How Television Charms the Modern Voter.* Thousand Oaks, Calif.: Sage, 1994.

Hartmann, Thom. *Unequal Protection: The Rise of Corporate Dominance and the Theft of Human Rights.* Emmaus, Pa.: Rodale, 2002.

Hawken, Paul. *Blessed Unrest: How the Largest Movement in the World Came into Being and Why No One Saw It Coming.* New York: Viking, 2007.

Heatherly, Charles L., ed. *Mandate for Leadership: Policy Management in a Conservative Administration.* Washington, D.C.: Heritage Foundation, 1981.

Hellman, John. *The Kennedy Obsession: The Myth of JFK.* New York: Columbia University Press, 1997.

Hersey, John. "Survival." *New Yorker Magazine,* August 1946.

Hertsgaard, Mark. *On Bended Knee: The Press and the Reagan Presidency.* New York: Farrar, Strauss and Giroux, 1988.

Hertz, Noreena. *The Silent Takeover: Global Capitalism and the Death of Democracy.* New York: Harper Business, 2003.

Hetherington, Marc J. *Why Trust Matters: Declining Political Trust and the Demise of American Liberalism.* Princeton, N.J.: Princeton University Press, 2005.

Hetherington, Marc J., and Michael Nelson. "Anatomy of a Rally Effect: George W. Bush and the War on Terrorism." *Political Science and Politics* 36, no. 1 (2003): 37–42.

Hetherington, Marc J., and Jonathan Weiler. *Divided We Stand: Polarization, Authoritarianism, and Contemporary American Politics.* New York: Cambridge University Press, 2009.

Hibbing, John R., and Elizabeth Thiess-Morse. *Congress as Public Enemy: Public Attitudes toward American Political Institutions.* New York: Cambridge University Press, 1995.

———. *Stealth Democracy: Americans' Beliefs about How Government Should Work.* New York: Cambridge University Press, 2002.

Hinckley, Barbara. *The Symbolic Presidency: How Presidents Portray Themselves.* New York: Routledge, 1990.

Hirschbein, Ron. *Voting Rites: The Devolution of American Politics.* Westport, Conn.: Praeger, 1999.

Holli, Melvin. *The Wizard of Washington: Emil Hurja, Franklin Roosevelt, and the Birth of Public Opinion Polling.* New York: Palgrave, 2002.

Holton, Woody. *Forced Founders: Indians, Debtors, Slaves, and the Making of the American Revolution in Virginia.* Chapel Hill: University of North Carolina Press for the Omohundro Institute for American History and Culture, 1999.

Horowitz, David. *The Art of Political War, and Other Radical Pursuits.* Dallas, Tex.: Spence, 2000.

Howell, William G. *Power without Persuasion: The Politics of Direct Presidential Action.* Princeton, N.J.: Princeton University Press, 2003.

Irons, Peter. *War Powers: How the Imperial Presidency Hijacked the Constitution.* New York: Henry Holt, Metropolitan Books, 2005.

Jenkins, John S. *Life and Public Services of Gen. Andrew Jackson, Seventh President of the United States, including The Most Important Of His State Papers.* Buffalo: Geo. H. Derby, 1852.

Jewett, Robert, and John Shelton Lawrence. *The American Monomyth.* 2nd ed. Lanham, Md.: University Press of America, 1988.

Kelley, Christopher, ed. *Executing the Constitution: Putting the President Back into the Constitution.* Albany: State University of New York Press, 2006.

Kelley, Christopher. "The Significance of the Presidential Signing Statement." Pp. 73–89 in *Executing the Constitution: Putting the President Back into the Constitution,* ed. Christopher Kelley. Albany: State University of New York Press, 2006.

Kelly, Marjorie. *The Divine Right of Capital: Dethroning the Corporate Aristocracy.* San Francisco: Berrett-Koehler, 2003.

Keltner, Dacher, Deborah Gruenfeld, and Cameron Anderson. "Power, Approach, and Inhibition." *Psychological Review* 110, no. 2 (2003): 265–84.

Kennedy, John Fitzgerald. *Profiles in Courage.* New York: Harper and Brothers, 1955.

Kerbel, Matthew Johnson. *Remote and Controlled: Media Politics in a Cynical Age.* Boulder, Colo.: Westview, 1999.

Khurana, Rakesh. *Searching for a Corporate Savior: The Irrational Quest for Charismatic CEOs.* Princeton, N.J.: Princeton University Press, 2002.

Knight, Keith, et al. *Beginners Guide to Community-Based Arts.* Oakland, Calif.: New Village, 2005.

Lessig, Lawrence, and Cass Sunstein. "The President and the Administration." *Columbia Law Review* 94, no. 1 (1994): 1–123.

Lewis, Anthony. "Making Torture Legal." *New York Review of Books,* July 15, 2004.

Lincoln, Abraham. *The Collected Works of Abraham Lincoln.* Ed. Roy P. Basler. Rutgers, N.J.: Rutgers University Press, 1953.

Liphart, Arend. "Presidentialism and Majoritarian Democracy: Theoretical Observations." In *The Failure of Presidential Democracy,* ed. Juan J. Linz and Arturo Valenzuela. Baltimore, Md.: Johns Hopkins University Press, 1994.

Lipman-Blumen, Jean. *The Allure of Toxic Leaders: Why We Follow Destructive Bosses and Corrupt Politicians, and How We Can Survive Them.* New York: Oxford University Press, 2005.

Lippmann, Walter. *Public Opinion.* 1922. New York: Free Press, 1997.

Lowi, Theodore J. *The Personal President: Power Invested, Promise Unfulfilled.* Ithaca, N.Y.: Cornell University Press, 1985.

Lummis, C. Douglas. *Radical Democracy.* Ithaca, N.Y.: Cornell University Press, 1996.

Madsen, Douglas, and Peter G. Snow. *The Charismatic Bond: Political Behavior in Time of Crisis.* Cambridge, Mass.: Harvard University Press, 1991.

Mailer, Norman. "Superman Comes to the Supermarket." *Esquire,* November 1960, 119–27.

Mann, Thomas E., and Norman J. Ornstein. *The Broken Branch: How Congress Is Failing America and How to Get It Back on Track.* New York: Oxford University Press, 2006.

Mansfield, Harvey C. "The Case for the Strong Executive." *Wall Street Journal,* May 4, 2007, http://opinionjournal.com/federation/feature/?id=110010014.

Mayer, Kenneth R. *With the Stroke of a Pen: Executive Orders and Presidential Power.* Princeton, N.J.: Princeton University Press, 2001.

McConville, Brendan. *The King's Three Faces: The Rise and Fall of Royal America, 1688-1776.* Chapel Hill: University of North Carolina Press, 2006.

McCormick, Richard P. *The Presidential Game: The Origins of American Presidential Politics.* New York: Oxford University Press, 1982.

McCullough, David. *Truman.* New York: Simon and Schuster, 1992.

McJimsey, George. *The Presidency of Franklin Delano Roosevelt.* Lawrence: University Press of Kansas, 2000.

Miroff, Bruce. "Monopolizing the Public Space: The President as a Problem for Democratic Politics." In Cronin, 218–32.

Moe, Terry M., and William G. Howell. "Unilateral Action and Presidential Power: A Theory." *Presidential Studies Quarterly* 29, no. 4 (1999): 850–73.

Mooney, Booth. *LBJ: An Irreverent Chronicle.* New York: Crowell, 1976.

Nace, Ted. *Gangs of America: The Rise of Corporate Power and the Disabling of Democracy.* San Francisco: Berrett-Koehler, 2003.

Neustadt, Richard E. *Presidential Power and the Modern Presidents: The Politics of Leadership from Roosevelt to Reagan.* Rev. ed. New York: Free Press, 1990.

Nichols, David K. *The Myth of the Modern Presidency.* University Park: Pennsylvania State University Press, 1994.

Nielsen, Jeffrey S. *The Myth of Leadership: Creating Leaderless Organizations.* Palo Alto, Calif.: Davies-Black, 2004.

"Nixon's Views on Presidential Power: Excerpts from an Interview with David Frost." *New York Times,* May 20, 1977.

Nofziger, Lyn. *Nofziger.* Washington, D.C.: Regnery Gateway, 1992.

O'Leary, Kevin. *Saving Democracy: A Plan for Real Representation in America.* Stanford, Calif.: Stanford University Press, 2006.

Ostrom, Elinor. "Polycentricity, Complexity, and the Commons." *The Good Society: A PEGS Journal/Committee on the Political Economy of the Good Society* 9, no. 2 (1999): 37–41.

Paludan, Phillip Shaw. *The Presidency of Abraham Lincoln*. Lawrence: University of Kansas Press, 1994.

Parton, James. *Life of Andrew Jackson*. 3 vols. Boston, 1859–60.

Patterson, Thomas E. *The Vanishing Voter: Public Involvement in an Age of Uncertainty*. New York: Vintage Books, 2003.

Percival, Robert V. "Presidential Management of the Administrative State: The Not-so-Unitary Executive." *Duke Law Journal* 51, no. 3 (2001): 963–1013.

Perret, Geoffrey. *Commander in Chief*. New York: Farrar, Strauss and Giroux, 2007.

———. *Lincoln's War*. New York: Random House, 2004.

Pestritto, Ronald J. *Woodrow Wilson and the Roots of Modern Liberalism*. Lanham, Md.: Rowman and Littlefield, 2005.

Phillips, Kevin. *American Dynasty: Aristocracy, Fortune, and the Politics of Deceit in the House of Bush*. New York: Viking, 2004.

———. *Wealth and Democracy: A Political History of the American Rich*. New York: Broadway Books, 2002.

Pious, Richard M. "Why Do Presidents Fail?" *Presidential Studies Quarterly* 32, no. 5 (2002): 724–42.

Pitkin, Hanna Fenichel. *Fortune Is a Woman: Gender and Politics in the Thought of Niccolò Machiavelli*. Chicago: University of Chicago Press, 1999.

Piven, Frances Fox, and Richard A. Cloward. *Why Americans Still Don't Vote: And Why Politicians Want It That Way*. Boston: Beacon, 2000.

Putnam, Robert D. *Bowling Alone: The Collapse and Revival of American Community*. New York: Simon and Schuster, 2000.

Reagan, Ronald, with Richard G. Huber. *Where Is the Rest of Me? The Autobiography of Ronald Reagan*. New York: Karz, 1981.

Reid, John, and John Henry Eaton. *The Life of Andrew Jackson*. Tuscaloosa: University of Alabama Press, 1974.

Relyea, Harold C. "Presidential Directives: Background and Overview." *CRS Report for Congress,* Order Code 98-611-GOV, updated April 23, 2007.

Remini, Robert V. *The Life of Andrew Jackson*. New York: Penguin, 1988.

Richardson, James D. *A Compilation of the Messages and Papers of the Presidents 1789–1908*. Washington, D.C.: Authority of Congress, 1896.

Richie, Robert, and Steven Hill. *Reflecting All of Us: The Case for Proportional Representation*. Foreword by Lani Guinier. Boston: Beacon, 1999.

Rogin, Michael Paul. *Ronald Reagan, The Movie: And Other Episodes in Political Demonology*. Berkeley: University of California Press, 1987.

Roosevelt, Theodore. *The New Nationalism*. New York: Outlook, 1910.

———. *Theodore Roosevelt: An Autobiography*. Charles Scribner's Sons, 1924.

Rosen, Jeffrey. "Power of One: Bush's Leviathan State." *New Republic,* July 24, 2006, 8–10.

Rozell, Mark. *Executive Privilege: The Dilemma of Secrecy and Democratic Accountability.* Baltimore, Md.: Johns Hopkins University Press, 1994.

———. *In Contempt of Congress: Postwar Press Coverage on Capital Hill.* Westport, Conn.: Praeger, 1996.

Rozell, Mark J., William D. Pederson, and Frank J. Williams, eds. *George Washington and the Origins of the American Presidency.* Westport, Conn.: Praeger, 2000.

Rubin, Gretchen. *Forty Ways to Look at JFK.* New York: Ballantine, 2005.

Ryan, Mary P. *Civic Wars: Democracy and Public Life in the American City during the Nineteenth Century.* Berkeley: University of California Press, 1997.

Schlesinger, Arthur M. *The Imperial Presidency.* New York: Houghton Mifflin, 1989.

Schudson, Michael. *The Good Citizen: A History of American Civic Life.* Cambridge, Mass.: Harvard University Press, 1998.

Schumpeter, Joseph. *Capitalism, Socialism, and Democracy.* New York: Harper and Row, 1976.

Schwartz, Barry. *Abraham Lincoln and the Forge of National Memory.* Chicago: University of Chicago Press, 2000.

Schwarz, Frederick A. O. Jr., and Aziz Z. Huq. *Unchecked and Unbalanced: Presidential Power in a Time of Terror.* New York: New Press, 2007.

Sharp, Roger. *American Politics in the Early Republic: The New Nation in Crisis.* New Haven, Conn.: Yale University Press, 1995.

Shultz, Jim. *The Democracy Owner's Manual: A Practical Guide to Changing the World.* New Brunswick, N.J.: Rutgers University Press, 2003.

Small, Melvin. *The Presidency of Richard Nixon.* Lawrence: University of Kansas Press, 1999.

Stenner, Karen. *The Authoritarian Dynamic.* New York: Cambridge University Press, 2005.

Sunstein, Cass. *Infotopia.* New York: Oxford University Press, 2006.

———. *Why Societies Need Dissent.* Cambridge, Mass.: Harvard University Press, 2003.

Surowiecki, James. *The Wisdom of Crowds: Why the Many Are Smarter Than the Few and How Collective Wisdom Shapes Business, Economies, Societies, and Nations.* New York: Doubleday, 2004.

Suskind, Ronald. "Without a Doubt." *New York Times Magazine,* October 17, 2004, 44–51, 64, 102, 106.

Tannen, Deborah. *The Argument Culture: Moving from Debate to Dialogue.* New York: Random House, 1998.

Taylor Jr., Stuart. "The Man Who Would Be King." *Atlantic Monthly,* April 2006, 25–26.

Tullis, Jeffrey K. *The Rhetorical Presidency*. Princeton, N.J.: Princeton University Press, 1987.

Tygiel, Jules. *Ronald Reagan and the Triumph of American Conservatism*. Pearson Longman, 2006.

Waldo, S. Putnam. *Memoirs of Jackson*. Hartford, Conn.: Silas Andrus, 1819.

Waldstreicher, David. *In the Midst of Perpetual Fêtes: The Making of American Nationalism, 1776–1820*. Chapel Hill: University of North Carolina Press for the Omohundro Institute of Early American History and Culture, 1997.

Wattenberg, Martin P. *Where Have All the Voters Gone?* Cambridge, Mass.: Harvard University Press, 2002.

Weems, Mason L. *The Life of Washington*. Ed. Marcus Cunliffe. Cambridge, Mass.: Belknap Press, 1962.

Weisberg, Jacob. "The Power-Madness of King George: Is Bush Turning America into an Elective Dictatorship?" *Slate,* January 25, 2006, http://www.slate.com/id/2134845/.

Wilentz, Sean. "Mr. Cheney's Minority Report." *New York Times,* July 9, 2007.

Wills, Garry. "At Ease, Mr. President." *New York Times,* January 27, 2007.

———. *Reagan's America: Innocents at Home*. New York: Doubleday, 1987.

Wilson, Woodrow. *Congressional Government: A Study in American Politics*. New Brunswick, N.J.: Transaction, 2004.

———. *Constitutional Government in the United States*. New York: Columbia University Press, 1908.

Winfield, Betty Houchin. *FDR and the News Media*. Urbana: University of Illinois Press, 1990.

Wolin, Sheldon. *Presence of the Past: Essays on the State and the Constitution*. Baltimore, Md.: Johns Hopkins University Press, 1989.

Wood, Gordon. *The Creation of the American Republic, 1776–1787*. Chapel Hill: University of North Carolina Press, 1998.

Woods, Randall B. *LBJ: Architect of American Ambition*. New York: Free Press, 2006.

Woodward, Bob. *Bush at War*. New York: Simon and Schuster, 2002.

Yoo, Christopher S., Steven G. Calabresi, and Anthony Colangelo. "The Unitary Executive in the Modern Era, 1945–2001." *Iowa Law Review* 90 (2004–5): 601–731.

Yoo, John. "Interview." http://www.press.uchicago.edu/Misc/Chicago/960315in.html (accessed June 9, 2007).

———. "War and the Constitutional Text." *University of Chicago Law Review* 69, no. 4 (2002): 1639–84.

Zukin, Cliff, et al. *A New Engagement? Political Participation, Civic Life, and the Changing American Citizen*. New York: Oxford University Press, 2006.

Index

ties of cabinet members and council appointments, 170–71; as "decider," 100–101; defense of wiretapping program of National Security Agency, 114; early-term refusal to explain himself to American public, 26; election of 2000, 204–5; image management, 105; job approval ratings, 6, 9–10, 145; as MBA president, 20, 170–76; "Mission Accomplished" speech (2003) aboard USS *Abraham Lincoln,* 140, 181; "monarchical" pretensions, 175, 176–79; NSA wiretapping controversy, 114, 135, 172; plebiscitary presidency, 176–78; president considered above rule of law, 172–73, 180; regulatory philosophy under, 171; Rehnquist Court decision against (2006), 5; signing statements issued by, 158, 173; spoof on superhero rhetoric of, 30; theory of presidential power, 3–4; unitary executive theory under, 27, 156, 170–76; war powers, 115, 173, 175

Bush Doctrine, 116–17, 172

Bush family, 170

business. *See* big business; corporation(s)

Business Ethics, 178

Butler, Pierce, 33–34, 111

Byrd, Robert, 148, 163

Cairo, Michael, 172

Calabresi, Steven, 156, 161

Cambodia, 131, 132

Camelot (musical), 57

Camelot mystique: Kennedy and, 57–58

campaigns, presidential: Bush (George H. W.) in 1988, 205; Bush (George W.) in 2000/2004, 20, 176; Clinton in 1992, 169; costs of, 177; expansion of primary season, 68; Johnson in 1964, 130; Kennedy in 1960, 56; party system and, 84, 89, 90; presidential candidates running on personality and charisma, 105–6; Reagan's tactics in 1980, 61

Campbell, Joseph, 48, 134

capitalism: corporate aristocracy in this era of market fundamentalism and, 178. *See also* big business; corporation(s)

Captive Public: How Mass Opinion Promotes State Power, The (Ginsberg), 102

Caro, Robert, 127

Carter, Jimmy, 133, 147, 153; executive orders from, 152–53; presidential control of bureaucracy and, 153; Reagan's radio addresses against policies of, 60–61; refusal to play part of hero, 59; voters' rejection of pessimism of, 61

cascades, 196–97

"Case for the Strong Executive" (Mansfield), 179–80

Center for Democracy and Citizenship, 211

centralized organizations, 190

CEO: Bush's MBA presidency in style of, 170–76; charismatic, corporate emphasis on securing, 20, 186–87; compensation, 169, 178, 187; president's role as, 27, 49; "unitary" corporate leadership model of, 155

Chait, Jonathan, 171

change agents: social entrepreneurs as, 209

charisma, 86, 94; business emphasis on securing charismatic corporate leadership, 20, 186–87; of Clinton, 164; consolidated first in relation to dead president, 42; of FDR, 51, 97; kingly executive, 176; presidential candidates running on, 105–6; of Reagan, 59, 65; as "relational phenomenon," 65; severed from evaluation of factually effective leadership, 65

Charles of England, King, 35, 110

checks and balances: Croly's critique of, 96; ignored during run-up to Civil War, 114–15; interbranch competition as healthy feature of U.S. government, 136; rewarding exercise of, 212; rising mystique of commander in chief and, 136–39; unitary executive and, 157; war powers of Congress and, 111–12. *See also* separation and balance of power, principle of

Cheney, Richard, 27, 29, 154, 171, 179, 180; minority response to Iran-Contra hearings, 174

Chevron, 171

China: entry into Korean police action, 124; most favored trading nation status of, 169

Christian Science Monitor, 123

Churchill, Winston, 122

CIA: under Reagan, 154

citizen agency, 205; government's retraction not only of services but also of, 208; open-system leaderless networks, 210–11; retaking democracy, methods of, 212–18; volunteerism, 205–8. *See also* civic agency

citizen assembly, 220–21

citizen-government partnerships in problem solving, 217–18

citizen heroism after 9/11, 7–8, 10; deactivated by Bush at Ground Zero, 9, 10

citizens: as consumers, 204–5; democratic realists' contempt for political abilities of, 203–4; informed and self-informing electorate, 218; New Deal and restructuring of government-citizen relationship, 49–50; presidentially conditioned habit of feeling "democratic" in moment of voting for president's power, 17, 68; as producers, 203–9, 210

citizenship: depoliticization of, 16, 18–19, 207–8, 211; exercised in private, Weems's lesson on, 45; linked to white manhood in 1800s, 80; as more than voting and volunteering, 203–9; overtaken by antidemocratic symbolics of military presidency, 136; presidential leadership fetishized at expense of, 66–68; rise and fall of, 204; universal citizenship service, 219–20

civic agency: cultivation of democratic skills, presidentialism working against, 18–19, 183; deactivated by Bush at Ground Zero, 9, 10; after 9/11, 7–8, 10. *See also* citizen agency

civic revitalization, 205–8

civic sector vs. nongovernmental organizations (NGOs), 209

civil service positions as political appointments: Reagan's use of, 155

civil service reform, 90

Civil War, 26, 87; checks and balances ignored during run-up to, 114–15; Lincoln's expansion of war powers during, 112–17

civil war, politics as, 200; lowered tolerance for disagreement and, 197–98

classified information, 153, 154

Clay, Henry, 81

Cleveland, Grover, 90, 91

Clinton, Bill, 3, 12, 64, 103, 149, 161–70; Bush's reversals of policies of, 171; ECHELON, global electronic surveillance action authorized by, 168–69; executive orders, 162–64; free-trade agreements and, 166–69; Project Podesta, 163; reversal on China, 169

Clinton v. City of New York, 158

Cloward, Richard, 90

Cold War, 121–26; end of, 165

Cole, David, 175

colonial power: United States as international, 91–92, 117

colonies: development and exercise of arts of self-governance, 71; founders'/elites' decision to declare independence, 71–72

commander in chief, president as, 26, 27; Bush (George W.) and, 135–36, 172, 173; changes in understandings of founders' "intent" regarding, 35, 36; crisis presidentialism and, 123; Lincoln's response to civil war creating role of, 112–17; mystique of, 133–39, 141, 142; title conferred on president by Constitution, 110–12

Commerce Department, 125, 150, 168

Committee on Administrative Management (Brownlow Committee), 49–50

common good among strangers, in model for democratic community, 202

common man: democratization of presidency in name of, 25–26; era of, 81–84

communism: Cold War and threat of, 121–26; Johnson's hard line against, 127–31; Reagan's plans to defeat communist Soviet empire, 62–63

community(ies): coproduced, 201; gated, 142; individualism vs., 201; knowledge, 191–94; lack of political mixing in, 215; Latin roots of, 202; as mutuality and service across differences, 202; without unity, 201, 203

Conaway, James, 65

conformists/conformity, 196

Congress.org (Web site), 212

Congress, U.S., 183; authority to suspend habeas corpus, 115; Bush's defiance of, 173–75; citizen assembly proposed for each member of, 220–21; Clinton's brinksmanship with, 163–64; Constitution on powers of, 37, 50, 110–12; as "democratic branch," 186; incentives for and ability to protect institutional interests, 137; Iran-Contra hearings, 63, 64, 174; job approval rating for Bush and, 9; Johnson and, 127; lack of incentive institutionally to unite against presidential unilateralism, 183; legislative debate portrayed as sign of governmental weakness, 16; media and polling used to campaign over heads of, 53, 134; misimpressions of, encouraged by presidents, 103–5; as "most dangerous branch," 157; powers lost to executive branch under FDR, 50; presidential mandate at expense of, 95; presidential powers and, 36–37; primary role in federal government maintained throughout nineteenth century, 87; public trust in and approval for, decline in, 138; reassertion of power after pardon of Nixon, 59; right to supervise war powers given to executive, 19; rising mystique of commander in chief and weakening of, 136–39; structural weakness compared to president, 137; Truman's deployment of troops in Korea without authorization of, 124; Vietnam War and, 128–29, 131, 132; war powers designated in Constitution for, 110–12, 113, 131; War Powers Resolution of 1973, 132–33

Congressional Authorization for Use of Military Force (2001), 175

Congressional Government (Wilson), 90

consensus, emphasis on, 18, 196, 197. *See also* disagreement; unity

Consequences of Consent (Ginsberg), 98–99

Constitution, U.S., 15; Article 2, 175; Authorization for Use of Military Force against Terrorists as counter to, 9; as "cost transaction model" in rational choice theory, 170; Croly's critique of checks and balances, 96; designed to remedy flaws of nation's original organization of government, 31; framers' conception of president in, 5, 35; legislative powers vested in Congress, 37, 50; Mansfield's redescription of three-branch constitutional government, 179–80; popular elections under, 32–33; presidential powers in, 35–38; representative system of, 13; separation and balance of powers under, 3, 4, 21, 37, 66, 148, 186; Seventeenth Amendment, 89; "take care" clause of, 92; on war powers, 110–12, 113, 131; Wilson's proposal for coordinating branch powers, 90–91

Constitutional Congress, 74–75

Constitutional Convention, 31, 111; debate over office of president, 34–36, 156

Constitutional Government (Wilson), 93–94

constitutionalism, venture, 157

Consumer Product Safety Commission, 149, 150

consumers, citizens as, 204–5

Coolidge, Calvin, 160

Cooper, Gary, 54

Cooper, Phillip J., 153, 157, 158, 159, 175

coproduced community, 201

coproduction, 191, 195; of commonwealth, 193; leadership vs., 188

Corlett, William, 201, 202

corporate aristocracy, 178

corporate executives: unilateral control of, 20. *See also* CEO

corporate state, project of transitioning political state into, 170–76

Corporate Watch (Global Policy Forum), 169, 176

corporation(s): adapting features of leaderless networks to competitive advantage, 191; Brownlow Committee reforms for administration patterned on, 49; Bush as MBA president and, 170–76; charismatic corporate leadership, emphasis on securing, 20, 186–87; dominance in rankings of worldwide largest economies, 169; downsizing, 161; ECHELON to procure industrial and trade negotiation secrets from U.S. competitors, 168–69; election of 2000 dominated by people tied to giant, 170–71; executive office powers in, expansion of, 20; foreign corporate investment, 166; free enterprise guaranteed by government, 97; innovation in early twentieth century of separating owners from expert managers, 96; political powers over citizens, 20–21, 27;

Reagan's 1981 tax cut bill for, 160;
with ties to Bush administration,
no-bid contracts to, 176; "unitary"
corporate leadership model, 155;
"Washington Consensus" and foreign
investments of, 166
counterstaffing, 155
covert activities under Reagan, 153–54
Cox, Archibald, 136
Craigslist, 191
creativity, democratic, 184, 198, 199, 203
Creek and Seminole Wars, Jackson in,
77, 79
Crenson, Matthew, 19, 126, 142, 147, 151,
162–63, 204, 205
crisis(es): Cold War, 121–26; Kennedy's
use of, 56; rhetoric of, 120; 1780s
commonly represented as time of,
31–32; strategy of overplaying, 26;
transition to modern presidency
through, 47–48
crisis presidentialism, 119–26
Croly, Herbert, 96
Cuba, independence of, 91
Cuban missile crisis, 56
culture: argument, 142–43; civil war atmosphere of U.S. democratic, 141; rank-
based, 188–89, 194, 208; shouting-
head, 141, 142, 184
culture wars, 142–43
Cunningham, Ward, 191

Dahl, Richard A., 94–95
Daily Show (TV), 15, 30
Dallas, Alexander, 73
Dames and Moore v. Regan, 179
Davis, Jeffrey, 73
dead presidential powers, 40–47, 48, 57
Deaver, Michael, 61

decentralized networks, 190–91
decision making: Bush as "decider,"
100–101; disagreement at heart of
good, 198; group, 194–95; leaders'
need to control, 189
decree, ability to legislate by, 148–49
Defense Procurement Authorization Act
(1971), 132
deliberative polling initiative, 218, 220
demagoguery, 17
democracy, 12–17; American colonists'
development and exercise of arts of
self-governance, 71; American monomyth undermining democratic ethos,
48, 55, 57–58, 63; definition of, 14, 17;
democratic energies aimed at public
sphere converted into private feelings
aimed at president, 42–43, 44; diminished by avoidance of public exercise
of politics, 199–200; direct modes
of self-governance under Articles of
Confederation, 32; early citizens'
desire and enthusiasm for "their darling democracy," 71–74; early official
attempts to quash enthusiasm for,
72–74; expansions of citizen power
and civic rights throughout U.S. history, 13–14; Habitat for Democracy,
200–203; linked to the vote in 1800s,
80; militarization of our politics as
aggressively antidemocratic, 139–43;
minimalist theory of, 204, 205; modern forms of voting as alienating and
discouraging to public, 99–101; normalized antidemocratic function of
president in United States, 11; as open
system, 183, 184–85, 214; party system and presidential "expansion" of,
84–87; Pavlovian, 98–102; plebiscitary,

electorate primed for twentieth-century transition from congressional to presidential government under, 76; era of common man and, 81–84; fabled spirit of independence, 79; legacy of, 77, 83–84; as military hero, 109; "personal" presidency of, 77; popularity of, 77, 80; president's representative authority under, 83; veto power used by, 78, 83

Jackson, Robert, 119, 126, 130

Japanese Americans: internment during World War II, 50–51, 119

Jay, John, 36

Jefferson, Thomas, 19, 40, 75–77; as "activist leader of Congress," 76; "second revolution," 76, 82; transition to presidency in 1800, 76

Jensen, Michael, 159, 160

Jewett, Robert, 48, 55, 57–58, 63

JFK. *See* Kennedy, John F.

job approval ratings, 9–10; of Bush after 9/11, 6, 9–10, 145; of Lyndon Johnson, 127, 130; of Reagan, 62, 64, 65; of Truman, 122, 124

Johnson, Andrew, 87

Johnson, Lyndon, 12, 59, 145, 146, 148; job approval ratings, 127, 130; negative media coverage of, 130; view of president as one chosen by American people to decide, 127–31

judiciary appointments: power to make, 36. *See also* Supreme Court

Justice Department, 179; arrogant assertion of executive supremacy by, 179; attorney-purging scandal, 174

Kelley, Christopher, 158

Kelly, Marjorie, 178

Keltner, Dacher, 188

Kenetech, 168

Kennedy, Jacqueline, 57, 58

Kennedy, John F. (JFK), 12, 25, 54–59, 64, 126, 148; assassination, 57, 59, 127; Camelot mystique, 57–58; campaign for president (1960), 56; congressional campaign, 55–56; as heroic leader, 56–57; public stature of, 58–59; voter turnout for, 97

Khmer Rouge, 133

Khurana, Rakesh, 20, 65, 186–87

King, Martin Luther, Jr., 130

king, prerogative power of, 175; originalist argument for granting president, 175–76

King's Row (film), 60

king's two bodies, Elizabethan doctrine of, 41–42; Reagan's invocation of, 62, 64

knowledge communities, 191–94

Korean police action, 122–24; China's entry into, 124

Kucinich, Dennis, 212

labor: free-trade agreements and, 167; neoliberal economic reform and corporate treatment of U.S., 166

Lady of the Lake (Scott), 109

lame-duck theory, 164

law, president considered above rule of, 172–73, 180

Lawrence, John Shelton, 48, 55, 57–58, 63

leaderless networks, open-system, 210–11; corporate adaptation of, to competitive advantage, 191

leaderless organizations, 190

leadership: of Bush in aftermath of 9/11, 6–10; charisma severed from evaluation of factually effective, 65;

coproduction vs., 188; expectations for, 21–22; fundamental necessity of some kind of, unquestionable assumption of, 187, 188–89; "great," 54; leader-follower dynamics, 188–89; myth of, 22; presidential leadership fetishized at expense of citizenship, 66–68; as "psychic prison" for group, 187–89; "unitary" corporate leadership model, 155; "weak" vs. "strong" president, 54

League of Nations, 138

Leahy, Patrick, 179

learned helplessness: cultural reliance on leaders and, 187

legislative branch. *See* Congress, U.S.

Lessig, Lawrence, 161, 164

Levy, Carly, 8

Lewinsky, Monica, 164, 178

Lewis, Anthony, 180

Libby, Scooter, 154

liberty, active, 203

Lieberman, Joe, 163

Lincoln, Abraham, 12, 58, 76, 87; heroic status cemented after assassination, 47; in military service, 112–13; opposition to Polk's claim to presidential war powers, 113, 116; presidential war powers under, 26, 112–17; as quasireligious symbol of national unification, 47; in state legislature and U.S. Congress, 113

line-item veto, 158–59

Liphart, Arend, 21, 66

loan packages to foreign countries: "Washington Consensus" and, 166

local representative institutions and agents, focusing on, 213

Locke, John, 110

lot, election by, 217

Lott, Trent, 140

Louisiana Purchase, 19, 76–77

Lowi, Theodore, 37, 47, 49, 89, 106

loyalty: loyalty oaths from federal employees, 148; to president as commander in chief, 123, 135, 136

Lummis, C. Douglas, 14, 217

machtpolitik, 139–43

Madison, James, 32, 37, 76, 80, 111, 112; concept of constitutional collaboration, 156

Madsen, Douglas, 65

Mailer, Norman, 56

Maine Lobster Fishery, 217–18

mandate, presidential, 25–26, 93–97; Jackson and, 83; Lincoln's claim of, 114; people's power garnished for unfettered use of president, 95; president at center of drama of American politics, 101; problem for democracy at heart of, 94; as "pseudodemocratization," 94–95; Wilson on, 93–94

"Mandate for Leadership" (Heritage Foundation), 155

Manichaean worldview, 141

Mann, Thomas E., 136, 142

Mansfield, Harvey, 172, 179

Mapuches: decentralized society of, 190

market fundamentalism. *See* neoliberalism

Marshall, John, 118–19

masculine variant of sentiment (patriotism), 43–45

Mason, George, 111

Mayaguez: 1975 retaliation for Khmer Rouge's capture of, 133

MBA president: Bush as, 20, 170–76

McCain, John, 173
McCarthy, Todd, 29
McConville, Brendan, 74–75, 84, 85
McCormick, Richard, 86
McCullough, David, 122
McDonnell Douglas, 168
McKinley, William, 88, 91, 117
media: centrality of president to coverage of government, 97; electronic forums and editorial space, using, 213; entranced by Reagan's storytelling abilities, 64–66; expansion from print into radio and television, 51–52; FDR's use of, 52; managing presidential image in, 56–57; savvy management of, 105–6; superheroes and, 47–54; television westerns and Kennedy's "New Frontier," 56; war coverage of Vietnam War, 130
Medicaid and Medicare, 127
Meese, Edmund, 155, 157, 159
merger and acquisition deals, 160
Mexican War, 91, 112, 113
mid-term elections: in 1994, 163; turnout for, 99
Mifflin, Thomas, 38, 73
militarization of our politics, 136–43; institutional consequences of, 140–41; machtpolitik and, 139–43; Manichaean worldview fostered by, 141; political consequences of, 141–42; social consequences of, 142–43
military: mystique of commander in chief and American democracy reimagined through lens of, 135–36; respect for presidency linked with authority of, 110; unilateral exercise of military force, 117. See also war powers
military heroes as presidents, 109

military-industrial complex, 170
military service, 219–20; draft for Vietnam War, 130, 132; volunteer, economic need and, 219. See also universal citizenship service
Milken, Michael, 160
minimalist theory of democracy, 204, 205
minorities: benefits of minority viewpoint to decision making, 194–95; proportional representation and, 215–16
Miroff, Bruce, 101, 106, 107
modern presidency, 11; ushered in by FDR's years in office, 47–48
Moe, Terry, 137
"monarchical" pretension of Bush (George W.), 175, 176–79
monomyth, American, 48, 55, 57–58, 63
Monroe, James, 76
Monroe Doctrine: Roosevelt Corollary to, 117
Montesquieu, 110
multichoice format, 219
multiple executive: debate in 1780s over, 34
myth, power of: American monomyth, 48, 55, 57–58, 63; Kennedy's experience in World War II and, 55–56. See also superhero, president as
myth of leadership, 22

NAFTA (North American Free Trade Agreement), 166, 167–68, 169
National Assembly, decentralized, 220–21
National Commitments Resolution, 131
National Economic Council, 162
National Election Study (1992), 141–42

National Environmental Policy Act (1969), 149

National Highway Traffic Safety Administration, 149

National Industrial Pollution Control Council, 150

National Industrial Recovery Act, 148

national initiative and referendum process, 219, 221

National Issues Convention (PBS), 218

nationalist mythology. *See* American monomyth

National Labor Board, 49

National Nuclear Security Administration (NNSA), 163

National Security Agency (NSA), 168; warrantless surveillance controversy, 114, 135, 172

national security bureaucracy: Cold War and, 121–22

National Security Decision Directive (NSDD) 189, 158

National Security Strategy of United States (Bush Doctrine), 116–17, 172

National Voter Registration Act (1993), 98

nation-state: weakening of protective capacity of, 177–78

Natural Capital Institute, 210

Negroponte, John, 172

"Neither Leaders nor Followers" (Barber), 67

Nelson, Michael, 46

Nemeth, Chandra, 194–95

neoclassical liberalism. *See* neoliberalism

neoconservatism. *See* neoliberalism

neoliberalism, 159–61; corporate aristocracy created by, 178; efforts to sell new political economy to public,

160; free-trade agreements, 166–69; Gore's overhauling of federal agencies and, 162; neoliberal corporatism gone global in 1990s, 165–66; rational choice theory, 102, 169–70; Reagan's presidency as platform for applying, 159, 160–61; unitary executive's advancement and consolidation of, 165; "Washington Consensus" and economic reforms, 166

networking, Internet, 190–91

networks, open-system leaderless, 210–11

Neustadt, Richard, 147–48

Neville, John, 73

New Deal, 49, 117, 153; Office of Information and Regulatory Affairs (OIRA) and pushback against, 153; rejection by 1990s, 161

New Democrat version of unitary executive, 161–62

New Engagement? Political Participation, Civic Life, and the Changing American Citizen, 205–7

"New Frontier," 56, 57

"new journalism" style, 55

New Republic, 96, 171

news agenda: president's influence on, 52

New York City: response to 9/11, 7–8

New Yorker: Hersey's "Survival" in, 55

New York Times, 176

New York Times/CBS News polls of Kennedy's popularity, 58–59

Nicaragua: Iran-Contra scandal, 138, 154; presidential interventions in, 117

Nielsen, Jeffrey, 187–88, 189

9/11. *See* September 11, 2001

Nineteenth Amendment, 89

Nixon, Richard, 9, 54, 59, 127, 131–32, 145, 146, 154; executive branch reorganizations by, 150–51; executive orders used by, 149–50; Office of Communications created by, 105; pardoning of, 59; people's condemnation of abuses of power, 12, 13; plebiscitary presidency and, 177; Saturday Night Massacre firings during Watergate, 136; views on presidential power, 146–47

Nofziger, Lyn, 60

nongovernmental organizations (NGOs): civic sector vs., 209

North, Oliver, 64, 138

North American Free Trade Agreement (NAFTA), 166, 167–68, 169

North Carolina Regulators, 71

NSA. *See* National Security Agency

Nullification Controversy of 1832, 77

Nupedia, 192

Oakley, Judith, 187

Obama, Barack, 219

Occupational Safety and Health Administration, 149

Office of Communications, 105

Office of Faith-Based and Community Initiatives, 171

Office of Information and Regulatory Affairs (OIRA), 152–53, 162

Office of Intelligence Liaison, 168

Office of Legal Counsel, 115; "torture memo" (August 2002), 173, 180

Office of Management and Budget (OMB), 150–51, 162; under Reagan, 153

O'Leary, Kevin, 220–21

Olson, Theodore, 171–72

Onion, 174

OPEC (Organization of Petroleum Exporting Countries), 165

open system(s), 196; active member-

ship elicited by, 193; free spaces as geographic locations for practice of, 213–18, 221; on Internet, 191–95; leaderless networks, 210–11; minefields in deliberative processes, 196–97; model for democratic community, 202–3; norms to make conflict and disagreement productive for group created by, 198–99; power of numbers in, 193; reimagining democracy as, 183, 184–85, 214; rewards in satisfaction of building something together that benefits everyone, 193–94; time banks, 191, 193, 195, 201, 202; wikis, 191–94, 195, 202

opinion polling. *See* polling

organizational models: centralized vs. decentralized, 190–91

Organization of Petroleum Exporting Countries (OPEC), 165

Ornstein, Norman J., 136, 142

Ostrom, Elinor, 217–18

Oz, story of, 109

Panama Canal, 92

Paperwork Reduction Act, 152

parliamentary systems, 210–11

participatory self-government under Articles of Confederation, 32. *See also* self-governance/self-rule

particle (insignificant) community, 201

partisanship: effect of authoritarian disposition on, 141–42

party system: presidential "expansion" of democracy in Jacksonian era and, 84–87. *See also* political parties

passivity of feeling politically involved watching president on television, 106

patriotism: masculine variant of

Populists, 88, 89

postpartisanship, 199; working model, 215

poverty, war on, 127

powers of presidency. *See* presidential power(s)

prediction markets, 195

preemptive model of presidential powers, 156–57

preemptive war, power of, 116–17

preferential balloting, 216–17. *See also* voting

prerogative power: Cleveland's reassertion of, by veto, 90, 91; Hamiltonian argument about, 156–57; originalist argument for granting president kingly, rebuttal of, 175–76

presidency: American myth about, 25; democratization of, 25–26, 82; "personal," 77, 106; plebiscitary, 176–78, 211; respect for, linked with authority of military, 110; rethinking our relationship to, 23, 24, 180–82, 182–85; symbolics around, 1–2, 6–7, 17, 38

president(s): beliefs in, as democracy's heart and its avenging sword, 1–2, 6–7; centrality of, to media coverage of government, 97; civically trained desire for powerful, 19; civic expectations for office of, 45–47, 48, 51–54, 97; constitutionally authorized foreign power, 26; constitutionally mandated dependency on legislative branch, 37; democratic power felt in election of, 4–5; domestic function as "commander in chief," 26, 27 (*see also* commander in chief, president as); expectations for leadership from, 21–22; framers' conception of,

in Constitution, 5; inventing, 31–37; misimpressions of government encouraged in speeches of, 103–5; as nation's representative agent, 4, 33; normalized antidemocratic function in U.S. democracy, 11; portrayal of legislative debate as sign of governmental weakness, 16; public perception of, 138; role in democracy, 10, 11; as source and center of democratic power and political action, belief in, 186; as symbol for strong federal reorganization, 31

presidential directives, 149. *See also* executive orders

presidential government, 26; FDR's presidency (1933–45) as turning point from congressional to, 47–48; symbolic force of office and inevitability of, 38; transition from congressional to, 37–38

presidential image, managing. *See* image, managing presidential

presidentialism, 4–10; Bush's activation of, 6–10; circumventing messiness entailed by equalitarian negotiation, 44; conditioning how citizens feel toward president, 5; crisis, 119–26; depoliticization of citizenship by, 16, 18–19, 207–8, 211; liberal containment of changed (self-disciplined) heart, 45; mesmerizing power of, 4; political participation discouraged by, 106–7; politics-as-war, winnertake-all model, 197, 198, 200; retooled for globalizing aims of "liberalized" economy, 165; solving problems ascribed to, 22–23; symbolic work of, 42; as threat to democratic skill-set

and spirit, 18–19, 183; Weems's mythical Washington consolidating emotive force of, 40–45
presidential mandate, 25–26, 83, 93–97, 101, 114
presidential power(s), 10–12; "ambiguity" or "paradox" of, 21–22, 66; boombust cycle of hope for presidential rescue fueling, 67–68; Constitution on, 35–38; dead, 40–47, 48, 57; fantasies about, influence of, 22; foreign policy powers, expansion of, 50–51, 91–93; foreign policy powers, in setting agendas, 21; foreign policy powers, "Sole Organ" doctrine and, 117–19; framers' conception of, 5; implied powers, 76, 92, 114; under Jefferson, 75–77; mobilization against occasional overreaching, 2–3; Nixon's views on, 146–47; opposing expansion on principle, 212; people's sovereignty condensed and unified in singular body of president, 83; performance paradox, 145, 164–65; preemptive model of, 156–57; under Roosevelt, 25, 26, 97; tradition of expanding, 1–4, 19–20; unitary executive, theory of (*see* unitary executive, theory of). *See also* war powers
Presidential Power and the Modern Presidents (Neustadt), 147–48
Presidential Power (Crenson and Ginsberg), 126, 147, 151, 162–63
presidential power tools, 27, 145, 146–52
presidential reform: drawn from organization and mind-set of big business, 97; Progressives on, 95–96; Wilson's call for, 93–94
Presidential War Powers (Fisher), 119–20

Presley, Elvis, 64
primary season, presidential, 68
priming, 53
problem solving: citizen-government partnerships in, 217–18
producers, citizens as, 203–9, 210
professionalization of politics, 211
Profiles in Courage (Kennedy), 56
Progressive Era, 26
Progressive Party, 96
Progressivism, 88, 89; on government intervention against big business, 92–93; reforms with pseudodemocratic results, 95–96
Project Podesta, 163
property ownership: battles in 1800s over traditional claims of property, 81; political participation associated with economic stability of, in founding era, 80–81
property rebellions, colonial, 71
proportional representation, 215–16
pseudodemocracy, 17; democratic voting for president as, 25; president's claim of mandate as pseudodemocratization, 94–95; Progressive reforms resulting in, 95–96
public actions, categories for, 149
public associations during Jacksonian era, 84–85
public democracy: modern forms of voting as alienating and discouraging to, 99–101
public disagreement: democracy as, 15–17, 34, 95, 139–40, 195–200
public opinion polling. *See* polling
public sentiment: activist groups' representation of, 52; polling for, 52–53; shaped by polls, 53

by which we live together, 200–203; democracy as power of collective, 12, 14, 15, 200, 221; democracy as public disagreement, 15–17, 34, 95, 139–40, 195–200; direct modes of, under Articles of Confederation, 32; free-trade agreements and local and national, 167–68; as public activity, citizens trained away from idea of, 99–101

separation and balance of power, principle of, 3, 4, 21, 37, 148, 186; longing for powerful president despite national pride in, 66. *See also* checks and balances

September 11, 2001, 19; Bush as commander in chief and, 172; Bush's presidential leadership in aftermath of, 6–10, 134–35; people's heroic response after, 7–8, 9, 10

Seventeenth Amendment, 89

shareholder democracy, 165

Sharp, Roger, 38, 72, 73

Sherman, Roger, 112

shouting-head culture, 141, 142, 184

Shultz, George, 150–51

signing statements, use of presidential, 132, 158–59; by Bush (George W.), 158, 173; by Clinton, 163–64; by Reagan, 158, 159; recent escalation in, 158

60 Minutes (TV), 65–66

Skoll Foundation, 209

Smith, H. Alexander, 124

Snow, Peter, 65

social enclaving, 142, 183, 200, 202

social entrepreneurship, 209, 210

Social Houses, 214

Social Security Administration, 49, 162

"Sole Organ" doctrine, 117–19

Southeast Asia Collective Defense Treaty, 129, 131

Southeast Asia (Gulf of Tonkin) resolution, 128–29, 131

sovereignty: act of sovereign authorization turned into act of deauthorization, 67; crisis presidentialism and crucial reversal of, 123; president's power as mystical transfer of power from rejected British sovereign, Sutherland on, 118; primary (people's) power vs. secondary (president's representative), 4, 33, 70; as radical promise of democracy, 26–27, 186

Soviet Union: Cold War and, 121–26; Korean conflict and, 123; Reagan's plans to defeat communist agenda of, 62–63; after World War II, 120–21

Spanish-American War, 91

split-ticket voting, 89

Stalin, Josef, 120

Star Wars (film), 48

steelworkers strike: Truman's response to threat of, 125–26

Stenner, Karen, 142

Stewart, Jon, 15

Story, Joseph, 111–12, 118

Strategic Defense Initiative (1983), 63

strong democracy, 203

Strong Democracy: Participatory Politics for New Age (Barber), 214, 218–19

strong government, 31

student volunteerism, 205–6

suffrage: expansion for white men after Revolution, 80, 86; history of, 69, 70. *See also* voting

Sunstein, Cass, 142, 161, 164, 192, 194, 195

superhero, president as, 25, 29–68; American monomyth and, 48; dead presidential powers, 40–47, 48, 57; inventing the president, 31–37;

Kennedy's Camelot mystique and,
57–58; leader of strength and unity,
37–40; leadership versus citizenship
and, 66–68; managing presidential
image, 38–39, 54–59, 102–7; media
and, 47–54; presidential action-figure
toys, 29–30; public primed for extralegal salvation of, 63–64; Reagan
and, 60–66; symbolic commander
in chief, 134; Weems's portrayal of
Washington as, 24–25, 40
"Superman Comes to the Supermarket"
(Mailer), 56
supply-side economic system, 62, 160
Supreme Court, 26, 183, 211; Burger
Court, 147; certification of executive
agreements, 92; challenge to Gramm-
Rudman-Hollings bill, 159; decisions
against presidency's domestic powers, 117–18; extremism of president
checked by, 178; FDR and, 49, 50, 119;
Hughes Court, 117; line-item veto
disallowed by, 158; presidential power
of "nonacquiescence" to decisions
of, 155; on presidential power to take
over steel companies in labor dispute,
125–26; Rehnquist Court, 5, 178–79,
180; Roberts Court, 179, 180; on
state laws banning import of products manufactured with child labor,
168; Taney Court, Lincoln's innovations on presidential powers upheld
as constitutional by, 116; unitary executive proponents on, 179, 180; unitary executive theory and, 4; Vinson
Court, 125–26
Surowiecki, James, 194, 195
surveillance: ECHELON, global electronic surveillance network, 168–69;

NSA wiretapping controversy, 114,
135, 172
"Survival" (Hersey), 55
Suskind, Ron, 1
Sutherland, George, 117–18

Taft, Robert, 124
Taney Supreme Court, 116
Tannen, Deborah, 142–43
Tax Almanac wiki, 191
tax cuts, 153, 160, 177
Taylor, Stuart, 176
television: false simplicity and false sense
of activity from viewing president
on, 106; war coverage of Vietnam
War, 130
terror, war on, 115, 126, 172, 173
Tet Offensive of 1968, 130
Theiss-Morse, Elizabeth, 138, 199
Thomas, Clarence, 4
Tiananmen Square massacre, 169
time banks, 191, 193, 195, 201, 202
torture: Bush administration policies on,
173; torture memo, 173, 180
Toyota, 191
transaction costs: Congress's diminishing standing due to, 137–38
treaties: bypassing treaty process, 92;
power to make, 36
Treaty of Ghent, 80
Truman, Harry, 50, 54, 112, 130, 145, 148;
Cold War and, 121–26; crisis presiden-
tialism under, 120–21; job approval
ratings, 122, 124; takeover of steel
companies, 125–26; troops sent into
Korea by, 122–24
Truman Doctrine, 121
Tullis, Jeffrey, 53, 120
Tygiel, Jules, 60–61

Tyler, John, 91
Tyranny of the Majority: Fundamental Fairness in Representative Democracy (Guinier), 216

uncertainty, myth of leadership in times of social or political, 22
UN Charter, 123
unilateralism, presidential: advocated by unitary executive theory, 3–4; Congress's tendency to support, 138
unitary executive, theory of, 3–4, 27, 152–82; achievements of, 165; from Athenian 500 to Forbes 400, 161–70; bureaucracy and, 155, 161–62, 179; Bush (George W.) and, 27, 156, 170–76; checks and balances and, 157; commander in chief, meaning of, 35; motivating logic for, 204; New Democrat version of, 161–62; people's tendency in general to approve of presidential power, 12; performance paradox of, 145, 164–65; questioning presidential and congressional candidates about position on, 212; rationales for, 11; of Reagan, 146, 152–61; realpolitik aim for presidential supremacy, 173–75; signing statement refined for purposes of, 159; threat to formal democracy within U.S. government, 181–82; throughout Clinton era of 1990s, 161–70
United Nations: Truman's commitment of U.S. troops in Korean conflict and, 123–24
United Nations Participation Act, 123–24
United States Code Congressional and Administrative News, 159
United States v. Curtiss-Wright, 117–18, 119

United Steelworkers Union, 125
unity: becoming more comfortable with less, 200–201; crisis presidentialism and, 123; president as an emblem of national, 42; presidentialism's overemphasis on, 16, 17, 18–19
universal citizenship service, 219–20
University of Chicago Law Review, 175
USA PATRIOT Act, 172
U.S. Bank, 78, 83
U.S.–Mexican–Canadian Free Trade Proposal, 166
U.S. Trade and Development Agency, 150
U.S. v. Nixon, 147
utopian possibility: Camelot mystique invoking fantasy of, 57, 58

Vanderbilt, William, 88
Vargas, Elizabeth, 64
venture constitutionalism, 157
veto power: Cleveland's reassertion of, 90, 91; Jackson's exercise of, 78, 83; line-item veto, 158–59; Nixon and, 132
Vidal, Gore, 98
Vietnam War, 57, 59; "Americanized" by Johnson, 129–30; Congress and, 128–29, 131, 132; draft for, 130, 132; as most censorship-free war in U.S. history, 130; Southeast Asia (Gulf of Tonkin) resolution, 128–29, 131; war coverage on television, 130
Vinson, Fred, 125
Vinson Court, 125–26
Virginian, The (Wister), 48
Voice of the People: Public Opinion and Democracy, The (Fishkin), 218
volunteerism, 205–8; federal cuts in services justified by soliciting, 208
volunteer organizations: members'

impulses toward political engagement stifled by, 207–8

voter reforms, 89

voter turnout, 98–102; expectations of president and, 97; fall-off by 1920, 26, 90; fall over last quarter century, 98; in local elections, 99; in mid-term elections, 99; during 1930s, 96; restrictive registration and poll requirements and, 90

voting, 69–107; Athenian scheme of election by lot, 217; cresting from 1880s through early 1900s, 87–92; history of suffrage, 69, 70, 80, 86; national initiative and referendum process, 219, 221; preferential balloting, 216–17; two rounds of, proposed, 219

voting age, 69

voting for president: centrality in U.S. democracy, 25; democracy linked to, 17, 24, 25, 47, 80, 83–84; era of common man, 81–84; historical reasons to be skeptical about association of democratic expression with, 75; miniaturization of citizen power and, 70; as partisan ritual of national belonging, 86, 87; party system and presidential "expansion" of democracy, 84–87; popular vote expansion in 1800s, 80, 81–82; as ritual of democratic faith, 102; sensation of democratic power from, 17, 68; split-ticket voting, 89

voting reforms, 89; alienation from public democratic practice and, 99–101; of early twentieth century, 99

wages, CEO compensation compared to real average, 178

Waldstreicher, David, 38–39

Wales, Jim, 192

Wall Street Journal, 172

war, rhetoric of crisis invoking, 120

war crimes tribunals: authority to set up, 5

WardsWiki, 191

War of 1812, 76; Jackson in, 77, 79–80

war on poverty, 127

war on terror, 115, 126, 172, 173; Iraq war, 138–39, 176; public and secret actions authorized by Bush in, 11. *See also* September 11, 2001

war powers, 26, 109–43; under Bush (George W.), 115, 173, 175; of Congress, 110–12, 113, 131–33; of Congress, negotiations over U.S. participation in UN charter and, 124; of Congress, War Powers Resolution and, 132–33; Constitution on, 35, 36, 110–12; crisis presidentialism and, 119–26; expansion of presidential, under Lincoln, 26, 112–17; Johnson's view of president as "chosen by the people to decide," 127–31; machtpolitik and, 139–43; mystique of commander in chief and, 133–39; Supreme Court and "Sole Organ" doctrine, 117–19; Yoo's monarchical genealogy for presidential, 175

War Powers Resolution (1973), 132–33

Washington, George, 1, 12, 31, 38–40; death of, 40; expressions of self-government treated as threats under, 72; Farewell Address, 45; father's lesson on truthfulness, 43; framers' invention of presidency based on admiration for, 33–35; image management by, 38–39; as military hero, 109;

national belonging through rituals celebrating, 38–39; as "nation's first action hero," 30; as quasi-religious symbol of national unification, 47; rituals and mythologizing of, 45, 46, 74–75; Weems's presentation as "superhero," 24–25, 40–41; Whiskey Rebellion and, 72–74

Washington Consensus, 166

Washington Rules, breakdown of, 179

Watergate scandal, 59, 147, 154; Saturday Night Massacre firings during, 136

weak government, 31

Weekly Standard, 155

Weems, Mason Locke, 24, 40–45; consolidation of emotive force of presidentialism in moral fiction about Washington, 40–45, 57; narrative approach, 44–45

Weiler, Jonathan, 141–42

Weisberg, Jacob, 176

western hero, mystique of lone, 56

West Publishing Company, 159

Where's the Rest of Me? (Reagan), 60

Whiskey Rebellion, 12, 72–74

White, Theodore, 57

White House Office of Faith-Based and Community Initiatives, 171

Whitewater, 164

Why Societies Need Dissent (Sunstein), 142, 195, 196

Wikipedia, 191, 192

wikis, 191–94, 195, 202

Wiki Wiki Web, 191

Wilentz, Sean, 174

Wills, Garry, 136

Wilson, James, 111

Wilson, Woodrow, 26, 90–91, 93–97, 138; description of ideal president, 93, 94

Winfrey, Oprah, 64

winner-take-all form of presidentialism, 197, 198, 200; exploring alternatives and alterations to, 215–17

wiretapping, NSA secret, 114, 135, 172

Wisdom of Crowds, The (Surowiecki), 194

Wister, Owen, 48

"Without a Doubt" (Suskind), 1

Wolin, Sheldon, 16

Wood, Gordon, 31

Woodward, Bob, 26, 135

World Bank, 165

World Trade Organization (WTO), 166, 167; China's admission as full partner in, 169

World War II, 47, 63, 119; FDR's justification of supplying military support to England during, 53; FDR's role as commander in chief during, 50–51; Japanese Americans' internment during, 50–51, 119; Kennedy's framing of experience during, 55–56

Yoo, Christopher, 156, 161

Yoo, John, 115, 139, 173, 175, 180

Youngstown Sheet and Tube Company, 125

Youngstown Sheet and Tube Co. v. Sawyer, 125–26, 130, 179

youth volunteerism, 205–6

Dana D. Nelson is a professor of English and American studies at Vanderbilt University, where she teaches classes in U.S. literature and history, and courses that connect activism, volunteering, and citizenship. She has published numerous books and essays on U.S. literature and the history of citizenship and democratic culture. She lives in Nashville and is involved locally with a program that helps incarcerated women develop strong decision-making skills and with an innovative activist group fighting homelessness in the area.